»   ISLAM: ORIGIN AND BELIEF   «

ISLAM
Origin and Belief

» EMORY C. BOGLE «

UNIVERSITY OF TEXAS PRESS

AUSTIN

Requests for permission to reproduce material from this work should be sent to
Permissions, University of Texas Press, P.O. Box 7819, Austin, TX 78713-7819.

♾ The paper used in this publication meets the minimum requirements of
American National Standard for Information Sciences—Permanence of Paper for Printed
Library Materials, ANSI Z39.48-1984.

LIBRARY OF CONGRESS CATALOGING-IN-PUBLICATION DATA

Bogle, Emory C., 1937–
Islam : origin and belief / Emory C. Bogle. — 1st ed.
p.   cm.
Includes bibliographical references and index.
ISBN 0-292-70861-0 (alk. paper). — ISBN 0-292-70862-9 (pbk. : alk. paper)
1. Islam—History.   2. Islamic Empire—History.   3. Shi'ah—History.
4. Islam—Doctrines.   I. Title.
BP50.B65   1998
297'.09—dc21   97-33934

For my sons,

RHETT AND ANDREW,

who bring me joy.

CONTENTS

ACKNOWLEDGMENTS
ix

INTRODUCTION
xi

CHRONOLOGY OF ISLAM
xiii

ONE
MUHAMMAD AND THE ORIGIN OF ISLAM
1

TWO
ISLAMIC BELIEF AND PRACTICE
26

THREE
ISLAMIC EXPANSION
570 to 1517
47

FOUR
SHI'I ISLAM
71

FIVE
CONFRONTATION WITH MODERN SECULARISM
95

SIX
SHI'I RESPONSE TO SECULARISM
118

NOTES
133

GLOSSARY
139

SELECT BIBLIOGRAPHY
149

INDEX
151

MAPS AND CHARTS

Maps

1. The Heartland of Early Islam   13

2. Islam in the Middle East   54

3. Persia (Iran): Center of Shi'i Islam   76

Charts

1. Genealogy of the Early Islamic Leaders   50

2. The Shi'i Imams and Their Rivals for the Imamate   74

ACKNOWLEDGMENTS

I must begin by thanking Dr. Ali Hossaini, my editor, for urging me to write this book. I would never have been bold enough on my own to presume to invade this area of specialization, since my own work had been primarily on secular topics. Islam, however, constitutes a great deal of the subject matter of my courses. Finally, I determined that I had a firm grasp of the level of knowledge of Islam that people need for a foundation. Writing this book was an enjoyable task. I did little else until it was completed.

Colleagues in the field of Middle Eastern studies offered their encouragement and suggestions. Years ago, Abu Hatim al-Khatib, a patient teacher, prepared me for seeking other knowledge of Islam by spending many hours answering my questions. Dr. Hafez Farmayan of the University of Texas History Department endorsed the idea and offered kind guidance in shaping the emphasis of the book. Dr. Robert Olson of the University of Kentucky History Department encouraged me constantly and offered crucial observations and suggestions. Dr. Mohammad Ghanoonparvar of the University of Texas Middle Eastern Languages and Culture Department performed his inimitable role of kind guidance and encouragement. Dr. Sulaiman al-Jarallah, director of the Institute for Islamic and Arabic Sciences in America, and his colleagues at that institution, Dr. Jaafar Shaykh Idris, senior research professor, Dr. Mustafa Mould, and Muhi al-Din al-Salih, offered their blessings and good will. James Clark, a doctoral candidate in history at the University of Texas, read the manuscript and offered helpful comments. Dr. William Rhodenhiser of the University of Richmond Religion Department, who is a devoted student of Sufi Islam, offered helpful observations and encouragement.

Departmental colleagues John Rilling and Barry Westin kindly read every page and made helpful observations. Michael Bell configured my computer and generally kept it capable of doing all the tasks I required. Dan Roberts, Ernest Bolt, John Treadway, John Gordon, Harry Ward, Barbara Sella, and Harrison Daniel continually expressed their best wishes for success with the project.

Some of the above-mentioned people gave me advice which I rejected for various reasons and to different degrees. They can, therefore, share in any value of this project, but I made all the decisions and bear all responsibility for the book's shortcomings.

Mary Ann Wilbourne and Debbie Govoruhk of the University of Richmond History Department helped upon request and covered for me when I neglected departmental duties to write. Janet Harris provided the best possible work environment.

The staff at the computer center—especially Rick Knight, Sergio Guillette, Ellis Billups, and Steve Zinski—met my computer needs and provided invaluable assistance. Michael Bell and Marvette Johnson were available for special computer problems. Bill Sudduth, Nancy Woodall, and Rochelle Colestock, reference librarians in Boatwright Memorial Library, cheerfully and competently guided me to answers.

Graduate students Lo Ann Fairman, Linda Hollett, Dana King, Sam Mottley, Beverley Marie Thurston, Jenny Pulley, Dave Waters, and Tayloe Wise read the manuscript and made their observations. Carol Wiegmann was especially helpful and considerate. Khalil Abu Rish, Bernarda Bandak, Habeeb al-Hajj, Arif Hajez, David Houghton, and Nabil Salam gave helpful comments on parts of the manuscript. Dimitrius Mavroudis, Joann McCracken, Mutasem Abu Jabr, Lee Camp, Kamal Mahmoud, Jameel and Sabah Abed, Nellie Texler, Hanah Bazuzzi, and Jerry Bogle demonstrated interest in the book.

My two sons, Rhett and Andrew, always had hearty inquiries about each stage of the project and expressed confidence that I should write the book.

INTRODUCTION

Several million of the world's more than one billion Muslims are at prayer during any half-hour period of any day. Islam, thus, constantly calls God's attention to its believers. This fastest growing religion in the world, which encompasses some unusually dynamic individuals and groups, also attracts increased earthly attention. While the Middle East, where it originated, continues to provide the impetus to Islam, more than half of the world's Muslims reside outside of that region. And although Islam's association with Arabs is well founded, it is in fact misleading in modern times. For instance, almost as many Muslims live in Indonesia as in all the Arabic-speaking countries combined. More Muslims live in Iran and Pakistan than in all of the adjacent Arabic-speaking countries. The dynamics of Islam's growth and invigorating experimental ideologies qualify it as one of the most influential forces in contemporary times.

This short introduction to Islam can best serve as an overview of the religion's history and major beliefs. It has, however, the advantage of being able to help the contemporary reader understand the development of aspects of Islam which most obviously influence contemporary affairs. Compared with similar works, this treatment places a far greater emphasis upon Shi'ism. The prominence of Shi'i influence on modern Islamic affairs and the popular perception of the role of Shi'ism justifies, or even compels, such an emphasis. The mere frequency of references in the public media and elsewhere to Shi'i or Shiite Islam is an indication of the increased popular awareness of the general topic of Islam. Most people who use the term cannot define it, but they know it is a form of Islam. "Militant" Islam and "Militant Shi'i" Islam have become virtually synonymous in popular parlance. This prevailing limited exposure to Shi'i activism has created the perception that Shi'i are by nature, if not by definition, the "radically militant" Muslims. This book's modest presentation should help the reader understand that some of modern Shi'i activism might well result from centuries of passivity. It should also make readers aware that Islam, in general, has only recently regained a central role in many societies, after a prolonged period of marginality.

The most sustained attention to detail in this book centers on the family relationships of the prophet Muhammad and his closest associates. Many readers will understandably resent having to plow through such minutiae to get to the bigger picture. I believe that this level of detail is necessary, however, to an understanding of how various movements later justified their efforts to control Islam or establish dissident alternatives. Some readers might feel more comfortable skimming the earlier parts of the book initially and returning to them later, when the importance of these family relationships in relation to later developments becomes apparent.

Some might also believe that too much valuable space for such a short treatment discusses conflicts between extremely small forces in the early years of Islam. But anything less is unconvincing. It almost defies credibility that the modest, almost inconsequential forces and resources available to Muhammad obtained control of the Arabian peninsula. This account attempts to explain how the efficient use of limited resources against the somewhat more plentiful resources of the opposition was sufficient for victory. Otherwise, an account of an orphan obtaining a message from God to revise and reform Judaism and Christianity by going to a strange city two hundred miles north of Mecca and fighting three major battles explains very little. Also, the roles of individuals in this entire series of events are critical; it is impossible to understand subsequent conflicts over attitudes and actions of individuals without knowing what they did or did not do in the earlier years.

The short text, chronology, chart of Shi'i Imams, glossary, and maps should serve as an entry-level introduction to the general subject of Islam. The focus on developments in the Middle East to the exclusion of all other regions is the result of the kind of unfortunate decision authors have to make. The best justification for this decision is that the introductory information presented in this book is a part of the development of Islam in all other parts of the globe. The significant differences in the development and practice of Islam in other regions are too important to receive marginal treatment. If this work can establish a satisfactory base, the reader should have less difficulty with more detailed studies of Islam in the Middle East and other regions.

CHRONOLOGY OF ISLAM

570
Muhammad is born in Mecca.

574
Abyssinian Empire rules Yemen.

574
Persians invade Yemen.

595
Muhammad marries Khadija.

597
Persians expel Abyssinians.

610
Muhammad receives first revelation during Ramadan at age of forty years.

615
A group of more than eighty Muslims migrates across the Red Sea to
Abyssinia (modern Ethiopia).

616
Most Meccan clans agree upon a communal economic and marriage boycott
of Muslims.
Major conflict begins among Yathrib tribes.

619
Following the deaths of Khadija and Abu Talib, Muhammad loses protection
in Mecca and decides to continue his mission in nearby Ta'if.

620
First seven residents of Yathrib (Medina) convert to Islam during
pilgrimage to Mecca.

621
Five more residents of Yathrib become Muslims.

622

622 C.E. becomes the first year of the Islamic calendar. Seventy-five Muslims
from Yathrib take oath of loyalty to Muhammad and his God in Mecca.
Meccan Muslim community *(umma)* participate in *hijra* to Yathrib.

623

Muslims begin to raid Meccan caravans. Attack on a caravan at Nakhla kills a
Meccan during a period of holy peace.

624

Muhammad changes the *qibla* from Jerusalem to Mecca.
March. Battle of Badr between Muslims and Meccans.
September. Muslims capture annual Meccan caravan to Syria at Qarda
in Nejd.
Muhammad expels Bani Qaynuqa Jews from Yathrib and confiscates
their property.

625

23 March. Battle of Uhud. Forces of Muhammad are victorious
despite total absence of any Muslim horse cavalry to match Mecca's
two hundred horsemen.
Muhammad expels the Bani Al-Nadhir Jewish tribes from Yathrib
in September.

626

March. Muslims go to Badr with 1,500 men, but Meccans do not appear.

627

Muhammad and the Muslims accuse the Bani Quraydha Jewish tribe
of complicity with their enemies and execute seven or eight hundred Jews.
March. Muslims victorious in the Battle of the Ditch
between Meccans and Muslims.

628

Muhammad decides to perform the *umrah,* or lesser pilgrimage.
March. Treaty of Hudaybiyyah provides for a ten-year truce between
Muslims and Meccans.
Prophet moves northward against three Jewish tribes at Khaybar, Fadak, and
Wadi al-Qura seventy to eighty miles northeast of Yathrib. Jews pay a fee
and are allowed to keep their possessions.

629

February. The Prophet and nearly two thousand Muslims perform the *umrah*
while the Meccans abandon their city to avoid conflict and fraternization.
September. Muslims are defeated at Battle of Mota by the Bani Ghassan in
southern Syria.
Zayd ibn Haritha, the Prophet's adopted son, and 'Ali's brother Ja'far ibn Abu
Talib die in battle at Mota.

630

During a ten-month period from January through October, Muhammad extends his control south to Mecca and north to Aqaba.

January. The Prophet moves militarily against Mecca, but Meccans decide not to resist. Muhammad gains control of Mecca.

February. Muslims are victorious at the Battle of Hunayn just northeast of Mecca.

October. The Prophet leads an expedition northwest toward southern Syria to meet a supposed attack from the Byzantines and wins many alliances along the way. He also extends his control almost 600 miles to the northwestern-most corner of the Arabian peninsula.

631

Spring. The city of Ta'if submits to the Prophet. Throughout the year, delegations arrive in Medina from all over Arabia to proclaim their loyalty to Muhammad and his God.

632

March. The Prophet performs the *hajj* ("pilgrimage").

June. The Prophet dies.

632–634

Caliphate of Abu Bakr

634–644

Caliphate of 'Umar

635

September. Muslims conquer Damascus.

636

Muslims' victory at the Battle of Yarmuk in August gives them control of most of Syria.

Muslims gain control of Iraq with victory at the Battle of Qadisiyyah.

638

Muslims obtain control of Jerusalem.

639

Muslims invade Egypt.

641

Muslims officially obtain surrender of Egypt.

642

Muslims gain control of Persia with victory at the Battle of Nihavand.

644

Persian slave assassinates Caliph 'Umar.

644–656

Caliphate of 'Uthman

656
Discontented Muslims assassinate Caliph 'Uthman in Medina.
656–661
Caliphate of 'Ali
657
Battle of Siffin in upper Euphrates between 'Ali and Mu'awiyah ends
in arbitration.
658
Caliph 'Ali destroys most Kharijites at Nahrawan.
661–680
Caliphate of Mu'awiyah, first of the Umayyad Caliphs, with capital
at Damascus
661
Caliph 'Ali defeats Aishah and her allies at the Battle of the Camel.
Kharijite assassinates Caliph 'Ali, last of the "Rightly Guided Caliphs" and
First Imam of Shi'i Islam, which he inspired.
669
Death of Hasan ibn 'Ali, son of 'Ali, brother of Husayn, half-brother of
Muhammad al-Hanafiyyah, grandson of Muhammad, Second Imam for
most Shi'i.
680
Husayn, the son of Imam 'Ali and the Prophet's daughter, Fatimah, known as
the Third Imam of Shi'i Islam, is killed at Karbala, where Umayyads remove
his head and send it to Damascus
680–683
Caliphate of Yazid, second Umayyad caliph and son of Mu'awiyah.
700
Death of Muhammad ibn al-Hanifiyyah, son of 'Ali and one of earliest
Shi'i leaders.
700–765
Great confusion in Shi'i circles follows the death of Muhammad
ibn al-Hanifiyyah, regarding line of succession and nature of the imamate.
Divisions remain large but among fewer viable candidates.
711
Tariq leads Muslim invasion of the Iberian peninsula. Gibraltar named after
him, the "Mountain (jabal) of Tariq."
732
Battle of Tours/Poitiers in what is now southern France.
740
Imam 'Ali's great-grandson Zayd stages a revolt in Kufa in behalf of his form
of Shi'ism and is killed in battle.

750–1258

The Abbasid Caliphate, previously centered in Baghdad, replaces
the Umayyad Caliphate, previously centered in Damascus. Abbasids forsake
earlier Shi'i leanings and become foremost advocates of Sunni Islam.

750–754

Reign of Abu al-'Abbas al-Saffah, the first Abbasid caliph.

754

Beginning of caliphate of al-Mansur, who founded the city of Baghdad
in 562.

763

Muhammad ibn 'Abdullah al-Nafs al-Zakiyyah and Ibrahim,
the last two Hasanids, die, leaving Fatimid Shi'ism in the Husaynid line.
Hanif line also dead by this time.

786–809

Reign of Harun al-Rashid of *Arabian Nights* fame.

796

Disappearance or death of Muhammad ibn Isma'il, who remains the central
figure of most Isma'ili belief and activities until the Fatimids split away in 899.

800 (circa)

Turks begin to emerge as the providers of personal safety for Abbasid
caliphs. Within a few decades Turks begin to fill the highest administrative
and military positions of the empire, and Turkish influence steadily
increases throughout Islam.

868

Beginning of Tulunid period in Egypt when Ahmad ibn Tulun becomes
governor of Egypt.

874

The Twelfth Imam, Muhammad al-Muntazar, disappears and goes
into occultation. Twelver Shi'i regard him as the Mahdi who will return
to signal Judgment Day and the domination of the righteous.

878

Ahmad ibn Tulun conquers Syria and makes it dependent upon Egypt.

899

'Ubayd Allah declares himself Imam to break with the other Isma'ilis and
begin the Fatimid movement.

900

Approximate beginning of the Qarmati movement to retain belief
in Muhammad ibn Isma'il as the Mahdi, in response to Fatimid claims
and interpretation of the imamate.

901

Zaydi Shi'i state is established in Yemen.

902

Salamiyyah in Syria ceases to be Fatimid center when 'Ubayd Allah goes to North Africa.

903

In Salamiyyah, Qarmatians destroy Fatimid base which 'Ubayd Allah had abandoned a few months earlier.

905

End of Tulunid dynasty in Egypt.

910

'Ubayd Allah establishes first Fatimid caliphate in Ifriqiyyah (Tunisia).

923–939

Period of intense Qarmatian attacks upon pilgrims and entirety of southwest Asia.

930

Qarmatians devastate Mecca and carry away the Black Stone, which they do not return until 951, after payment from the Abbasids.

930s

The Buyids emerge from the Caspian Sea area and establish a series of loosely connected kingdoms throughout Persia and eastern Mesopotamia.

945

Buyids take control of Baghdad and the Abbasid Caliphate until 1055, when Seljuks remove them. (Buyids were Shi'i who dominated a caliphate that remained Sunni.)

952–975

Reign of al-Mu'izz, the first Fatimid caliph in Egypt, who modifies Fatimid concept of the imamate to make it more compatible with most other Isma'ilis.

969

Fatimids (Isma'ili Seveners who reject the entire premise of the Abbasid caliphate) conquer Egypt and move the Fatimid caliphate from Tunisia to Egypt.

969

New Fatimid regime begins construction of a new city called Cairo.

970

Fatimids begin construction of al-Azhar to serve as a religious center for Isma'ili Islam.

1019

Muhammad al-Darazi, namesake of Druze religion, disappears in Egypt.

1021

Al-Hakim (Fatimid caliph in Egypt), who inspired the Druze religion, disappears at age 36.

1025

Seljuk Turks who have become Sunni Muslims begin to sweep into
northeastern Persia.

1055

Seljuks capture Baghdad and restore full authority of the Abbasid Caliph
and Sunni Islam.

1055

Buyids lose control of the Abbasid caliphate they have held since 945.

1058

Qarmatians lose control of Uwal (modern Bahrain) to Abbasids.

1058–1111

Life span of Abu Hamid al-Ghazali.

1064

First Turkomans enter Syria. Seljuks push Fatimids out of most of Syria
and Palestine.

1071

Seljuk Turkish victory over Byzantine Empire at the Battle of Manzikert
in eastern Anatolia lays the basis of a Seljuk dynasty in Anatolia
and the transformation of Anatolia into a predominantly
Turkish society.

1073

Fatimid administration in Egypt falls under control of Armenian (Christian)
military element. Turks soon replace them.

1077

After 150 years of controlling much of the Arabian peninsula,
Qarmatians lose control of the city of al-Hasa to Abbasids and cease
to be important.

1099

Crusaders capture Jerusalem from Fatimids.

1127–1154

Seljuk Turks capture much of Syria from the crusaders.

1154

Seljuk Turks capture Damascus from crusaders.

1163

Saladin arrives in Egypt as a subordinate Seljuk officer.

1170

Saladin repels crusaders from Egypt.

1171

Last Fatimid caliph dies, and Saladin restores Egypt to Sunni Islam.

1187

Saladin captures Jerusalem.

1192

Saladin completes the defeat of the Third Crusade, which attempted to restore crusader holdings.

1250

Mamluks create their own dynasty for Egypt-Syria when they begin to choose the sultan from among their ranks.

1252–1334

Life of Safi al-Din, the originator of the Safavid religious movement in Persia, which evolves into Twelver Shi'ism.

1256

Mongols, under the leadership of Hulegu, invade Persia and begin their sweep to the west.

1258

Abbasid Caliphate in Baghdad ends when Mongols execute the last caliph. Baghdad falls to Mongols.

1260

Mongols capture Aleppo and Damascus.
Egyptian Mamluk army defeats the Mongols in northern Palestine at the Battle of 'Ayn Jalut, thereby stopping Mongol penetration to southwest Asia and Africa.

1261

Mamluks establish a Sunni Abbasid Caliphate in Cairo that lasts until the Ottoman takeover of Egypt in 1517.

1291

Egyptian Mamluks defeat crusaders at Acre and end crusader presence in the Holy Land.

1295–1304

Reign of Ghazan Khan, leader of the Mongols, who converts to Sunni Islam.

1326

Ottomans conquer Bursa.

1352

Ottomans conquer Gallipoli.

1387

Ottomans conquer Salonika.

1379

A new spate of Mongol invasions of southwest Asia begins under the leadership of Timur.

1405

Death of Timur.

1453

Ottoman Turks conquer Constantinople after a siege of fifty-five days.

1501

A Safavid, Esma'il, wins the Battle of Sharur. Proclaiming himself Shah in Tabriz, he founds the Safavid dynasty, which lasts until 1736.

1514

23 August. Ottoman Empire defeats the Safavid Persians at the Battle of Chaldiran.

1516

24 August. Ottomans defeat the Mamluks at the Battle of Marj Dabik near Aleppo and take control of Syria and Palestine. Kansu al-Gauri, the Mamluk sultan, dies of shock.

1517

23 January. Ottomans capture Cairo and end both the Mamluk dynasty and the Mamluk Abbasid caliphate. The Turks take the last Mamluk Caliph to Istanbul, where they claim he has assigned his caliphal powers to Selim I, the Ottoman Sultan. The Hejaz, previously under Mamluk control, also comes under Ottoman control with the victories in Syria and Egypt.

1520–1566

Reign of Suleiman the Magnificent in the Ottoman Empire.

1534

Persian capital moves from Tabriz to Qazvin.

Ottomans capture Baghdad from Persian Safavids.

1536

Alliance between France and the Ottoman Empire, which establishes French as an influence superior to any other Western power.

1571

Pope Pius V organizes a Holy League against the Ottomans.

1572

Naval Battle of Lepanto in which the Western Christian coalition of the Holy League defeats the Ottomans.

1597

Persian capital moves from Qazvin to Isfahan.

1638

Ottomans take Baghdad from Persia.

1683

Christians under the leadership of John Sobieski of Poland turn back the Ottoman armies at Vienna.

1687

In Second Battle of Mohacs, Christian forces regain control of most of Hungary in behalf of the Austrian Hapsburgs.

1699

Treaty of Karlowitz ends prolonged war between the Ottomans and the Holy League, giving Austria the remainder of Hungary and marking a reversal of Ottoman expansion westward and the gradual decline of the Ottoman Empire.

1703

Birth of Muhammad ibn 'Abd al-Wahhab, advocate of a strict adherence to the most traditional beliefs and practices of Islam. The movement he inspires transforms life and religious practice over most of the Arabian peninsula. The success of Wahhabism is closely associated with that of the al-Saud family, which supports the movement and establishes the modern kingdom of Saudi Arabia.

1739

With the Treaty of Belgrade, Ottomans lose part of Serbia to the Austrian Empire.

1774

With the Treaty of Kuchuk Kainarji, Russia makes considerable territorial gains from the Ottomans and also gains the right to interfere in the affairs of Ottoman Christians.

1792

With the Treaty of Jassy, Russia gains additional Ottoman territory.

1805–1849

Reign of Muhammad 'Ali in Egypt.

1849

Birth of Muhammad 'Abduh, a noted Egyptian scholar closely associated with Jamal al-Din al-Afghani and Muhammad Rashid Rida in their efforts to help Islam meet the challenges of the Western nations and culture.

1854

Birth of Syrian Islamist 'Abd al-Rahman al-Kawakibi.

1876

Egyptian finances are placed under the control of the European administrators of the Egyptian Debt Commission.

1881

Ottoman Empire finances are placed under the direction of European administrators of the Ottoman Public Debt Administration.

1882

Great Britain invades Egypt and controls most of Egypt's affairs until the end of World War II.

1896

One of Jamal al-Din al-Afghani's disciples assassinates Shah Nasir al-Din of Persia.

1898

'Abd al-Rahman al-Kawakibi publishes *Mecca: Mother of Cities* and soon thereafter publishes *Attributes of Tyranny* before he dies in 1902 at the age of forty-eight. His basic thesis is that Turkish backwardness and ignorance have prevented Islam from preparing to meet the challenges of modern times.

1906

Birth of Hasan al-Banna, founder and "Guide" of the Muslim Brotherhood, in Egypt.

1906

9 October. Birth of Sayyid Qutb in Musha, Egypt.

1923

Muhammad Rashid Rida publishes *The Caliphate or the Supreme Imam.* He advocates an Arab caliphate with assistance through consultation *(shura)* and interpretation *(ijtihad)* to help Islam adapt to modern times while retaining its identity. He also initiates a weekly magazine, *Al-Manar* ("The Lighthouse").
Birth of Jalal al-e Ahmad, an important Iranian intellectual of the 1950s and 1960s who wrote both history and fiction.

1928

Hasan al-Banna establishes a chapter of the Hasafiyyah Sufi brotherhood in Isma'iliyyah which quickly evolves into the Muslim Brotherhood *(Jamiyyat al-Ikhwan al-Muslimun),* the most important politico-religious organization in modern Egypt.

1933

Muslim Brotherhood moves its headquarters to Cairo.
Birth of 'Ali Shari'ati, the Iranian intellectual who probably did more than anyone else to prepare an atmosphere receptive to the Iranian Revolution. His popularizing of the Husayniyyah Irshad movement spread the idea that laymen should play an active role in establishing justice to prepare for the return of the Hidden Imam.

1938

Al-Nadhir ('The Warning'), weekly newspaper of the Muslim Brotherhood, begins publication.

1940s

The Muslim Brotherhood registers as a religious and charitable organization in the 1940s and becomes an integral part of Jordanian life with a steady proliferation of schools, clinics, hospitals, religious centers, and mosques. The Brotherhood's greatest influence outside of Egypt probably occurs in Syria, where a fully developed Brotherhood organization is strong enough in the late forties to battle the Baath, Communist, and Syria Social Nationalist parties with strong organization and ideological agendas.

1948

The Brotherhood's armed element proves relentless and effective in the Palestine war of 1948 and never acquiesces to the truce accepted by Egypt and other Arab governments.

6 December. The Egyptian government outlaws the Brotherhood for its general political effectiveness in colluding with a spectrum of other groups from communists to fascists.

1949

12 February. A Muslim Brotherhood member's assassination of Egyptian Prime Minister Mahmoud Nuqarshi leads to the secret police's assassination of al-Banna. Hasan al-Hudaybi becomes new "Guide" of the Muslim Brotherhood, which has grown to two thousand branches and half a million active members.

1952

23 July. The Free Officers' coup, which initially appears favorable to the Muslim Brotherhood, soon relegates the latter to an inconsequential role for nearly three decades.

1953

The Revolutionary Command Council (RCC) abolishes the Wafd and other political parties.

Sayyid Qutb becomes the Muslim Brotherhood's principal theoretician and editor of the Brotherhood's weekly newspaper, *Jamiyyat al-Ikhwan al-Muslimun.* He also directs the newly established Liberation Rally, which the RCC has created to replace all political parties.

1954

26 October. A Brotherhood member's attempt on the life of Gamal Abdel Nasser signals the end to an uneasy relationship with the RCC. Six Muslim Brothers die on the gallows for the deed.

Sayyid Qutb is sentenced to prison, where he remains until 1964 and suffers torture as a prominent leader of the Brotherhood.

RCC negotiates treaty with Great Britain, which the Muslim Brotherhood condemn.

Egyptian government again outlaws the Brotherhood, who return underground in Egypt and move their headquarters to Damascus.

1955

January. The RCC co-opts Islam as an issue through creation of the International Islamic Congress (IIC).

1956

The Suez Canal crisis and war.

1958

Musa al-Sadr, an Iranian of Lebanese lineage, gradually emerges as the most revered Shi'i leader after arriving in Lebanon in 1958.

1960

Mild efforts of respected Iranian clergymen to address contemporary issues in the Monthly Religious Society in 1960–1961 attract government retaliation. Authorities force the termination of the group's public lectures and their subsequent publication.

1960

Al-e Ahmad adopts the term *gharbzadegi,* which his friend Ahmad Fardid coined, meaning "Occidentosis" or "Weststruckness," which becomes a theme of Iranian revolutionary efforts to eliminate Western cultural domination in Iran.

1960s

Al-e Ahmad's novel emphasis early in the decade upon creating a Shi'i-oriented Iranian society becomes a popular theme among Iranian dissidents. By the mid-1970s, it will dominate their discussion.

1962

Mehdi Bazargan, a respected layman, criticizes Iranian clergymen for staying out of politics in a speech to the Second Congress of Islamic Societies.

1962

Ayatollah Khomeini's vivid public opposition to the White Revolution in 1962–1963 is an anomaly, while his exile warns others with similar intentions that his fate is the least that could happen to them.

1963

Khomeini, whose opposition to the Shah reaches back to the 1950s, is exiled to Iraq, causing little protest among the higher clergy, who generally do not regard him as a first-rate intellectual.

1964

Sayyid Qutb publishes *Milestones,* which calls for true Muslims to fulfill their duties to wipe out governments which support *jahiliyyah.*

April. The Muslim Brotherhood has the best organization for coordinating the nationwide uprising in Syria. Rioting, demonstrations, and violent confrontations occur in most larger population centers, but the heaviest fighting and greatest bloodshed is in the city of Hama, where the Brotherhood is strongest.

1965

Initiation of the Husayniyyah Irshad movement, of which Shari'ati soon becomes and remains the most popular and important spokesman.

1966

August 29. Sayyid Qutb, foremost activist of the Muslim Brotherhood, is executed in Egypt.

1969

Mu'ammar Gadhafi adopts an Islamist stance soon after seizing control of Libya.

Musa al-Sadr gains respect and a large following with his establishment of a Shi'i Higher Council expressing dissatisfaction with traditional Shi'i subservience to Lebanese Sunni Muslims.

Muhammad Rashid Rida dies.

1970s

Abu al-Hassan Bani-Sadr writes and speaks in behalf of an Islamic republic to replace the monarchy in opposition.

The Husayniyyah Irshad becomes an important subculture throughout Iran and among expatriate Iranians worldwide.

1973

The Iranian government closes the Husayniyyah Irshad and arrests Shari'ati.

1974

Musa al-Sadr's establishment of the Movement of the Disinherited strongly states the Shi'i demand for full access to Lebanon's political and economic bounty.

1975

Outbreak of civil war in Lebanon.

1977

The Syrian Muslim Brotherhood, which maintains a strong underground organization, increases resistance to the Baathist regime.

'Ali Shari'ati's mysterious death shortly after going to England enhances his reputation as another Shi'i martyr in the struggle for equality and justice.

1978

Iranian expatriates around the world manifest the hope that they can arouse enough unrest in Iran and public support abroad to overthrow the Shah.

September 16. Shah flees in response to a general outcry against his rule.

October. Iraq expels Khomeini in response to Iranian pressure. No regional state accepts him, so he goes to France.

1979

Islamic militants occupy the Grand Mosque in Mecca, and Shi'i unrest is manifested in the eastern provinces of the Kingdom of Saudi.

February 1. Khomeini returns to Iran and installs a government under the control of members of Mossadegh's 1950s National Front who intend to establish a secular republic based upon the 1906 constitution.

June 16. An attack by the Muslim Brotherhood on the Aleppo Artillery School results in thirty to eighty-five cadets' perishing, while many others suffer wounds.

November 6. Mehdi Bazargan resigns as prime minister of Iran two days after activists seize the United States embassy.

1980

January. Bani-Sadr becomes president of Iran.

March–April. Ten thousand Syrian troops with heavy tank support kill approximately two thousand Muslim Brothers in the process of subduing Aleppo.

September 22. Iraq attacks Iran.

1981

The Muslim Brotherhood's bombings and shootings in Damascus dictate a life of limited activities and pervasive security precautions.

1982

3 February. Violence breaks out in Hama and more than 10 thousand troops with artillery, tank, and aerial support battle the Muslim Brotherhood for a month.

1983

Sudan, long a center of activist Sufi Islam, experiences dramatic change when President Ja'far Nemeiri suddenly imposes a harsh *salafiyyah* approach on the law.

1987

Islamic Jihad emerges under the leadership of Shaykh 'Abd al-Aziz Awdah.

December. The Intifada begins in Gaza after a traffic accident, generating large demonstrations of Palestinians.

1988

January. The Muslim Brotherhood initiate a movement called Hamas (Movement of Islamic Resistance) to oppose PLO leftist elements and the Islamic *Jihad.*

August. Hamas publishes its covenant.

1990

The U.S. Gulf War against Iraq begins, ending the *Intifada* and changing the entire region and its relationship with the world.

1993

While not a majority, Muslim Brotherhood members constitute the largest group in the Jordanian legislature.

13 September. Yasser Arafat shakes the hand of Israeli Prime Minister Yitzhak Rabin in Washington, D.C., to symbolize his acceptance of an Israeli state, in return for the right to administer the civil affairs of the isolated enclaves of Gaza and Jericho.

» ISLAM: ORIGIN AND BELIEF «

ONE

MUHAMMAD AND THE
ORIGIN OF ISLAM

The popular association of nomadism with Arabia often leads to the assumption of a pastoral origin for Islam, which in fact developed in an urban environment. No less an observer than the Prophet Muhammad said, "We are an urban people." This urban orientation shaped the outlook and nature of Islam. The complicated private property considerations and business contracts of its earliest adherents in Mecca addressed issues that did not concern most of the rural population in the region. Their participation in sophisticated international trade also accustomed Meccans to address concerns of a universal nature. Mecca's commerce, therefore, gave the city and its residents a global orientation that transcended parochial restraints.

Mecca's centuries-old tradition as a sacred religious center also provided it with an aura and outlook commensurate with cosmic speculation. Mecca was holy. There was a sense in Mecca of the confluence of spiritual powers in the rocky valley. Believers in all known gods of the region placed their gods, or symbols of their gods, in a common temple, called the Kaaba, and ecumenically gathered there to worship. The depiction of Christian holy symbols in the Kaaba, a cube-shaped structure containing the sacred Black Stone, indicates either that Christian monotheists shared the sense of holiness in Mecca or that polytheists placed manifestations of Christianity there because they respected and revered the One God of Christians.

Annually all conflicts, including blood feuds, ceased in a specified region for a period of time that allowed pilgrims to benefit from the special aura at the Kaaba. Lest cynics say that this pilgrimage to the Kaaba resulted from commercial considerations, there are indications that religious practice preceded commerce. It is true that the temporary fairs that accompanied the annual pilgrimage gradually grew into a permanent commercial settlement. The inextricable connection between the economic health of Mecca and pilgrimage to the Kaaba is beyond dispute, but it was the gravitation of pilgrims to the holiness of Mecca that determined its development as a center for commerce.

The values of Mecca, rather than those of Yathrib (later Medina), shaped Islam even though it thrived in Yathrib after expulsion from Mecca. Muhammad, a Meccan, perceived the world from the perspective of his native city. There is no evidence that his personal relationship with God changed his basic nature in any significant way, and God used him as he had developed within the culture of his city and its surroundings. Since they had not shared in his elevation to prophecy, however, Meccans initially perceived no advantage in accepting or even tolerating Islam. The Prophet and his followers obtained haven in Yathrib as mediators among its quarreling factions rather than as missionaries teaching a new religion and a new way of life. While Yathrib had to serve as his base of operations, the success of Muhammad's movement as a religion depended upon the city of Mecca's acknowledgment of Islam as the legitimate fruition of its centuries of holiness.

The dual role of Mecca as an ecumenical religious center and as a thriving center for international trade helps explain how it could create, sustain, and spread a religion that was globally applicable and compatible. Islam's initial success, however, depended upon acceptance of the city-born religion by rural, polytheist bedouin tribesmen. Despite the commonalities in attributes and attitudes of urban and rural Arabs, there were enough differences between them to test Islam's potential for universal appeal. City life and social structure differed drastically from rural life and social structure, regardless of their common language and considerable economic interdependence. Tribal concerns that dominated rural Arabs became blurred in cities where even clans within a tribe tended to operate independently from each other. Individuals had myriad opportunities in cities to establish different kinds of relationships, affinities, and preferences, some of which were totally unrelated to family or tribal considerations. The financial disparity between the wealthy 'Abd Shams clan and the economically marginal Hashim clan, both of the Quraysh tribe, illustrates the effects of centuries of city life upon a tribe. In very important matters, urban peoples of different cultures had more in common with each other than with rural people who spoke the same language. For instance, religion, law, morals, ethics, customs, marriage practices, and land-tenure practices that developed in urban settings were frequently inapplicable to rural settings.

It was, of course, untenable that the One God would reveal religious practice suitable exclusively for one kind of life, in one place, at one time. It had to be for all people, in all places, for all times. From the outset, urban-born Islam successfully met the challenge of fulfilling the religious needs of the rural Arabs who constituted most of the population of the Arabian peninsula.

Perhaps Islam's simplicity accounts for its acceptance initially in urban and rural Arabia and then across the globe. The omnipresence and omnipotence of the One God constituted the essence of Islam. Acceptance of a single divinity gave unity to all things for all time. A harmony of interdependence throughout the universe had to follow from such an outlook. This belief unified all people and obliterated the significance of tribe or locality. Converted polytheists immediately became the brethren of Jewish and Christian monotheists. Acknowledgment of Muhammad as God's prophet was also essential for Islam, as his teachings and God's words in the Qur'an constituted amendments to earlier monotheistic revelations.

Hesitancy to accept a mortal messenger was a problem for many, but belief in a single God who cared about human welfare required a level of faith that relegated everything else to the province of details. According to Islam, only God was divine. Everything else, including prophets, was subject to His universal and unchanging laws. Islam taught that human behavior within God's law determined rewards and/or punishments during earthly life and throughout eternity. While some have tried to make Islam more complicated, it spread and endured because of the simple, practical teachings of Muhammad.

THE SETTING

Islam emerged in a remarkably brief time in a fairly small area about halfway between the two extremities of Yemen and Syria on the Arabian peninsula. While polytheism dominated the vast region in the middle of the peninsula, both ends were steeped in monotheism. The region of Islam's birth became important because of its extensive intercourse with Yemen and Syria.

At the beginning of the sixth century, Yemen, which already had a Christian element, was under the control of a Jewish ruler by the name of Dhu Nuwas. Under Byzantine instigation the Abyssinian Empire gained control of and ruled Yemen from 525 to 574. Since the Abyssinians practiced Monophysite Christianity, most Arabs in the region were unfamiliar with the concepts of the dual nature of Christ as man and deity and the Trinity, which were found in other Christian communities.

Persians invaded Yemen in 574 and war ensued, continuing until Persians expelled the Abyssinians in 597. Soon thereafter the Persian conflict with the Byzantine Empire left Yemen unattended, and it devolved back to the control of indigenous elements composed of native Yemenites as well as Abyssinians and Persians. Polytheists dominated Yemen from that time on, but a large number of Jews and a small number of Christians also resided there.

Mecca, which is about halfway between Yemen and Syria, evolved into an important city as the disarray in Yemen reduced the capacity of that region to handle its affairs. Mecca is located in a flat, rocky valley a mile and a half long by less than half a mile wide with sheer rock walls, where nature precluded agriculture or even animal husbandry. It was, however, an ancient site for worship. The Kaaba contained many idols of the polytheists of the region and, as mentioned earlier, probably also contained some Christian icons or other religious representations.

The Quraysh tribe, composed of several major clans, dominated Mecca from early in the fifth century. Meccans became the principal middlemen in trade between Yemen and Syria in the second half of the sixth century. Trade of this magnitude required considerable knowledge and skill. Perhaps of most importance to its continued success was the ability of the Quraysh to maintain safe passage for their cargo over more than one thousand miles of trails that passed through numerous tribal territories. Armed Meccans and mercenaries accompanied the caravans, but agreements with the tribes, which often required payment for protection, provided the greatest security for the safe passage of trade.

By the sixth century most trade transpired from two annual caravans. One went south to Yemen to obtain goods from India, China, and other points eastward for sale in Syria and Egypt. Most of the goods carried on the return trip from the north met the needs of the Hejaz—the strip along the west coast of the Arabic peninsula comprising Mecca and Yathrib. Smaller caravans also accounted for some portion of Mecca's trade. All caravan activity and military activity, however, depended upon the availability of adequate water and grazing for camels and horses, as well as upon favorable weather conditions. Unusually harsh weather prevented or delayed merchant and military operations.

MUHAMMAD'S BACKGROUND

Muhammad was born in Mecca in 570 to Amina of the Zuhra clan and 'Abdullah of the Hashim clan of the Quraysh tribe. His paternal grandfather, 'Abd al-Muttalib, was the only son of Hashim, founder of the Hashim clan. Hashim was the son of 'Abd Manaf and the grandson of Qasi, who elevated both the Quraysh tribe and Mecca from obscurity to prominence.

'Abd al-Muttalib, Muhammad's grandfather, was important for his illustrious lineage and his right to provide the pilgrims with food and water. He obviously had a strong vested interest in the polytheist pilgrimage traffic to Mecca. The fact that he gave Muhammad's father the name of 'Abdullah, which means "servant or slave of God," indicates that he had a strong affinity for "The God," represented by the Black Stone in the Kaaba. Given the general religious tolerance among most polytheists, there is no reason to believe Hejaz Arabs concluded that the existence of "The God" or "The Supreme God" precluded the existence of other gods. Each god had a particular function. Individuals could choose any combination of gods to satisfy their needs. The entire experience of Mecca had religious significance. Mecca, in general, and the immediate area of the Kaaba were sacred and had been for longer than anyone could say and for reasons that worshipers no longer remembered. Consequently, people from all over Arabia could make pilgrimages to Mecca at specific times without fear for their safety or their property. Since the worship of many gods was an ancient practice, it was understandable that the sacred area of Mecca accommodated these known gods.

Many Arabs knew about the concept of monotheism, but few had received instruction in such beliefs. Interestingly, however, most of the Arab Christians insisted upon the Monophysite approach to Christianity, which rejected the confusing concept of the Trinity. Apparently there was something in the Arab temperament receptive both to the notion of a god for every function and to that of a single god who had no partners and needed no help. Arab polytheists observed that Christians and Jews generally lived more bountiful lives than themselves, which perhaps led them to the conclusion that Christians and Jews pleased the One God. It would be difficult to underestimate, however, the trauma involved for tradition-bound Arabs to embrace a religion from an outside culture, with the attendant way of life. Some Arabs, who were known as *hanifs*, became monotheists but did not embrace any particular religion. The heart and/or mind that led them to monotheism also held them to the culture of their forefathers. Their numbers were few, but the rapid and zealous spread of monotheism among the Arabs in one decade hints at a deep and widespread yearning for a monotheism based upon Arab culture. Arabs needed to be true at once to their traditions and to the One God.

The central role of the Black Stone in the Kaaba, the large Jewish communities in and near Yathrib, a sprinkling of Christians in Yemen, and the domination of Christianity among the Ghassanid, Lakhmid, and other Arab tribes in the north acquainted the Arabs of the Arabian peninsula with monotheism. Caravans of a thousand camels and their accompanying merchants, soldiers, and other functionaries traveled annually from Mecca to Syria. Such efforts involved a large percentage of the population of that small city. Some branched off to Egypt. Orthodox Christianity dominated the entire region which these Meccans visited for weeks annually to conduct commerce. Caravans of similar size went annually to Yemen, where Judaism remained strong following its militant hegemony in the early sixth century. Fifty years of Abyssinian Monophysite Christian domination had followed the Jewish period. Persian and polytheist forces did not regain control of Yemen until after Muhammad married Khadija. Christianity was widespread among the Lakhmid Arabs of the al-Hira region on the Euphrates before Muhammad received his first revelation. Meccans traded with their Lakhmid brethren by a route that passed through the Nefud. Understanding how extensively Arabian peninsula residents interacted with monotheists makes it less surprising to learn that at least one male and one female cousin of 'Abd al-Muttalib were reputedly very familiar with Christian scriptures.

Since 'Abdullah, Muhammad's father, died before the boy was born, the future prophet of Islam became the ward of his grandfather, 'Abd al-Muttalib. In keeping with prevailing custom, he lived most of his first six years in the countryside among the Bani Saad tribe, in the care of his wet nurse, Helema. When his mother died within a year after he returned to Mecca, Muhammad went to live with his grandfather. But 'Abd al-Muttalib died within two years and the eight-year-old boy went to live with Abu Talib, his paternal uncle (not to be confused with Abi Talib, a latter-day caliph).

We know little about Muhammad until he joined the merchant enterprise of his female cousin Khadija. Most scholars agree that Muhammad was twenty-five years of age when he married the forty-year-old widow in 595, after she proposed marriage to him. For any era, that would have been a fairly advanced age for her to bear six children with him. Their two sons died in infancy, and only one of his daughters, Fatimah, lived to be of historical significance as the wife of 'Ali and the mother of Hasan and Husayn. Apparently Muhammad brought no estate of his own to his marriage with Khadija. Unaccountably, Abu Talib experienced financial difficulties, while Muhammad's marriage provided him a comfortable living. Abu Talib's young son, 'Ali, joined Muhammad's household, and the two cousins established a relationship more akin to that of father and son or uncle and nephew. Muhammad also formally adopted a Christian former slave boy by the name of Zayd ibn Haritha, who was close in age to 'Ali. In their earliest years of manhood, Muhammad called on each of them to fulfill important tasks that required exceptional character and bravery.

For the most part, only anecdotal material of questionable accuracy is available about Muhammad for the fifteen years following his marriage. There is no doubt of his involvement in Khadija's commercial enterprise. The fact that many addressed him by the acquired honorific name of al-Amin ("the trusted one") indicates he had a reputation for honesty and integrity.

At some point Muhammad adopted the practice of meditating alone in a cave on Mount Hira, adjacent to Mecca. While this activity indicates a personal spiritual search, evidence that other Meccans engaged in similar meditations manifests a pronounced spirituality and receptivity to nontraditional religious expression that may have been inherent in their culture.

THE CALL TO PROPHECY

During the month of Ramadan in 610, when Muhammad was forty years old, a heavenly messenger, later identified as the Archangel Gabriel, interrupted his meditations and said, "Oh Muhammad, you are the Messenger of God." The experience shocked and horrified him because he feared he might be insane or controlled by an evil spirit. He fell to his knees, in terror rather than from reverence. The spirit ordered Muhammad to "Recite!" three times before he composed himself well enough to receive his first revelation, which became the first part of sura 96 of the Qur'an. He decided to throw himself off the mountain to end the insanity or curse, but the spirit moved closer and repeated "Oh Muhammad, you are the Messenger of God."

Reassured by the second appearance of his heavenly visitor, he accepted the burden of prophecy. Scholars disagree, usually along sectarian lines, about which of his associates first learned of his experience, endorsed his call to prophecy, and embraced Islam. Apparently Khadija, 'Ali, Abu Bakr, and Zayd converted without hesitation and encouraged Muhammad to accept his mission and fulfill God's role for him. Since 'Ali and Zayd were only ten years old, many question whether they were mature enough to make any decision other than to follow the lead of the man who functioned as their father.

The passage of two or three years before he received additional revelation aroused doubt and uncertainty in the new prophet. The next revelation instructed him to inform the Hashim clan that he was the Messenger of the One God. His Hashim clan was not impressed, and most members of the family, like other Meccans, apparently assumed he was suffering from some type of spell or dementia. Initially, the converts beyond Muhammad's immediate household and friends were slaves and others without family connections in Mecca. As early as 613, however, the tiny Muslim group was causing enough of a stir in Mecca that Meccans warned pilgrims to avoid the new, misguided element.

When some younger members of Meccan families gradually began to affiliate with Muhammad, the new Muslim community (umma) caused rifts in families and resentment toward Muhammad. Anything that weakened family ties generated strong reaction in a society that placed family solidarity above all else. Muslim converts, upon embracing monotheism, usually adopted a strident antipathy toward polytheism. Their treatment within the community and their families usually depended on how much of that outlook they communicated to others. Belief in the Final Judgment and the reality of the horrors of Hell led many converts to disdain their pagan forefathers and zealously urge their family members to abandon the errors of their polytheism.

Fortunately for Muhammad, his mentor, Abu Talib, not only led the

Hashim clan but also enjoyed a good reputation in the wider Meccan society. For several years he managed to protect Muhammad from the more severe repercussions he could have experienced for sowing dissent. His uncle's protection did not extend to the slaves, non-Meccans, and other "unconnected" Muslims, however, and some of these less fortunate Muslims experienced indignities in the first twelve years of the Muslim movement. The young converts from "good" Meccan families could also obtain protection, but, especially after the earliest years, some converts adopted homicidal intentions toward their unrepentant brethren.

Within five years Muhammad had attracted converts from most of Mecca's prominent families. These conversions increased animosity toward Islam in Mecca. In 615 a group of more than eighty Muslims migrated across the Red Sea to Abyssinia (modern Ethiopia) on the correct assumption that the Christian society would protect fellow monotheists. Since many of the emigrants belonged to prominent families, Meccan leaders unsuccessfully implored the Abyssinian emperor to return them. Most of them, including Abu Sufyan's daughter and 'Ali's brother Ja'far, remained in Abyssinia until the entire Muslim community found a safe haven.

It is essential to understand that the close-knit relationships within Meccan clans and their kinship clans, with whom they conducted most marriages, provided large numbers of people with knowledge of their kin's intimate lives and behavior. Since conversations centered on family gossip, news of aberrant behavior spread rapidly and demanded appropriate family response. Meccans determined that the Islamic blight which was denigrating their traditional gods and condemning their ancestors to Hell had stemmed from the Hashim and al-Muttalib clans' refusal to discipline Muhammad and his following.

Most of the Meccan clans agreed upon a communal economic and marriage boycott of those two clans to quarantine against further contamination. The boycott, which began in 616, was an inconvenience, however, and some elements of Mecca apparently did not adhere to it. Also, with a combined population of at least several hundred, the two quarantined clans constituted a fairly viable economy in a city of approximately ten thousand. The conversion of two of Mecca's most notable warriors during this period gave the movement credibility and an additional capacity for self-defense. One was Muhammad's uncle, Hamza ibn 'Ali, and the other was 'Umar ibn al-Khattab. Only the foolhardy dared risk the wrath of either of these warriors.

Muhammad's status declined in 619 following the deaths of Khadija and Abu Talib in close succession. His uncle Abu Lahab had always been openly hostile to Muhammad's teachings, while his uncle 'Abbas demonstrated a personal affection for Muhammad but disapproved of the latter's disruption of

Mecca. Muhammad's other uncle, Hamza, had professed Islam, rendering him useless as a bridge to the Meccan mainstream. In short, the leaders of the Hashim clan were now unable or unwilling to protect Muhammad. His predicament illustrates the loving relationship that had existed between Abu Talib and Muhammad; his uncle had forced the entire clan to suffer financially, and he had withstood heavy personal pressure within the Hashim clan in order to protect Muhammad. His behavior is all the more remarkable when we consider that Abu Talib rejected Muhammad's prophethood and died refusing to forsake the religion of his ancestors.

Without protection in Mecca, Muhammad decided to continue his mission in nearby Ta'if in 619. The Messenger of God, who had acquired a certain level of fame in Mecca after nine years of effort, was surprised that the leaders of Ta'if knew nothing about him. Ta'if residents drove the audacious Meccan out of their town in a hail of stones soon after he expressed his intentions. His experience underscores how tiny and defenseless the Islamic movement was even when the Prophet was almost halfway through his short mission. Unwelcome in his own clan, unwelcome in his native city, and unwelcome and unknown in Ta'if, he accepted the terms offered in Mecca by his cousin Mutin ibn 'Adi of the Nawfal clan of the Quraysh. This clan, whose progenitor was the brother of Hashim, had a history of tolerating members who had affiliated with Christianity. Muhammad had to agree to cease proselytizing among Meccans in return for ibn 'Adi's protection, but apparently their agreement did not prevent him from approaching non-Meccans. This arrangement, which other Meccans evidently found agreeable, allowed him to remain in the city of his birth.

THE SITUATION IN YATHRIB

Conflict among the tribes of Yathrib provided Muhammad the opportunity to escape the limitations of Mecca. A mixture of Arab and Jewish tribes had amicably inhabited this oasis for generations. Predominantly a date palm–growing center 250 miles north of Mecca, Yathrib also sustained other forms of agriculture and animal husbandry. Its fertility contrasted sharply with the rocky nonproductivity of Mecca. Also, well inland from the main caravan route, it had only marginal trade and little industry. While the two large Arab tribes of Aus and Khazraj owned most of the land, three Jewish tribes also owned land and supplemented their incomes with trade, manufacturing, and money lending. As was typical of the region, relations among the five principal tribes and the smaller groups in and around the oasis reflected the vagaries of close association over generations, and alliances never followed the demarcations between Arab polytheists and Jewish monotheists. The two religious groups shared cultural similarities, in part because many of the Jews were probably Arabs who had adopted Judaism.

Yathrib did not appear to offer the capacity to accommodate a persecuted group of outsiders. The wells and soil of Yathrib could sustain its modest population, but there was no potential to produce significant individual or communal wealth. Matters of tribal honor and pique, rather than economic or cultural differences, ignited a conflict among Yathrib tribes in 616. Jews and Arabs participated on all sides of a sometimes violent squabbling that defied solution. This level of conflict persisted over a number of years.

In the year 620 seven residents of Yathrib talked with Muhammad when they were in Mecca performing their pilgrimage. They embraced Islam, and these seven Yathrib Muslims added five fellow townsmen the following year, to give that community a base of twelve Muslims. Muhammad sent a Muslim by the name of Musa'ab ibn 'Umayr to solidify the converts and proselytize in Yathrib. By 622 the Muslim community of seventy-five in Yathrib was close to the size of the Muslim communities in Mecca and Abyssinia.

Early in 622 Muhammad received an invitation from residents of Yathrib to live among them and arbitrate the differences that had led to constant unrest and some violence. Although Muhammad's success in Mecca had been marginal by most standards, the situation was worsening; people who resented his fracturing of their families and those who resented his attacks upon the status quo had decided to act collectively against him. Good evidence indicates that a group of Meccans was planning to assassinate Muhammad at the time he decided to accept the Yathrib invitation. His Muslim community *(umma)* secretly exited from Mecca in small groups to go to Yathrib in June 622, with little more than the clothes on their backs. They and their descendants would always enjoy special status within Islam as the *Emigrants* or *Companions* of the Prophet. They were always revered as the most reliable sources for accounts of what the Prophet did and said. The early Yathrib converts acquired almost equal status and obtained distinction as *Helpers* of the Prophet and the Meccan refugees.

Muhammad, Abu Bakr, and 'Ali did not immediately join the other Muslims on the *hijra,* or flight, to Yathrib. 'Ali remained in Mecca, while the two foremost leaders of Islam hid in a cave for three days before making their way north to Yathrib. Only a full appreciation of the emphasis upon family unity in Arabia allows comprehension of the efforts then made by some Meccans to repatriate the Muslims who chose to flee. The loss of people was equated to a loss of strength, and a large reward was even offered for the return of Muhammad to Mecca. Preservation of family strength was the principal reason that

Arabian society, like many others, customarily arranged marriages between cousins. Conflicts over normal family relations, such as those recorded in the Old Testament, had led to both temporary and enduring cleavages, but nothing like the unprecedented ideological challenge of Islam had ever before split Arabian families.

For Muhammad, the custom of affiliating with a family and obtaining full family rights added to the challenge of moving to Yathrib. Since his relocation was based on the assumption that his wisdom could help resolve the internecine conflicts among the families of the oasis, it was necessary for him to remain unaffiliated with any particular tribe. Muhammad, in fact, had blood kinship with the Khazraj tribe of Yathrib. His paternal great-grandmother, Selma, was from the Bani al-Najjar clan of that prominent tribe. Another relative, Asad ibn Zurara, not only was chief of the al-Najjar clan, but also had been one of the first Yathrib converts to Islam in 620. It is unclear, however, whether anyone outside the clan knew of Muhammad's kinship with the al-Najjar.

As those in Yathrib anticipated his arrival, Muhammad took special care to plan the first impressions he would make upon his new community. His three-day pause at Quba, just south of Yathrib, provided adequate time for word to spread that he might enter the oasis at any time. When he finally entered, he allowed everyone to see that he moved without the purpose of reaching any particular destination. He had decided to live where his camel stopped. There was plenty of open land in the agrarian setting of Yathrib, which was more a collection of adjacent agricultural settlements than a city. The guardian of the two orphan boys who owned the property where his camel stopped, in the compound of the al-Najjar, agreed to sell the land to the Prophet. There was plenty of land on which to construct a house and a mosque and accommodate his guests.

Muslims date the beginning of their religion from Muhammad's transfer to Yathrib. Therefore, 622 C.E. became the first year of the Islamic calendar because it represented such a major change in the status of Muslims. Meccan Muslims soon joined their fellow believers in Yathrib, as did the refugees living in Abyssinia shortly thereafter. The Prophet and his *umma* now had a solid base from which to operate, and Yathrib became known as Medina, the City of the Prophet.

Although the Muslim situation improved after the move to Yathrib, there was little reason to predict anything more than survival. The Prophet's possession of his own dwelling was unique among the Emigrants, most of whom lived with Yathrib hosts. They were unskilled in agriculture and owned no land to farm. The skills they did possess required capital they did not have. Also, some Yathrib residents resented the Muslims in general as intruders and

Muhammad in particular as an unwelcome meddler in their affairs. Consequently, Muhammad never trusted the sincerity of any significant element of the Yathrib population, even after they avowed conversion to Islam. Foremost among the "hypocrites" was 'Abdullah ibn Ubayy, who probably assumed that only the presence of Muhammad prevented him from being the most influential person in Yathrib. The tension increased when Muhammad became the chief of the al-Najjar clan once Asad ibn Zurara died, shortly after the *hijra*. The Muslims obviously needed their own source of wealth, and Muhammad needed to avoid becoming embroiled in petty Yathrib affairs.

RAIDING AND THE BATTLE OF BADR

Early in 623 the Muslims began to raid Meccan caravans. It is unclear whether they adopted this direct approach to improve their impecunious conditions or to accomplish some political goal. The failure of their early attempts at raiding Mecca's northernmost caravans reflected not only Muslim ineptitude but also, perhaps, an initial discomfort with raiding their families and former neighbors. This failure was also predictable for the mostly urban Muslims, who had ventured for the first time into the bedouin practice of raiding.

The Prophet, however, concluded that the raids had failed because the Meccans had received advanced warning of Muslim plans. As a remedy, Muhammad took the unusual precaution of giving the next raiding party sealed written orders, which they could not open until they were out of town and away from all nonparticipants. These orders instructed the Muslim raiders to fulfill an unusual task. Their mission was to go more than 250 miles south to Ta'if, south of Mecca, and disrupt Meccan trade with Ta'if. This approach was doubly provocative because the Prophet ordered the raid during the period of peace that customarily accompanied pilgrimage to Mecca. The surprise tactic succeeded all too well, as the attack on a caravan at Nakhla killed a Meccan.

No other early raid matched the success of Nakhla, however. While Meccans could conclude that Muhammad was the worst kind of outlaw, one who violated civilized restraints, they were not impressed with initial Muslim efforts at raiding. Nor did Muslim skill improve appreciably until the movement attracted more bedouin converts, who regarded raiding as a sport.

Despite earlier failures, Muhammad set out on March 8, 624, to raid the annual caravan from Syria to Mecca. The caravan of one thousand camels represented a large percentage of Mecca's annual trade. The Prophet planned to engage the caravan at the wells of Badr, about eighty miles southwest of Yathrib. His slightly more than three hundred men, composed of eighty-three Emi-

» MAP I «

The Heartland of Early Islam

grants and the rest Helpers, had seventy camels and two horses with which to confront the escort of the valuable caravan. This force probably represented the Muslims' entire military capacity.

Abu Sufyan ibn Harb, the leader of the caravan, learned of the Muslim threat and sent word to Mecca for reinforcements. Most of the able-bodied men in Mecca rushed to assist the caravan, which represented a significant investment for a majority of Meccan families. Close to one thousand Meccans moved toward Badr to protect the city's interests.

The caravan passed Badr and continued southward before the Muslims arrived. Although the caravan was out of danger, the Meccan force proceeded north and engaged the Muslims at the wells of Badr. The Muslims obtained and kept the initiative. Muhammad had positioned his forces to take advantage of the elements of nature; the Meccans had to look into the morning sun through a swirl of blowing dust and sand. The three Muslim champions, including 'Ali—the best champion the Muslims had for single combat—killed their opponents in one-on-one contests. When the Meccan forces fled the battlefield, they left approximately seventy dead and a similar number of prisoners. Years of frustration and resentment had impelled the Muslims to victory and revenge. Individuals, including Muhammad and his servant Bilal, had retaliated against old enemies, and some spiteful acts during the burial of the Meccan dead also reflected the bitterness and hatred that permeated the Muslims' relations with their polytheist families and neighbors.

The Battle of Badr, which involved only about fifteen hundred combatants, was a major military engagement for families unaccustomed to full-fledged war. Abu Jahal and most of the other leaders of Mecca, except Abu Sufyan, perished at Badr. By contrast the Muslims lost only fourteen, and their leadership remained intact. The Prophet's largely youthful following demonstrated great satisfaction following victory over their tormentors. Their zeal, born of a sense of moral superiority, injected fervor atypical of Arab armed confrontations of that time.

Tragic family cleavages abounded, as attested by the presence of one of Muhammad's sons-in-law among the prisoners. In addition, the daughter of Abu Sufyan, Mecca's most important leader, was a Muslim who had gone to Abyssinia with her husband. After her husband died, she returned to Yathrib and married Muhammad in 629, long before the Prophet and Abu Sufyan reconciled their differences.

This relatively small battle at Badr was one of the most important steps toward establishing Islam as a major force in the world. It helped validate Islam as a religion because believers and opponents alike could easily conclude that God alone could award such a decisive victory to the weaker Muslim force. Following Badr, every facet of Muslim life improved. Division of the booty, one fifth of which went to Muhammad, provided the formerly impecunious Muslims with some dignity and financial independence. The vital role of the Helpers in the battle proved their sincerity and worth. Also, bedouin, who gravitated toward successful and charismatic leaders, were more receptive to Muhammad's message following the success at Badr. If human factors were going to be important in the establishment of Islam, the marginal Muslim re-

sources obviously needed reinforcements to meet expected Meccan retaliation. The Muslims, therefore, needed to attract bedouin allies, just as the Meccans had cultivated them for many years to protect their caravans.

After Badr, Muhammad had his first opportunity to demonstrate his behavior in triumph over vanquished foes. Out of all his prisoners, he singled out
a few critics from Mecca and two poets from Yathrib for execution. His modest retaliation helped create a reputation which thereafter allowed his opponents to surrender without fear of annihilation.

AFTER BADR

Six months after Badr the Meccans suffered another devastating blow. They attempted to send their annual caravan to Syria in September 624 by an eastward
route through Nejd, rather than northward along the Red Sea coastal route.
Zayd, the Prophet's adopted son, led an expedition that captured the caravan
at Qarda.

The apparent all-out Muslim attack on Meccan trade threatened to doom
the city. Mecca's stark landscape precluded any other means of earning a living. Its very existence depended upon trade between Greater Syria to the
north and Yemen in the south. Cooperation from the tribes along this long
route of more than a thousand miles was essential. The tribes derived much of
their income from either protecting the trade or agreeing not to attack it.
Bedouin from time immemorial had raided each other on a small scale in pursuit of honor and to obtain women, slaves, livestock, and other possessions. In
several respects, the bedouin depended upon the safe transit of trade. The
Muslim frontal attack on trade was different from traditional Arabian raiding.
It represented a threat not only to the economy, but also to all kinds of relations among the urban and rural tribes of the region. Whatever the long-range
effects of this innovation might be, the short-range effects would include competition between Muslims and Meccans for loyalty among the rural tribes. The
fact that the first successful Muslim attack had occurred south of Mecca ensured that the conflict would not be limited to the region north of the city.

THE BATTLE OF UHUD

Meccans pooled their resources and raised an army of three thousand to destroy the Muslim threat in Yathrib. Under the command of Abu Sufyan, the
Meccans and their allies proceeded to Mount Uhud on the northwest outskirts

of Yathrib, where they could obtain easiest access to the city. The Prophet led about seven hundred men to confront the Meccan forces before they could enter the oasis. An additional disparity in their forces on March 23, 625, was the total absence of any Muslim horse cavalry to match Mecca's two hundred horsemen.

The confrontation began with the traditional praise and insults from the poets, the shrill, baleful yells of the women, and single contests—calculated to infuse each army with courage and zeal. An overwhelming victory of one side in such preliminary activities sometimes eliminated the need for battle. Although 'Ali and four other Muslim champions triumphed in single combat, they could not deter battle between two forces who had begun to understand that they were fighting to shape the course of the future.

As at Badr, the smaller Muslim force seized the initiative and forced the Meccans to yield ground. The Prophet's battle plan disintegrated, however, after some archers that he had placed strategically to counter the Meccan cavalry disobeyed his instructions and joined in pursuit of the retreating Meccan infantry. The Meccan cavalry maneuvered behind the Muslims and changed the course of the battle. Belief among some that Muhammad had already died in the battle also helped wilt the Muslim effort. The Prophet, indeed, lost a tooth and experienced blows which his helmet and armor deflected. He survived, but later had to explain how God, whom he had credited for victory at Badr, had allowed defeat at Uhud. The Meccans settled for victory on the field and did not attempt to eliminate the Muslims, who were in disarray and separated from their leaders. The Muslims suffered seventy-four deaths and inflicted twenty-two deaths upon the Meccans. Abu Sufyan promised to meet the Muslims the following year at Badr.

In March 626 Muhammad took fifteen hundred men to Badr to meet Abu Sufyan's challenge of the previous year. The Meccans did not show, but the Muslims' acceptance of the challenge demonstrated that they were not afraid. In fact, it allowed them to exhibit their numbers, which had doubled since the year before. It was also a good demonstration to the bedouin tribes that the Muslims were still vying for ascendancy.

The continued presence of the Muslims astride the northern Meccan trade routes prevented anything close to normal business in Mecca. Muslim posturing as powerful was an effective menace until the Meccans would call their bluff and send an army to confront them.

While the Muslims' new military force held the Meccans at bay, Muhammad pursued an active policy to win the support of the rural tribes. The Prophet, in fact, gained considerable stature by moving from place to place with small armies for the apparent purpose of raiding sundry foes. These forays, which involved very little actual conflict, gave Muhammad the opportunity to meet tribesmen in the region, who offered their hospitality and accepted his. In the course of his lifetime most of the bedouin he met allied with him and eventually professed to accept him as God's Messenger.

THE BATTLE OF THE DITCH

In March of 627 Meccans raised an army of ten thousand to deal with Yathrib and the Muslims. Their increased numbers were largely the result of additional alliances with bedouin tribes, foremost among whom were the Ghatafan and the Bani Kinana. The Muslim army had more than quadrupled in strength since Badr, reaching three thousand through conversions. The Muslims decided to dig a ditch in front of the houses on the perimeter of Yathrib as a defensive measure to compensate for their numerical weakness. Introduced by a Persian convert named Salman, this innovation in the warfare of that part of the Arabian peninsula made conventional fighting impossible. Some on both sides regarded "The Ditch" as an unmanly and unsporting dodge of the issue. It was effective, however, because the attacking Meccans had no means of breaching the walls or dealing with the ditch. They also had no capacity to sustain themselves for a prolonged period without access to the Yathrib oasis.

A month of siege ensued with only a few individual heroics to break the boredom, including 'Ali's killing of another man in single combat. Horses and camels needed more food and water than the besiegers could obtain. Also, the need to prepare for the pilgrimage season, accompanied by a traditional ban on violence, turned the attention of the Meccans southward. Abu Sufyan finally admitted there was no possibility for victory and returned to Mecca.

The Battle of the Ditch reduced the importance of the failure at Uhud. The Muslims had avoided defeat in the face of overwhelming odds. The Meccans, by contrast, had failed to win, although their numerical advantage was as large as they could expect at any time in the future. Success against an army of such unprecedented size, albeit a victory of tactics, enhanced Islam's appeal. Fascination with Muhammad attracted a flow of new chiefs to him. Few could resist his message, charm, gifts, and success. Expansion of the Prophet's movement in the hinterlands increased Mecca's isolation and further endangered its life-giving commerce.

RELATIONS WITH YATHRIB'S JEWS

Muhammad's attempt to be a prophet to all monotheists had to confront the challenge of the Yathrib Jews, who lived beside the developing Muslim movement. Some Yathrib Jews apparently enjoyed exposing discrepancies in Muhammad's accounts of Old Testament stories. They contended that a prophet must possess accurate knowledge of God's past actions to be entrusted with His future plans. Muhammad rejoined that Jews had a long tradition of altering history and rejecting prophets. Continued Jewish criticism of Muhammad's grasp of the monotheist tradition became even less acceptable to him after his success at the battle of Badr in 624. Consequently, he expelled the Bani Qaynuqa Jews to Syria and divided their wealth and property among the Emigrants. Their confiscated wealth provided the Meccan refugee Muslim community with some relief from their two years of total dependence upon their Yathrib hosts.

Muhammad's change in the direction of prayer *(qibla)* from Jerusalem to Mecca at this time was even more important than his expulsion of the Bani Qaynuqa Jews. His continued efforts to communicate with Jews indicated, however, that the expulsion had responded to a perceived problem with particular Jews rather than an impasse with all Jews. While the change of the *qibla* became permanent, it had the short-range effect of convincing Arab polytheists that Islam incorporated a pronounced reverence for and continuation of traditional Arabian religious practice.

Islam's increased appeal in Yathrib and the region led some Jews to perceive the movement as a threat to all Judaism in the area. In response to their resentment, Muhammad expelled the Bani al-Nadhir Jewish tribe in September 625, after accusing them of plotting his assassination. The confiscation of their fairly extensive lands again provided a pronounced improvement in the Emigrants' economic welfare.

Following the Battle of the Ditch in 627, the Prophet addressed the problem of the Bani Quraydha, the last remaining Jewish tribe in Yathrib. They had refused to participate in the defense of the city. Furthermore, the Muslims believed that the Bani Quraydha had intrigued with the expelled Jewish tribe of Bani al-Nadhir and the Meccans during the prolonged siege that had threatened to destroy the Muslims. The Prophet allowed a wounded and dying Muslim whose tribe had once enjoyed good relations with the Bani Quraydha to pronounce judgment. In compliance with his verdict, the Muslims executed the seven to eight hundred men of the condemned tribe.

Some Jews continued to live in Yathrib even after the Muslims expelled or executed the three main Jewish tribes. Jewish rejection of Muhammad's mission never altered his respect for them as monotheists. Throughout his life, Jews and Christians, as "People of the Book," enjoyed his protection unless they overtly opposed him and threatened his mission to the polytheists. The Prophet married a Jewish widow from the Bani Quraydha in 627, and a little more than a year later married another Jewish woman of the vanquished Khaybar tribe, who accepted him even though her father, brother, and husband had lost their lives to the Muslims.

CONQUEST BY PILGRIMAGE

Early in 628 Muhammad decided to perform the *umrah,* or lesser pilgrimage. Traditionally, no violence was supposed to occur during this period of formal pilgrimage. Approximately seven hundred lightly armed Muslims accompanied him. Lacking their full complement of arms, his contingent could not have fared well against a better-armed group of similar or greater size. The Muslims did not go entirely unarmed, however, because there was no way of predicting the Meccan response to the bold action that would place them in the heart of Mecca—the very city that had fielded ten thousand soldiers against them a year earlier at The Ditch.

The Meccans, in fact, alerted a sizable army and prepared to prevent the Muslims from entering their city. Muhammad paused near Mecca at Hudaybiyyah and allowed the Meccans to send a series of envoys to evaluate his intentions and strength. Clearly, neither side wished to fight. The Meccans expressed their discomfort with allowing a large Muslim group to enter Mecca and asked for a year to make preparations. In March 628 they negotiated the Treaty of Hudaybiyyah, which provided for a ten-year truce in their conflict. It allowed the Muslims to return for the next *umrah* pilgrimage. The agreement permitted both sides to ally with rural tribes, who would, in turn, comply with the terms of the treaty between the two principals. A provision that reflected Mecca's apparent advantage required the Muslims to return any Meccans who tried to join them. The treaty hardly seemed like a success to the Muslims as they returned to Yathrib.

But Meccans continued to convert, despite the restrictions of Hudaybiyyah. To comply with the treaty, a significant number of the men left Mecca and inhabited the countryside, raiding Meccan trade from outlying bases. Thus, the new converts did the work of Muhammad without being under his direct supervision. Moreover, after the Prophet received a revelation that Believers should not return women to unbelieving husbands, the Muslims refused to return newly converted women to Mecca. The Muslims did, however, monetarily compensate the former husbands for their losses.

Since the Treaty of Hudaybiyyah forbade or restricted Muslim activities to the south, the Prophet moved northward against three Jewish tribes in 628. The Jews at Khaybar, Fadak, and Wadi al-Qura were located seventy to eighty miles northeast of Yathrib. Khaybar was a prosperous agricultural center whose

Jewish population was closely allied to the Ghatafan Arab allies of the Meccans. The wealth of the Khaybar Jews and their sympathy for the Meccans provided adequate provocation for a campaign. After a prolonged siege, the beleaguered Jews yielded, retaining their lives and homes by pledging an annual payment of half their income to the Muslims. To avoid similar experiences, the Jews at Fadak and Wadi al-Qura also agreed to pay the Muslims half of their annual incomes.

Shortly after the surrender of the Jews, the Prophet and nearly two thousand Muslims performed the *umrah* at Mecca over a three-day period in February 629 while the Meccans abandoned their city to avoid conflict and fraternization. From this cooperation, Meccans and other polytheists could determine that the new religion did not threaten either the pilgrimage or the trade fairs associated with the Kaaba. Fear of economic repercussions from Islam declined, and non-Muslims could also observe that Islam embraced a large part of their traditional customs. Knowledge that Mecca, rather than Jerusalem, was the *qibla* for the Muslims must have assured many polytheists that Islam was truly based on Arab traditions and was not just a new form of Christianity or Judaism.

After the successful pilgrimage, the Prophet and his following seemed firmly established as the strongest political, military, and economic force in the Hejaz, and perhaps the strongest in the entire Arabian peninsula. Success accelerated converts to Islam. Khalid ibn al-Walid and Amir ibn al-As, two of Mecca's foremost military leaders, as well as 'Uthman ibn Talha, keeper of the keys to the Kaaba, joined the Muslim movement during the pilgrimage. The Prophet's uncle, 'Abbas (the progenitor of the Abbasid dynasty), who had remained a polytheist, reconciled with Muhammad during the pilgrimage. 'Abbas pursued a fairly safe course, remaining in Mecca, while others also positioned themselves to establish favorable relationships with Muhammad.

Indicative of Islam's new strength and vision, the Prophet sent envoys beyond the western part of Arabia to invite distant peoples to embrace Islam. An affront from the Bani Ghassan in southern Syria in response to an overture of submission to God's Messenger inspired a small Muslim campaign in September 629. A battle at Mota, near the modern Jordan town of Kerak, resulted in victory for the Bani Ghassan over an outnumbered Muslim force of three thousand. Among the sixteen Muslim dead were the expedition's leaders, Zayd ibn Haritha, the Prophet's adopted son, and the Prophet's nephew, Ja'far ibn Abu Talib, brother of 'Ali. The remote location of the Muslim defeat at Mota reduced its adverse effect upon the movement. Clearly, however, the expedition indicated Muhammad's intentions to expand beyond the Arabian peninsula.

Important as it was to expand Islam over a wider area, the spread of Islam within Mecca was even more crucial. Mecca was not only the birthplace of the

Prophet; astride the trade route from Yemen to Syria, it was also the center of talent, tradition, trade, finance, and learning for the entire Hejaz. Yemen at this time provided not only its own goods but also the products of eastern Asia and east-central Africa to many locations in the north.

Control of Mecca seemed essential to Islam. Following the successful pilgrimage early in 629 and the subsequent growth of Islam, the provisions of Hudaybiyyah became unacceptable to some of the Muslim community. For them, compliance with the treaty unnecessarily impeded Islam's new momentum for growth.

Conflict between a tribe allied with the Muslims and one allied with the Meccans altered the status quo and provided justification for the Muslims to move militarily against Mecca. On January 1, 630, the Prophet led an army of ten thousand against Mecca, and additional warriors joined them as the Muslims marched toward the holy city.

The Meccans decided not to offer any resistance in the face of the overwhelming Muslim force. A large percentage of the Meccan population had, in fact, already embraced the new religion. 'Abbas ibn 'Abd al-Muttalib and Abu Sufyan ibn Harb, the progenitors, respectively, of the Umayyad and Abbasid dynasties, intercepted the Muslims before they reached Mecca and negotiated the terms for the Muslims to enter Mecca virtually unopposed.

Thus, the orphan Muhammad, who had left Mecca in secret and under duress with about a hundred believers eight years earlier, returned amid great pageantry, endowed with the capacity to impose any conditions he wished upon the city of his birth. His impositions were few beyond the demand for a pledge of loyalty from every man and woman of Mecca, the expulsion of all idols from the Kaaba, and the execution of four persistent critics, two of whom were female entertainers. After establishing Muslim authority in Mecca, Muhammad returned to his family, property, and seat of power in Yathrib. Although he was born and reared in Mecca, he chose to live the remainder of his life in his adopted city, which changed its name to al-Medina, City of the Prophet.

ISLAM TRIUMPHANT

Muslim control of Mecca prevented the traditional polytheistic religious practice among the Arabs who had centered their worship on the Kaaba. Pilgrimage to the Kaaba and expression of reverence for its idols and the Black Stone seemed essential to validate the multifaceted polytheism and provide it unity. While there apparently was no belief that the panoply of gods could or should offer worshipers any type of afterlife, the entire spectrum of gods, from the smallest household idols to the Black Stone, was essential to provide protection in this life.

Muhammad, as the Messenger of God, had the mission of establishing the supremacy of the One God. Within a year after his triumph over Mecca, the Prophet forbade polytheists to perform the pilgrimage. The Prophet also declared his obligation to use force to convert polytheists to the worship of the One God. Jews and Christians, as believers, did not have to alter their worship, but each person was obligated to pay a one-dinar poll tax annually. Muslim converts also had to pay taxes to support the growing Islamic community *(umma)*. Financial obligations of the converts to their new overlord were both normal and essential to meet expenses. Also, in keeping with contemporary political relations among Arabian tribes and tribal alliances, the taxes were important not only as additional revenue but also as tribute and acknowledgment of the payers' submission to the Prophet and his God.

The steady growth of the Islamic community interjected a new and indomitable force into Arabian affairs. Each tribe normally obtained intertribal status commensurate with its numerical and military capacity. The kinship nature of tribes and the demographics of the time prevented significant sudden changes in tribal strength or status. Tribes customarily could improve their status only through alliances with other tribes. Normally, alliances were forged to meet mutual immediate needs and involved mercenary arrangements to achieve avaricious goals. Such alliances, therefore, were frequently mercurial. The uncommon enduring alliances usually reflected relationships between unequal partners.

The new Muslim force, by contrast, grew from the hundred or so who accompanied the Prophet to Yathrib in 622 to the ten thousand who marched on Mecca in 630. An additional two thousand converts shortly after the acquision of Mecca provided Muhammad with unprecedented power in numbers that did not rely upon traditional, transitory arrangements.

The large Islamic force gave every appearance of being permanent. The Muslims were united around an idea and a mission which transcended tribal identities and allegiances. Entire tribes followed the leadership of chiefs who pledged loyalty to God's Messenger. Individuals also continued to defy tribal loyalty and join the Prophet. No doubt, some such "conversions" lacked conviction and opportunistically allied tribes and individuals to Muhammad as a highly successful leader who provided honor and bounty. Traditionally, alliances of this nature dissolved with the death of the leader or a decline in his fortunes. A surprising percentage of Muhammad's allies, however, submitted themselves to him as their earthly leader and to the will of God. This *umma* became the force that swept everything before it.

The Prophet had vowed to rid the region of polytheism. While there are well-documented cases of individuals who incurred the wrath of Muhammad, he generally preferred to achieve his goals without using force. Given the customs of his times, however, success usually required force or the threat of force. Concomitantly, loyalty of the brave and honor-seeking Arab tribesmen usually required assurance that sufficient action could enforce all threats.

Muhammad had the opportunity to use major force against Arabs one final time when the Hawazin and Thaqif tribes defied his leadership and his message. Fortunately for him, the large army that had intimidated Mecca into submission was intact. The three-to-one numerical advantage of the Muslims brought them victory at the Battle of Hunayn just northeast of Mecca early in February 630. Soon after the battle, Malik ibn Auf, the chief of the Hawazin, announced his submission to God and his loyalty to Muhammad. The Thaqif, however, who owned the stronghold of Ta'if, stubbornly resisted conversion to Islam and demonstrated a commitment to the pagan goddess al-Lat that was uncharacteristic of most polytheists.

After returning to Medina, the Prophet led an expedition toward southern Syria in October 630 to meet a threatened attack from the Byzantines. The leisurely trek provided him opportunities to exhibit his strength and employ his diplomacy. Tribes in the region gravitated to him and swore their allegiance. By the time his expedition reached Tabuk, which is about 350 miles north of Medina, it became obvious that no Byzantine forces threatened the region. This, like the expedition to Mota the previous autumn, indicated the Prophet's interest in expanding his influence northward. Knowledge of his achievements spread beyond his physical location by the efficient methods of intertribal communication. In fact, emissaries from as far north as the predominantly Christian town of Aqaba negotiated a pact that put them under Muslim protection after they agreed to pay a poll tax. With a show of force and a penchant for diplomacy, Muhammad extended his control almost six hundred miles to the northwesternmost corner of the Arabian peninsula during October 630.

Muhammad controlled the Hejaz. During a ten-month period in 630 he extended his control south to Mecca and north to Aqaba. No adjacent population center or regional leader could match his resources. Trade of any kind between Syria and Yemen required the consent of the Muslims because they dominated the strategic lands in between.

Its strong base and strategic location helped Islam spread very rapidly in 631. Even Ta'if, which had been more obdurate in accepting Islam than any other part of the Hejaz, submitted to the Prophet in the spring of that year. Throughout the year delegations arrived in Medina from all over Arabia. Bani Temim and Bani Hanifa delegations from the Nejd region; Bani Ta'i from the Nefud; Zubayd, Bajila, Himyar and lesser tribes from Yemen; Kinda from the

Hadraumaut—all sent expressions of alliance and requested instruction in Islam. In keeping with the policy the Prophet had instigated with the Jews in Khaybar in 628, the numerous Jews and Christians in Yemen retained their ways of life in return for payment of a poll tax.

Whether acceptance of Muhammad's leadership was politically or religiously motivated, Islam, the new monotheism, endorsed a unity of all on earth to match the unity of the One God. According to the new teaching, there could be no separation of religion from everything else. The will of God should prevail in all realms. In compliance with this approach, the sincerest and most hypocritical Muslims alike owed immediate allegiance to God, to God's Word (the Qur'an), and to God's Messenger.

The Prophet performed the *hajj* ("pilgrimage") in March 632. Although he was only sixty-two years old, there was an air of finality at the end of his long sermon to his believers. His apparent good health and the increased veneration many had for him did not hint of death; however, the Prophet died in June in the quarters of Aishah, his favorite wife, after a short illness which had not seemed life threatening.

The question of succession had never arisen during his life for several understandable reasons. First, he generally enjoyed good health. Second, his leadership of a viable and effective following had lasted only ten years. Third, the preponderance of Islamic expansion had occurred over the last three years of his life. Dramatically, Islam had spread as a new movement with no sense of the mortality of its earthly founder. Although he had emphasized his humanity, some believers had deified the Prophet and had thus ruled out the possibility of his death. From a practical point of view, it would probably have been unwise to address the question of his death and succession, considering that it was only in the final two years of his life that the movement had seemed indomitable.

The fabric of Islam seemed almost too weak to withstand the Prophet's death. Nothing in the Arab past portended unity. In fact, the Arab experience was full of individual pride and tribal loyalty. Intense tribal loyalty, almost by definition, led to tribal rivalries. Intertribal wars of near infinite memory permeated tribal relations, although the Prophet had decreed that Muslims were to give up blood feuds. Most Muslims were very recent converts. Muhammad had enjoyed the mantle of prophecy for only twenty-two years. For twelve of those years, in Mecca, he had suffered derision and obtained very few converts. Most "Muslims" had never met Muhammad, and many had little foundation for absorbing anything close to the fullness of his teachings. A large percentage of the converted were too new to have received instruction on Islamic belief and practice. For many reasons, therefore, the death of Muhammad seemed to signal the demise of Islam.

The Prophet's closest associates believed in the authenticity of his prophecy and rallied to continue his mission. Understandably, even those close to Muhammad were in despair when they heard of his death. The Prophet's oldest friend—and one of his earliest converts—asserted himself to explain their leader's sudden and unexpected departure. These oft-quoted words attributed to Abu Bakr help explain Islam's endurance: "O Men, if anyone worships Muhammad, let him know now that Muhammad is dead. But if anyone worships God, let him know that God is alive and immortal for ever."

Abu Bakr obtained the role of leadership at this crucial juncture in the development of Islam. His elderly status, his prolonged and close association with the Prophet, and the fact that God's Messenger had insisted that Abu Bakr lead the prayers when the former was sick provided sufficient justification to proclaim him Caliph, or successor to the Prophet.

ISLAMIC BELIEF
AND PRACTICE

Islam's emphasis upon faith and behavior reflects its lack of sacraments and ritual. The invisibility of faith prevents all but the professed believer and God from judging sincerity of belief. And while behavior is more readily discernible, proper outward behavior has no validity without sincere faith. In general, Muslims must earn salvation through living their faith in their daily lives, rather than through some cathartic process, spontaneous revelation, or intercession from earthly or heavenly helpers. This emphasis might lead to the conclusion that Islamic doctrine must consist of a body of regulations for the behavior of its adherents. But, contrary to widespread belief, Islamic doctrine does not directly address vast portions of human activity. While practicing Muslims are expected always to think and behave in a manner compatible with direct religious teachings, individual believers must rely on their own judgment, prevailing custom, and guidance from respected leaders to govern much of their lives.

A spectrum of permissibility has characterized Islam from the earliest times, with a small number of obligations at one end and a small number of forbidden activities at the other. There was never any doubt, however, that a significant number of "recommended" activities bore something close to obligatory status for Muslims. Likewise, doctrine did not forbid—but did label as "reprehensible"—numerous activities that were therefore very close to the "forbidden" end of the spectrum. Most human activities lay somewhere between the two poles and allowed individuality of style and approach, which permitted groups and individuals to create singular yet legitimate Islamic practices.

While this absence of direction intrinsically provided flexibility to Islam, local practice sometimes became entrenched and assumed the authority of doctrine. Prevailing practice in a limited area often became accepted there as an authentic, universal standard. Such attitudes have in places led to rigidity and intolerance toward Muslims of different views as well as toward non-Muslims. Assumption of the guise of orthodoxy allowed—even impelled—behavior among Muslims contrary to the spirit of the religion. Such behavior is understandable since most believers presumed that the religious practice of their locality was the genuine, if not the only, Islam. The dominance of local custom veiled the reality that, while Islamic doctrine demanded the performance of a few specific acts and forbade the performance of a few specific acts, it allowed believers to determine their fate so long as they lived according to general Islamic guidance.

THE FIVE PILLARS

Even the most individualistic Muslims must practice their religion within the framework of five obligatory duties, which are commonly called the Five Pillars of Islam. Reliable *hadith*[1] quote the Prophet Muhammad as saying, "Islam has been built upon five things." Accordingly, all Muslims are expected to (1) profess their faith *(shahadah)* at all times; (2) perform five daily prayers *(salat)*; (3) annually contribute alms *(zakat)*; (4) annually perform a thirty-day fast *(siyam)*; and (5) make at least one pilgrimage *(hajj)* to Mecca during the believer's lifetime. Muslims could meet the minimal demands of all of these duties except the *hajj* with a modest effort. It would be misleading, however, to imply that all Muslims limit their practice to the minimum or that all Muslims fulfill all duties.

Profession of Faith

Acceptance of Islam begins with the profession of faith and has no meaning without it. Believers state, simply, "There is no god but God and Muhammad is His Prophet."[2] The seemingly unnecessary length of this *shahadah* indicates that it emerged after the concept of more than one deity existed. It also addressed any confusion relating to the possibility that God could assume human form. It clarified any doubt regarding Muhammad's mission in behalf of the One and Only God, while it exposed the error of belief in gods that uninformed minds created with their imagination. The prevalence of polytheism required the accompanying disclaimer rather than the bold monotheistic message of Islam that "Muhammad is the Messenger of God."

Within the main body of Muslims, belief in God and willingness to profess that belief constitute the one incontrovertible duty.[3] Conversely, the unwillingness to acknowledge belief in God constitutes *shirking,* the one unforgivable transgression of God's law. Acceptance of Muhammad is also essential to distinguish Islam from Judaism and Christianity, as preexisting and errant monotheistic religions, although Muhammad was generally tolerant and indulgent of those religions and always afforded them special status as People of the Book.

According to Islam, Muhammad came to mend and revise earlier teaching and to expunge deviant practice. He was God's vessel for revealing not only His latest word but His Last Word. Muhammad was the Seal of the Prophets, meaning that he represented God's final attempt to convey His wishes to His human creations, who repeatedly strayed from His instructions. Muhammad's acknowledgment of the validity of the Old Testament prophets, and of Jesus as a prophet, amply indicates his commitment to and association with mainstream monotheism. But one gets the impression that Muhammad strove to spread the simple obedience of Abraham to God's will, rather than the juristic approach of Moses, the humanist approach of Jesus, or that of any of the prophets in between. However he might resemble or differ from the other prophets, there was no doubt that Muhammad was unique in more than time and place: he was also an inseparable part of Islam. It was unthinkable for God's new message to be valid unless Muhammad was genuinely God's Messenger.

Prayer

Formal Islamic worships centers on five daily prayers, which are scheduled for daybreak, noon, mid-afternoon, sunset, and night. This frequency of prayer does not dampen the ardor of sincere Muslims. On every occasion of prayer, Muslims realize they are communicating with God, before Whom they bow in awe. No amount of repetition can diminish God's majesty or engender anything approximating casual familiarity. In fact, believers must prepare themselves for each prayer with an outward cleansing of their body that symbolizes a more important spiritual purification. Ideally, mosques provide clean, running water to enable worshipers to perform their ablutions; however, the absence of running water or any other kind of water does not prevent the performance of a worshipful ablution. The fact that worshipers are permitted to cleanse themselves with unpolluted sand or soil is the clearest indication that the emphasis is upon spiritual rather than physical purification. Real or imaginary water must pass over all parts of the head, neck, hands and arms up to the elbows, and the feet and legs up to the knees in preparation for prayer.

While it is ideal for worshipers to pray in mosques, prayer elsewhere is not only acceptable but expected. Obviously, believers often spend much of the day and night at considerable distance from any mosque and also have duties that do not allow them to be away for prolonged periods of time. Worshipers are nevertheless supposed to fulfill specific requirements wherever they pray. They align themselves with the *qibla,* which is easy enough in any mosque that contains a *mihrab* indicating the direction to Mecca. A *mihrab* can be as simple as a single, differently colored tile or as elaborate as the ornate constructions that accompany the world's grandest mosques. Worshipers use a carpet, a piece of fabric, or even some leaves to provide a special surface upon which to pray. Even crude and not so clean accouterments of prayer serve to remind them of the extraordinary importance of prayer. All worshipers must remove their shoes before entering a mosque and make the first step into a mosque with the right foot.

A strong and bold announcement of the time for prayer has been a part of Islam since the earliest days, when the first *mu'adhdhin,* or muezzin[4]—Muhammad's Abyssinian servant, Bilal—called the first Muslims to prayer. Nothing seems more singular to Western consciousness or more typical of a Muslim community than the *mu'adhdhin*'s sonorous elongation of each word of the invitation to prayer from atop a *minaret.*[5] The calls near sunrise, at sunset, and in the middle of the night have a special poignancy in the near or total darkness. In large cities the almost plaintive sounds seem to echo from one neighborhood to another as the various *mu'adhdhin* call the faithful to their duties at almost the same time and in almost the same way. The symphonic merging of one *Allahu akhbar* ("God is great") with an adjacent proclamation, "I testify that there is no god but God," while a nearby *mu'adhdhin* is saying "I testify that Muhammad is the Messenger of God," provides a verbal expression of the unity of Islam and God. At slightly different times all the calls end with "Come to prayer," "Come to security," and an operatic *Allahu akhbar* to provide the impression of a single musical performance that announces to God in the Heavens that the multitudes are awake and about to prostrate themselves in praise for Him.

Worshipers within a mosque or in a group praying elsewhere follow the leadership of an imam. This is not a clerical position, as mainstream Islam professes to have no clergy. The vast majority of the world's mosques are, in fact, tiny neighborhood facilities which do not need, and could not provide a livelihood for, anyone involved in full-time religious activities. Since it is a distinction to serve as the imam, however, men of special esteem and influence usually fulfill the duties.

While each circumstance provides some uniqueness, Muslim prayer is remarkably the same in all places. Worshipers usually engage in some personal devotions when they arrive for prayer, while awaiting the assembly of others. In most cases their preliminary worship will be at least in part the same as the later collective worship. Virtually all individual or collective prayer includes a recitation of the first chapter *(sura)* of the Holy Qur'an, called the *Fatihah,* which is the most widely known passage of the Islamic holy book. Emphasis on the praise for God in the *Fatihah* exemplifies the nature of Islamic worship:

> In the name of God, the Merciful, the Compassionate.
> Praise belongs to God, the Lord of all Being,
> > the Merciful, the Compassionate,
> > the Master of the Day of Judgment.
> Thee only we worship, and Thee only we ask for help.
> Guide us in the Straight Path,
> The Path of those whom Thou has blessed,
> Not the path of those who incur Thine anger,
> Nor of those who go astray.[6]

Beginning in a standing position, Muslim worshipers drop to a kneeling position and proceed from there to as many as four prostrations. Each sequence that results in prostrate worshipers on hands and knees with forehead and nose against the ground or floor is a *raka.* Each move is deliberate and accompanied by phrases of prayerful praise to God or recitation from the Holy Qur'an. Most prayers will repeat the *Fatihah* after the last *raka* and end with each worshiper looking over the right shoulder and saying, "Peace be on you and the mercy of God," then turning to repeat the same blessing over the left shoulder.

While working and sleeping habits of believers create variety in the other thirty-four weekly prayers, the Friday noon prayer has more uniformity. All Muslims are required to worship at a mosque with fellow believers at the Friday noon prayer. The assemblies for such prayers are therefore much larger, in part because people who neglect other prayers congregate with their fellow believers at this time. On these occasions the imam, or perhaps a specialist, will publicly recite passages from the Holy Qur'an in a rhythmic fashion that many would call chanting. The lyrical presentation reflects a literary style similar to that used with the Torah. The entire prayer is usually longer on Fridays because of additional *rakas,* prayers, and Qur'anic recitations. In addition, the imam must deliver a sermon *(khutba)* that traditionally includes a favorable comment about the head of government. Failure to do so, or derogatory comments, can cause conflict. On this one day the imam mounts to the pulpit *(minbar),* which consists of a set of steps with a platform at the top. Passages from the Holy Qur'an and/or selections from the *hadith* supply the text for the sermon that the imam relates to some contemporary issue. Islam's permeation into every aspect of life means that no issue need be excluded as a possible topic for the sermon.

All of these factors help explain why the time immediately following the

Friday noon prayer is often especially important. A sermon in the mosque or the mere assembly of like-minded people sometimes inspires demonstrations or other expressions of political, social, and economic concerns. Traditionally, the large assembly provides the perfect audience to witness punishments handed down by Islamic courts on the assumption that public punishment and embarrassment are major deterrents to misbehavior.

While in the past believers usually returned to their normal duties after the Friday noon prayer, in recent years in some parts of the Islamic world, the entire day and Saturday have increasingly taken on an identity close to the Western concept of a weekend.

Alms Giving

Islam embraced the long-standing Arab custom of generosity but redirected it toward care for the needy and away from acts of excessive self-aggrandizement. Admonitions in the Holy Qur'an and *hadith* which implored Muslims not to deprive their families through lavish munificence addressed the Arab tradition of sharing. The concomitant Arab opprobrium toward stinginess facilitated the development of a sense of community responsibility for the welfare of all believers. Many of the earliest Muslims, after all, lost the customary support from their tribes and families when they espoused Islam. The early Islamic movement experienced conflicts that produced many widows and orphans, and in time it also acquired the normal proportion of elderly, blind, crippled, and otherwise dependent individuals. While the Holy Qur'an mentions such needs, it also justifies using alms for obtaining converts, caring for travelers, and freeing slaves, hostages, and debtors.[7] In short, the obligatory alms *(zakat)* provide the revenues of each *umma*. The rate of 2.5 percent of a believer's net worth annually is a modest levy that most can bear without difficulty, but the Holy Qur'an recognizes that some will be unable to contribute anything but their faith and services.[8] Islam also encourages additional contributions *(sadakat)* from believers with the promise that " . . . it will be doubled for them, and theirs will be a rich reward."[9] *Sadakat* contributions have enabled Islamic communities to establish both grand and modest mosques, schools, hospitals, and other institutions of social and cultural importance.

Ramadan Fast

Fasting during the month of Ramadan is one of the five things every Muslim must do. This ninth month, like all other months of the Islamic lunar calendar, will occur in every season of the year during the lifetime of most mature Muslims, because the length of time between the new moon and the full moon of the twelve lunar months does not correspond to the 365 days required for the earth to revolve around the sun.

Long summer days in hot climates inflict extraordinary demands upon fasting Muslims during Ramadan, but spiritual demands in any weather and climate are a real test of commitment to the fast. Lack of emphasis upon the spiritual and aesthetic elements of the fast frequently causes even well-meaning Muslims to keep some of the form while ignoring the substance.

Keeping the fast requires a commitment to reading or listening to reading of the Holy Qur'an for extended periods, additional prayer and meditation, exhibiting faultless behavior, having pure thoughts, and banishing such feelings as lust, envy, or greed. In addition, during the approximately thirty days of Ramadan fasting, believers are not to drink, eat, smoke, or engage in sexual activity from the time they can see a white thread of daylight in the morning until they can no longer see it at dusk.[10] Muslims who might suffer damage to their health are exempt from the physical part of fasting. The very old, the very young, the sick, travelers, and soldiers at war or fulfilling demanding duties can desist from fasting. If their status should change, however, the latter three are expected to fast for some thirty-day period during the year.

The entire experience of fasting is a time for renewal which emphasizes recommitment to service to God and all of His creation, including fellow humans. While the overtly religious aspects of the fast obviously serve this purpose, the religious value of physical deprivation is less discernible; however, the restraints upon nourishment and physical pleasure are supposed to make believers aware of the simple pleasures of life which they often take for granted. People who normally experience little discomfort can, during the days of fasting, feel hunger pains, become thirsty, and feel the urge to pursue pleasures customarily available to them. Fasting believers can choose to obey the dictates of Islam or to relieve their discomfort and trust the "Merciful and Compassionate" God to forgive the transgression sometime before Judgment Day. Perceptive believers, especially those with proper guidance, will realize that many fellow humans suffer real pain and deprivation of life's basic needs virtually every day of their lives, and that the pain and torment of the truly needy do not result from a religious exercise that will end at sunset. These realizations should move believers to feel a more profound gratitude to God for their good fortune. In addition, the fasting experience should induce a more willing payment of *zakat,* which communities usually collect at the end of the Ramadan fast. This is also frequently the time when people of wealth, power, and influence bestow their largess upon their families, neighbors, employees, and the less fortunate. Their *sadakat* of money, food, clothes, and other gifts impresses others, confirms their importance, and, according to Islam, pleases God when their intentions are charitable instead of vain.

Compliance with the Ramadan fast has always varied with time and place. Few Islamic societies have had the capacity or the desire to enforce even the most outward manifestations of the fast; however, most predominantly Islamic societies have statutes or customs that encourage the physical restraints of this intrinsically personal obligation. Almost all Islamic areas experience a major decline in production during Ramadan, and in some places work virtually ceases. Extensive visiting among family and friends and the preparation of special foods to break the fast can easily lead to a practice in which some communities virtually reverse the activities of day and night to sleep much of the day in order to enjoy themselves after sunset. The custom of exchanging small gifts and acquiring fine clothes and other non-necessities develops into a festive atmosphere for the Ramadan feast *(Id al-Fitr)*, which is one of the two major feasts of Islam. The elaborate celebration is special, even for those who refrained from fasting, whether through permissible exemption or apostasy. The feast diminishes regrets of any inconveniences from the fast, while it engenders anticipation of beginning to fast again in eleven months.

Pilgrimage to Mecca

Distinctive as they are to Islam, the four obligations listed above bear considerable similarity to practices of other religions. There is, however, no confusing a fifth Islamic duty—the pilgrimage to Mecca—with those of other major religions. Granted, most religions have shrines of particular appeal, some of which venerate sites of miracles and even provide miracles for pilgrims. Pilgrims of other religions, however, generally undertake their pilgrimages as a matter of choice or to fulfill an ecclesiastical or self-imposed penance. All Muslims *must* fulfill the *hajj* if they are physically and financially capable of doing so. Since most are aware of this obligation from early in life, part of their religious responsibility is to work and plan to make the *hajj,* rather than leave it to chance that their finances and health will permit them to fulfill this duty.

Islamic doctrine makes a persuasive case for this practice, even though it imposes an unusual hardship upon Muslims. Muslims believe that Adam, the first human, built the first shrine to God on the site of the Kaaba. They further believe that Ibrahim (Abraham) and his son Isma'il rebuilt Adam's temple on the location of the present Kaaba. Since all religion and worship thus began in Mecca, all believers should worship there to acquire its special aura.

Until the second half of the twentieth century, obstacles to performing the *hajj* were so overwhelming that the vast majority of Muslims, including those within a few hundred miles of Mecca, had to view it as a wish rather than as an obligation. Virtually no one overtly expressed such a conclusion, because it contradicted a central Islamic doctrine. Common sense confirms the observation, however, to explain why millions of sincere Muslims did not become insane with grief when they realized that circumstances in the world, the region, and their own lives made the pilgrimage impossible. War, brigandage, piracy, plague, villainy, bigotry, poverty, distance, bad roads, no roads, unsafe seas, family obligations, military service, broken bodies, and sick dependents were among the both blatant and imponderable reasons why most Muslims never performed this duty. Many of those who tried to go never made it to Mecca, and many who got there never returned to their place of origin. The obstacles that made fulfillment of this duty impossible tested the faith of those who believed the major tenet of Islam: "God does not expect more than His people can do."

Mecca is always holy, and theoretically Muslims can obtain permission to worship there at any time, but a period from the eighth to the thirteenth day of the twelfth month *(Dhu al-Hajja)* is the only time for performing the *hajj*. Pilgrims should prepare themselves spiritually for this experience and settle all their debts and disputes, plus establish a sound financial base for their dependents, before beginning the journey to Mecca. Pilgrims who prepare properly and possess a penitent attitude will be free from sin following the pilgrimage. They acquire the title of *hajji* and bear the responsibility of living exemplary lives.

The increased financial and logistical support that the Saudi Arabian government began to provide in the 1970s facilitated performance of the pilgrimage, but produced new challenges. By the 1990s approximately two million people were descending upon Mecca each *hajj* season, all requiring visas and the various accommodations and services occasioned by their visit. As the Saudi government assumed much of the expense of facilitating the *hajj*, the logistical demands became almost as challenging for that government as other concerns had been in the past, when few pilgrims could get there and when the Saudis counted on every pilgrim to add to their meager revenues. The monumental task of providing transportation, food, water, hygiene, sleeping arrangements, waste disposal, and all the special services related to the *hajj*, including ritual slaughtering of animals, defies description. Duties for the pilgrims, however, have not changed since the earliest days of Islam.

The equality of all before God is a major theme of the pilgrimage, even though the size of the multitude emphasizes the diminutive stature of each individual and the magnitude of God. Men wear two single unsewn pieces of white fabric *(ihram)*, a costume that destroys any differentiation of rank or wealth among them. During the course of the pilgrimage, most shave their heads, which provides even greater uniformity to the assembled masses from every race and continent, and almost every nation. Although there are no prescribed garments for women, concerns for modesty require that they be fully covered except for their faces, hands, and feet. A large percentage of the women wear a white gown and scarf. Female pilgrims from societies that require veiling are permitted to perform the *hajj* unveiled.

Repetition of the short pilgrim song "Here I am, O God" from the time they approach Mecca reflects pilgrims' belief that God has expected to see each of them in Mecca some day. Most pilgrims go straight to the Grand Mosque, which accommodates close to half a million people, and proceed to circumambulate the Kaaba seven times in a counterclockwise direction, just as Abraham did. Each *hajj* season the Kaaba receives a new covering *(kiswa)*,[11] which is a specially woven black fabric decorated with Qur'anic verses in gold and white thread. All pilgrims attempt to work their way to the wall of the Kaaba and kiss the Black Stone that Gabriel gave to Abraham. The multitude participate in prayers in the only place on earth where the *qibla* requires worshipers to form concentric circles instead of straight parallel lines. This is another indication of the special quality of Mecca, where Muhammad walked and talked and where humans first worshipped the One God.

Just as the *hajj* occurs at a prescribed time of year, pilgrim activities follow a prescribed schedule. After the initial prayer at the Grand Mosque, pilgrims spend their first night of the *hajj* in prayer and meditation at Mina, a town about five miles south of Mecca which is unoccupied the rest of the year. Even so, Mina's housing is limited and can accommodate only a small percentage of the pilgrims; the rest obtain shelter in the huge tent city that the government provides. The following day, pilgrims proceed another ten miles south to the Plain of Arafat and the Mount of Mercy to commemorate Muhammad's last sermon during his farewell pilgrimage. Prayers and a rendering of the Prophet's final sermon occupy some of the time, but most pilgrims spend much of the day in private meditation, a ritual referred to as "the standing" *(wuquf)*. In this observation, they repeat the experience of those who heard the Prophet's last sermon, which emphasized that Muslims in all times and places constitute one community *(umma)*. At the end of the day pilgrims collect stones at Muzdalifah to throw the following day at the three masonry pillars at Mina, which represent the Devil and his two helpers who tempted Abraham to disobey God's command to sacrifice Isma'il. The stoning signifies the pilgrims' willingness to make any sacrifice for God. Pilgrims sacrifice sheep, goats, or camels to symbolize God's granting relief to Abraham through a similar substitution.[12] Muslims throughout the world join the pilgrims in this three-day feast, which is the largest of the Islamic year *(Id al-Adha)*.

The huge multitudes, the differences in the stamina of individual pilgrims, and numerous other factors dictate that parts of the *hajj* occur at the pilgrim's discretion. After the feast, all will attempt to circle the Kaaba seven times again and touch or salute the Black Stone. Each pilgrim will attempt to spend some time in the spot within the Grand Mosque where Abraham prayed, and to run seven times between the hills of Safa and Marwa to emulate Hagar's panicked search for water for herself and Isma'il after Abraham banished them to the wilderness to satisfy Sarah. Pilgrims drink from the Zamzam well that Gabriel discovered to relieve their plight. Most will return to Mina and once again stone the pillars that symbolize the Devil. A journey to Medina and worship at the Prophet's Mosque are not part of the *hajj*, but many pilgrims manage to include these desirable activities as an extra blessing. Muslims who make the *hajj* fulfill a duty that most Muslims never achieve, and they invariably regard it as the highlight of their lives.

Muslims who can perform the *hajj* should have no difficulty fulfilling all five obligations to their faith. These duties, however, do not occupy a major portion of believers' time, and they do not directly touch upon great portions of believers' activities. Any believer who lives under the guiding spirit of the Five Pillars will avoid all forbidden behavior and, with guidance from the Holy Qur'an, *hadith,* and the *shari'a* (Islamic law), will live an Islamic life.

THE ROLE OF LAW

The simple religion which Muhammad received and practiced changed as time passed and the religion spread. For numerous reasons it soon became impossible to make a categorical statement of "Muslim belief." New influences from the myriad civilizations Islam encountered altered Islamic practice regionally, in differing degrees. Families, tribes, and nations imposed their proclivities upon Islam. Early deviations by a few in the religious community managed to endure and obtain legitimacy through longevity. (Extensive treatment of deviations from mainstream practice lies beyond the scope of this work.)

All Islamic belief and practice must center on the Qur'an as the word of God, the *sunna* as accounts of the life of the Prophet of God, and the *shari'a* as the law of God. The centrality of God, to which all else is subservient, essentially defines *Islam,* which means submission to the will of God. One who submits to God's will is a *Muslim.* God's revealed words and the life of His Prophet constitute the foundation of His law. Obedience to God's law is the primary manifestation of submission and a guarantee to enter Paradise. Conversely, the violation of God's law puts transgressors at His mercy and raises the possibility of eternal damnation in the fires of Hell. Islam requires belief in the reality of Paradise and Hell. Good behavior to humans, animals, and the natural world are legal duties to God, rather than ethical conduct believers owe to the society in which they live. Human law and God's law, therefore, should be the same.

The Holy Qur'an

Muslims believe that the Holy Qur'an,[13] which God revealed to Muhammad intermittently from the time he was called to prophecy in 610 until he died in 632, is a replica of the original Qur'an in Heaven. God speaks directly in the first person in the Qur'an, whereas in the Hebrew and Christian scriptures others relay the message of God and the behavior of His prophets. This message from God is in Arabic. Muslims do not regard translations into other languages as authentic because of the impossibility of conveying exact meaning from one language to another. In the view of Muslims, therefore, translations are at best interpretations or commentaries. All acknowledge that the names of chapters and their arrangement from longest to shortest result from human activities. This fairly small book, which is comparable in size to the New Testament, is arranged in 114 *suras,* or chapters.

Muslims regard the language of the Qur'an as extraordinary beyond emulation. The Prophet observed that the Qur'an was his only miracle, since nothing else could explain how something so divine in content and literary beauty could come from a humble, illiterate man like himself. There was a marked difference between his language for conducting his ordinary affairs and the language he uttered as the instrument of God's revelation. Muhammad, who could neither read nor write, recited his revelations to companions, who in turn committed them to memory. While some companions transcribed sundry passages on objects such as stones, bones, and palm leaves, believers preserved the corpus of the Qur'an by memory throughout most of the first generation. The prodigious capacity for memorization Arabs had developed for centuries to perpetuate their poetry helps explain why such talent was available. The quasipoetic style of the Qur'an and the practice of chanting it aloud also lightened the task. The Prophet's insistence on reciting the Qur'an slowly became customary, as did his practice of reciting it in no fewer than three days. Seven different acceptable ways of reciting the Qur'an developed, but all are variations on the simplest reading to ensure the exact sound and meaning of each letter and pronunciation mark. The most highly skilled and best trained chanters produce lyrical, operatic reverberations which can move even the hardest souls.

'Uthman, the Third Caliph (644 to 656), commissioned the official written version. Down through the ages, believers have striven to embellish the pages and binding of this unchangeable sacred text in the most beautiful fashion possible. Islam's prohibition against depicting humans, animals, or plants in a zealous avoidance of idolatry inspired the extraordinary use of calligraphy, colors, geometric figures, and precious stones and metals. Just as art has embellished the written Qur'an, passages from the Qur'an have embellished art. Frequently the only art on display in Muslim homes, offices, or public buildings consists of framed passages from the Qur'an. The depiction can vary from simple and inexpensive to elaborate and costly beyond expression. Some of the most phenomenally complex decorative designs in Islamic buildings are passages from the Qur'an which only the practiced eye can detect and the even more practiced eye can read. Even the illiterate often find comfort during dire sickness from drinking the water used to dissolve Qur'anic passages written in ink on a saucer. Believers count among their most prized possessions whatever part of the holy writ they know.

This revealed word of God requires special handling. Readers or reciters must be ritually clean and must align themselves with the *qibla* when reading from the Qur'an. Readers are expected to turn each page, even if they are reciting by memory. One must never eat, drink, or smoke while handling or reading the Qur'an. No object should ever be placed upon it, nor should it be put in situations which might subject it to desecration. These stipulations express reverence for the revealed word of God as an instrument to use in worship, rather than an object to worship. Sophist arguments among rival Islamic intellectuals about the origin and nature of the Qur'an have never swayed the masses of the faithful from their conviction that it is the word of God. That confidence ensures compliance with regulations for handling the Qur'an.

Any brief commentary on the *Qur'an* is inadequate and misleading. The dominant single theme is the demand for obedience to God. While the many attributes of God, including ninety-nine different names for Him, receive attention, "Compassionate and Merciful" receives greatest emphasis. God promises great reward for the righteous, but He also acknowledges that Satan provides strong appeal. In juxtaposition to the steady exhortation to do God's will is the frequent assurance that God forgives all but the most vile behavior. There is a strong implication that believers with weaker constitutions, in particular, can take comfort that God does not expect more than they can do. In short, while the demands are heavy, they are neither impossible nor unbearable.

The frequent reference to God as omnipotent raises the question of whether His human creations have free will. Reference to the Qur'an cannot answer this question because almost as many passages imply that humans control their fates as imply that God controls every aspect of life. The Mu'tazila theological movement in Baghdad in the early ninth century countered a strong prevailing tendency to attribute everything, including sin, to God's will. While their efforts to infuse Islam with the controversial philosophical and theological issues which divided Christianity failed to gain widespread approval, they succeeded in emphasizing the concept of a God who was indulgent of human frailties. Ultimately, the overriding evidence points to free will, however, since the Qur'an clearly states that each person's Book of Life, which records one's deeds, determines one's eternal destiny.[14] All people, therefore, control their fate through their choices and behavior. There is no concept of souls tainted at birth with the sins of Adam or any other ancestor. There is, therefore, no concept of the need for the sacrifice of a messiah to make salvation possible for others.

In keeping with the contention that Islam is a modifying correction of existing monotheism, the Qur'an assumes that the reader has knowledge of the Hebrew and Christian scriptures. It refers to the creation of Adam, Noah and the flood, Abraham, David, Solomon, and other Old Testament figures and incidents as though the reader will understand without extensive elaboration. Demonstrative of this is the following passage:

> Say, O Muslims: We believe in God and that which is revealed unto us and that which was revealed unto Abraham, and Ishmael, and Isaac, and Jacob, and the tribes, and that which Moses and Jesus received, and that which the Prophets received from the Lord. We make no distinction between any of them, and unto Him we have surrendered.[15]

The numerous Qur'anic references to food merely state that Muslims should follow the law of the Jews. Unlike Judaism, however, Islam forbids the drinking of wine.[16]

Likewise, the Qur'an does not present a history of the development of Islam but refers to many particular incidents related to Muhammad's life on the assumption that the reader knows about them. The emphasis is often upon the correction of deviant behavior, the temptations of Satan, the obstacles of unbelievers, and the obligation of the strong to care for the weak.

The portions of the Qur'an which deal with legal matters, however, have heavily shaped the belief and practice of Islam. Many statements, including those most clearly articulated, have required specific commentary or elaboration in Islamic law. The Qur'an addresses such vital topics as the avoidance of idolatry, the restriction of the number of wives to four at one time, grounds and rules for divorce, estate division, the role of witnesses, the nature of contracts, the prohibition against charging interest on loans, and modesty for women. Virtually no subject, except the need to adore and obey God, receives more attention than the obligation to care for the weak, especially widows and orphans. In the same vein, the Qur'an urges believers to share their good fortune generously, but given the Arab proclivity for generosity, it also cautions believers not to deprive their families through extravagant almsgiving. Believers should also be beneficent in forgiving wrongs and injustices. While murder deserves the severest punishment, the scripture implores believers to accept an amicable monetary settlement instead of shedding more blood. The Qur'an urges kindness to slaves, including leading them to Islam and giving them their freedom.

Many additional subjects in the Qur'an address most of the issues and circumstances which might have been expected to arise among the Arab communities of early Islam. The scripture generally defines believers' relationships with God, family, and community. The earliest Muslims could assume that their traditional way of conducting their lives was correct unless the Qur'an or the Prophet specified otherwise.

The Tradition (Sunna) of the Prophet Muhammad

Islam acquired an empire before it acquired a system of law to govern it. Consequently, like everything else in the early empire of the Umayyads, the laws were a combination of Islamic principles, Arabic traditions, and local customary laws. Under the Abbasid caliphs in the late eighth and early ninth centuries, four scholars who worked separately in different parts of the empire laid the foundation of most later Islamic law. While Abu Hanifa, Malik ibn Anas, Muhammad ibn Idris ash-Shafi'i, and Ahmad ibn Hanbal agreed that a unified law had to be based upon the Qur'an, they differed on how to supplement the relatively sparse amount of law in the holy writ. Their honest disagreements were no cause for serious schism; they accorded each other recognition. Each region of the Islamic world developed laws in the tradition of one of these four approaches or schools. All had in common the assumption of building a legal structure on the life of Muhammad. The Meccan born ash-Shafi'i (d. 819), whom most regard as the father of Islamic jurisprudence, established that the component parts of Islamic law had to be the Qur'an, the *hadith, ijma'* or consensus of the most knowledgeable scholars, and *qiyyas,* or analogy.

The conduct and comments of Muhammad became a vital supplement to the Qur'an as a source of Islamic law. Contemporaries of ash-Shafi'i, no doubt, followed his example in many matters they believed conducive to Islamic life and life in general. Direct comments he made on specific subjects assumed the stature of law even when he was not voicing God's revelations. Like most scholars, however, ash-Shafi'i did not attempt to explain why the Prophet did the most ordinary things in his life, probably because both he and his contemporaries took such behavior for granted. These matters had to be authenticated by memory when later generations desired to pattern a genuine Islamic life through emulating the Prophet.

Accounts of the Prophet's comments and behavior, known as *hadith,* began to circulate from the time of his death. The entire body of *hadith* constitutes the *sunna,* or tradition, of Islam, meaning the accepted account of how the Prophet lived. Islam's rapid spread over vast areas made authentication of all accounts virtually impossible, even if suspicion arose that anyone might fabricate information related to such a serious subject. Accident, design, greed, ignorance, and malice all played a part in the proliferation of fabricated *hadith.* The reality of forgery and gross misrepresentation became apparent as *hadith* of all kinds emerged, including some that ascribed deity to Muhammad. Although the establishment of the validity of specific *hadith* was often vitally important to the efforts to build an Islamic society, conclusive proof was not always possible.

Scholars attempted to establish an *isnad,* or chain of transmission back to the Prophet, for every *hadith.* In other words, scholars tried to authenticate by verifying that all sources who said that the Prophet did or said a particular thing could have known each other and that one of them could have known the Prophet or one of his Companions. The chain of transmission might well be longer than the *matn,* or content of the *hadith.* The deluge of false *hadith* made this a daunting task.

The Shari'a

Isma'il al-Bukhari finally provided some order to the law in the middle of the third Islamic century, assiduously building his approach upon the work of some predecessors. He identified 600,000 *hadith* in circulation and decided that authentication required gathering biographical information on all of the principal transmitters of *hadith* in order to determine whether they could have been present at the crucial junctures each *hadith* specified. Few scholars would have attempted such an extensive research. Correlating the locations of transmitters at the time they supposedly obtained their information from predecessors was an even greater task. Al-Bukhari's demanding analysis resulted in his accepting the validity of fewer than 3,000 *hadith.* His and other valiant attempts to expunge false precedent defined the foundation upon which the Islamic law, or *shari'a* ("path"), developed.

Even after all the adjustments, scholars acknowledged that the *sunna,* which passed as Muhammad's teaching through living, might contain some inaccuracies and additions. It could not be otherwise. Since enough unquestionable precedent did not exist to comprise a comprehensive legal system, the learned scholars adopted *hadith* compatible with those which bore the mark of authenticity. This, in fact, became the basic guide to Sunni law, as jurists agreed to amend the legal base of the Qur'an and the *hadith* by the principle of consensus, or *ijma'*. While this approach was the result of necessity, the Sunni mainstream justified cautious change on the basis of the Prophet's observation that his community could not err. He meant simply that those who understood the Qur'an and the personal example of Muhammad would not adopt any practice which was incompatible with these two manifestations of God's will. Consensus, then, of the learned scholars *('ulama)* became the principal means for Sunni Muslims to amend the law. The limited number of precedents and the need for consensus provided continuity and stability for Sunni law, but also made it difficult, if not impossible, to adapt to dramatically different circumstances. On a limited scale, however, Sunni judges could employ the practice of analogy *(qiyyas)* to adjudicate distinct but similar cases.

While a fuller discussion of the Shi'i approach to law exists elsewhere in this work, a few comments are appropriate in the present context. The *shari'a* in Shi'i law begins with the Qur'an and the *hadith* of the Prophet, but also includes *hadith* from 'Ali, Husayn, and the other imams. Shi'i believe that the imams were exempt from providing any justification or precedent for their rulings, since they were special manifestations of God's will. Also, the recognized erudition of all members of the Shi'i *'ulama* provides them the authority to exercise their personal judgment *(ijtihad)* without seeking consensus. The Shi'i approach allows considerably more flexibility and the capacity to alter the law to accommodate social changes and needs.

Islam is a way of life for its followers, rather than one of life's many efforts. Muslim belief that the end of life on earth leads either to Paradise or to Hell ensures a high priority for religion and places a premium on obeying God and emulating the life of His Prophet. Islam allows a full enjoyment of the good things in the earthly life within the constraints of respect for God, fellow human beings, and the environment. The temptations of Satan are strong, but there is the assurance that the one true God, for all of His might, is Compassionate and Merciful.

THE SUFI EXCEPTION

The Sufi element of Islam is the best illustration of the difficulty of categorically defining "Muslim belief." Further exemplifying this problem is the difficulty of making a commentary which can encompass every manifestation of Sufism itself. The term *Sufism,* which derived from early Islamic ascetics' practice of wearing rough woolen garments, has to encompass a spectrum as diverse as the entirety of Islam. Sufism varies from adherents who sit quietly reading the Qur'an to wildly gyrating illiterate dancers. While some Sufis wholeheartedly embrace the *shari'a*, others regard all customary practice of Islam as banal. The difficulty of having such disparities share the same label is akin to the problem posed by having diametrically contrasting elements of Sunnism and Shi'ism both claim to be Islamic.

Sufis, although diverse, have in common the desire to achieve spiritual unity with God. Many believe that human souls can and should merge to become one with God. Their perception that human souls are part of God often appears to their uninitiated fellow Muslims as direst heresy. The most convincing Sufis usually relate a specific conversion experience in which they typically see the light of God. They invariably express that the dramatic changes in their lives ruled out a return to their former ways. In fact, they relate feeling compelled to follow the Sufi Way. One of the earliest prominent Sufis, Mansur al-Hallaj—a Baghdad resident of Iranian birth—exclaimed in his ecstasy, "I am the Truth." While other Sufis recognized he had experienced spiritual union with God, the authorities crucified him in 922. His fate was instructive to Sufis, who realized that nonmystics could not comprehend Sufi spiritualism. Sufis therefore learned to express their feelings in veiled terms and symbolism, primarily through poetry. Although Sufism spread throughout the tenth and eleventh centuries, it sometimes experienced an uneasy relationship with mainstream Islam, which it intended to augment rather than supplant.

Generally Sufism developed and thrived in predominantly Sunni regions. Muslims of outstanding piety and discipline frequently attracted others who desired similar religious accomplishment. The practice developed of young men devoting themselves to spiritual training under the tutelage of a spiritually gifted *shaykh,* or honored leader. Disorder and confusion were common in the early stages of Sufi development, when practitioners did not know exactly what to do and had not justified their right to exist. By the twelfth century, however, Sufi orders developed which were composed of the *shaykh*s and their followers, called *faqir*s (Arabic) or *darwishe*s (Persian). Trained Sufis became *shaykh*s in their own right and opened new branches, but they usually maintained an affiliation with the original *shaykh* to provide a laying on of spiritual hands from the first *shaykh* to the newest initiate. Large networks of Sufi orders often became important in almost every aspect of life in areas where they were strong. The unquestioned authority of the *shaykh* determined the exact orientation and practice of each Sufi order. Some *shaykh*s stressed the Qur'an and mainstream Islamic belief, while others adopted esoteric means of transporting the spirit beyond the confines of normal worship. Rhythmic chanting, physical exercises, whirling, and other forms of dancing were as much a part of Sufi expression and the quest for spiritual realization as were elements of the *shari'a*. Music, which other forms of Islam shunned as anathema, was often central to Sufi worship. Some individuals excelled to reach unfathomable heights of grace, endurance, strength, and technique. Credible witnesses swear that whirling *darwishes* were known to achieve levitation in their exercises, which lasted for hours.

For some, the temptation to fame and fortune was too great to keep the blessing of spiritualism private. Public display of unusual Sufi talents attracted attention and converts. Whether by magic or by spiritual power, some Sufis performed feats which appeared miraculous. Miracles and fanciful display appealed to people who could not relate to the essentially law-based mainstream of Islam. Sufi missionaries, therefore, converted rural regions, and their approach influenced large numbers of the urban poor to profess Islam. As the reputations of the Sufi founders spread, accounts of their influence in helping devotees acquire Paradise and in healing the afflicted kindled outright veneration. Elaborate festivals to celebrate the birth or death of these founders became annual highlights among their followers. Some Sufi "saints" inspired their followers to construct elaborate shrines surrounding their tombs, which attracted pilgrims. Believers visited such shrines to obtain blessings and healing of all kinds. Some believers regarded pilgrimages to Sufi tombs as a legitimate substitute for the *hajj* to Mecca; in fact, some *shaykhs* only allowed such pilgrimages and specifically forbade their *darwishes* to perform the *hajj* or other traditional Islamic duties. The entire panoply of activities surrounding such Sufi worship was anathema to traditional practitioners of Islam. Rarely, however, did suppression of Sufism succeed for any extended period. Numerous holders of political power, including the Safavid dynasty of Persia and the janissaries of the Ottoman Empire, depended upon Sufi support.

In truth, it was impossible to know or measure the extent of Sufism. Such manifestations as dancing wildly to raucous music, handling snakes, eating fire or glass, or walking on red-hot coals were easy enough to detect and eliminate if authorities were sufficiently determined. But the deeply spiritual individuals who sought union with God in solitude or in small groups could go undetected in the midst of the strongest orthodox communities. This often-silent stream of Sufism provided most of the literature and spiritual guidance which not only met the metaphysical needs of a certain type of Muslim but also appealed to non-Muslims with similar spiritual inclinations. Islam has obtained some influential intellectual non-Muslim sympathizers among people who initially found solace in Sufism.

Most scholars recognize that the prominent Islamic scholar Abu Hamid al-Ghazali not only defended the legitimate role of Sufism in Islam but also obtained veneration for its highest practitioners. His work prior to addressing the Sufi issue especially suited him for such an undertaking. He had provided intellectual stability to the entire Islamic civilization, which was under attack from many quarters, when he arrived in Baghdad in 1091. This native of Tus, in the northeast of Persia, had received an outstanding education in law, theology, and philosophy at Nishapur. He could deftly move from the Qur'an and *hadith* to all the early Islamic legal and theological commentators, to the Greek philosophers, mathematicians, and physicians, to Islamic philosophers like ibn Sina and al-Farabi, and to the early formulators of Sufi practice. His combination of wisdom and erudite mastery of subject matter uniquely equipped him to address any intellectual subject. There is no denying that his was the superior intellect of his time in both law and theology. His unusual understanding of both the Greek and the Muslim writers culminated in a work entitled *The Incoherence of the Philosophers,* which effectively refuted the materialistic approach to life and the universe which Islamic philosophers had adopted from the Greeks. He demonstrated an equally thorough understanding of the Shi'i concept of theology, law, and history in his rebuttal of Shi'i efforts to replace traditional Sunni dominance. In all his arguments he was able to defend Sunni practice through his firm stand in behalf of the work of the Prophet Muhammad. This approach demonstrated the strength of Sunni Islam in conflict with the mightiest competing beliefs. His strong reliance upon Muhammad in his explanation of Sufism validated proper Sufism as compatible with, and perhaps necessary for, traditional Sunni Islam.

Al-Ghazali's prestige and fortune skyrocketed as a result of the intellectual services he performed in behalf of Sunni Islam at Nizamiyyah Madrasa in Baghdad. The masterful ingenuity of his writings put the formerly aggressive philosophers and Shi'i itself on the defensive. His entourage seems to have matched that of any other public figure in the Islamic capital of Baghdad. Al-Ghazali himself, however, in middle life began to doubt the very tools of reason and argument which had brought him fame and fortune. He had become familiar with the works of the Sufis during his extensive studies, but now he assiduously consulted Sufi leaders such as al-Makki, al-Muhasibi, al-Junayd, al-Shibli, and al-Bistami in a search for answers. He expressed conviction that their approach of asceticism was correct, but his efforts to forsake his own good life failed. The dependence of about three hundred students upon him also helped prevent him from following his new inclination.

Al-Ghazali suddenly became mute at the age of thirty-seven and at the apparent height of his career. His general health declined due to an inability to consume adequate food or drink. After he decided in 1095 to give up his position, fortune, family, and friends, his health and his confidence in the validity of reason returned: "But that was not achieved by constructing a proof or putting together an argument. On the contrary, it was the effect of a light which God Most High cast into my breast. And that light is the key to most knowledge."[17] He left his career and Baghdad to follow a quest for spiritual fulfillment through isolation and meditation at the Umayyad Mosque in Damascus, the Dome of the Rock in Jerusalem, the Mosque of the Prophet in Medina, and the Grand Mosque in Mecca. His visit to Muhammad's tomb seems to have been particularly meaningful to him, as he always expressed an extraordinary acknowledgment of both the intellect and the spirit of the Prophet. For eleven years he pursued his spiritual destiny away from the pursuits and places which had provided his fame.

This great synthesizer of the use of reason and the metaphysical in Islam confessed that he could never retain the level of abandonment of earthly concerns some Sufis achieved. Concern for his family and his compulsion to teach and write led him to return to teaching in Nishapur in 1106. He never seemed to regard himself as a bona fide Sufi, despite having experienced God's "lock on his tongue" and the light cast into his breast. Al-Ghazali presented his most laudatory comments about Sufism in the third person, writing that because

the Sufis are those who uniquely follow the way to God Most High, their mode of life is the best of all, their way the most direct of ways, and their ethic the purest. Indeed, were one to combine the insight of the intellectuals, the wisdom of the wise, and the lore of scholars versed in the mysteries of revelation in order to change a single item of Sufi conduct and ethic and to replace it with something better, no way to do so would be found. For all their motion and quiescence, exterior and interior, are learned from the light of the niche of prophecy. And beyond the light of prophecy there is no light on earth from which illumination can be obtained. . . . The Sufis see the angels and the spirits of the prophets and hear voices coming from them and learn useful things from them.[18]

He confided that only Sufis can know their vivid experiences because words are incapable of expressing their insightful visions.

Despite his self-declared inability to depend totally upon spiritual insight, al-Ghazali acknowledged that his Sufi efforts served an important function. He confessed that his vanity and search for glory had driven him to his early academic achievements. He had gloried in his distinctions and fame, and he had instructed others in the art of self-aggrandizement. He professed that all of his earlier assumptions had been wrong; his Sufi experience had convinced him that there was "no might for me and no power save in God . . . and it was not I who moved, but He moved me; and that I did not act, but He acted through me."[19] Thus humbled, he was thankful for the opportunity to serve God, and he implored God to provide him direction for further service for the remainder of his life.

THREE

ISLAMIC EXPANSION

570 to 1517

People in the West frequently equate *Arab* with *Muslim* and use the words interchangeably. While this misconception honors the tremendous contribution of Arabs to Islam, it indicates the general ignorance of Islam in the West. Only about 10 percent of the Islamic population of the world is Arab, and about 10 percent of the world's Arabs are Christian. In the time of Muhammad, the ancestors of most modern Arabs were Greeks, Egyptians, Phoenicians, or other Mediterraneans. They or their offspring adopted the Arabic language and much of the Arabic culture, and many adopted Islam to become Arabic-speaking Muslims, in much the same way that people from all over the world migrated to North America and became English-speaking Americans.

The cultural stream ran both ways, however, and as Arab domination spread, many Arabs quickly adopted the ways of the colonized areas. And, much more significantly, the Islamic belief in a genuine and total monotheism compelled Arabs to share their concept of the Only God with all who would accept it. Their success in expanding their territory and their religion eventually relegated the Arabs to a minority status in the religion and culture they initiated. Soon Persians, Turks, Kurds, and other non-Arabs were providing leadership for the Islamic religion and culture. The Islam of Muhammad rapidly exploded into a profusion of sometimes contradictory beliefs as proponents of virtually every existing belief system and numerous political agendas attempted to alter Islam.

The simple culture of the Prophet's homeland became amazingly enriched with knowledge and skills that spanned the known world to create a syncretic culture unparalleled in scope until the latter half of the twentieth century. Islamic dynamism arose from Islam's ability to give focus to a wide range of knowledge from many cultures. Islam pushed far. It pushed fast. Nothing could control it. Nothing could define it over a significant area for any prolonged period.

The desire to impress God with beauty inspired dazzling buildings, furniture, fabrics, books, fountains, jewelry, vases, weapons, and other objects. The prohibition against depicting people or animals stimulated the creation of every abstract design possible for the human brain and soul. These designs and geometrical figures, which usually accompanied elegant and complicated calligraphy, defined the clarity, majesty, simplicity, complexity, and infinity of the God they glorified. A level of beauty that might be considered sinful in other religious cultures expressed adoration of God and the success of His believers.

The Islamic culture surpassed anything that had ever existed, in large part because it contained elements of all the outstanding cultures that had preceded it. In short, Islamic culture emerged from the universality of religious expression. At its height it even transcended many subsequent cultures that would borrow from it; however, it proved unable to sustain its own standard of excellence.

ISLAM UNDER THE PROPHET'S SUCCESSORS

Initial reaction of the Arab tribes to the Prophet's death and Abu Bakr's elevation as caliph was less than propitious. Tribes under strong leaders confessed to belief in God, in His Messenger, and in the Prophet's message, but denied any obligation to obey or pay taxes to a successor selected by a small number of Muhammad's associates. Abu Bakr subdued the tribes and initiated excursions into Syria and Iraq, but he died after two years and two months as caliph.

Leaders of Islam selected 'Umar ibn al-Khattab as caliph in accordance with Abu Bakr's recommendation. While his election kept the caliphate among the Quraysh, it denied the contention of 'Ali's supporters that only Hashimite[1] blood relatives of the Prophet should provide leadership for the Islamic community. 'Ali, as the closest male blood relative and husband of the Prophet's only living offspring,[2] should by this reckoning have succeeded Muhammad. Likewise, the supporters of 'Ali (the *Shi'i*)[3] contended that leadership of Islam should always devolve to descendants of Muhammad through 'Ali's lineage. No stronger or more provocative thread runs through Islamic development than this question of succession that emerged immediately following the Prophet's death.

Once the Arab tribes were under control, they provided additional resources to intensify Islamic expansion into the Byzantine and Persian empires. The Greek-based Byzantine Empire controlled the lands on all shores of the eastern Mediterranean Sea. The Persian Empire abutted the Byzantine empire in eastern Anatolia and in eastern Syria, and stretched eastward into Afghanistan and to within two hundred miles of the Indus River. The Euphrates River formed the southwestern border of the Persian Empire, but the area from there westward to the Byzantine Empire was essentially unclaimed, as the Lakhmid and the Ghassanid Arabs in the region were weak and disorganized. The fact that neither of the formerly great empires had the energy or resources to occupy this large region indicates the existence of an opportunity for Islamic expansion.

Medina served as capital of the developing Arab empire, but Meccans dominated Arab and Islamic policy-making. The two major campaigns that began in 632 under Abu Bakr and the two most important Arab commanders, Khalid ibn al-Walid and Amir ibn al-As, yielded dividends in September 635, when Damascus fell, and the following August, when most of Syria surrendered to Arab control after the Battle of Yarmuk. Jerusalem remained under Byzantine control until 638. Victory over the Persians south of Najaf at Qadisiyyah in 636 gave the Arab army control of Iraq. A second and decisive battle with the Persians at Nihavand in 642 eliminated organized resistance to Arab control of the Persian Empire. General Amir ibn al-As, who had led the attack on Byzantine Syria, also led the invasion of Egypt in 639. Within a year Egypt was under Arab control, but official Byzantine surrender did not occur until 641. When Arab armies defeated the Byzantines in Tunisia in 647, Islam had spread halfway across North Africa. By 675 the Arabs had pushed eastward into Asia, north of the Oxus River and east of the Indus River, to finish a remarkable forty years of expansion.

Arabs and concerns related to the Arabs dominated the Islamic policies of the first few decades following the Prophet's death. The conquered lands were an Arab empire. Time would prove whether it could or would become an Islamic empire. Although 'Umar was a military man, he also proved to be an excellent administrator when he became caliph at the prime age of forty-three. He directed and encouraged expansion, but made no attempt to impose either Arab ways or Islamic belief upon the conquered lands. Christians and Jews, as *dhimmi* ("protected ones"), or People of the Book, kept their religions, and the Arabs conducted most of their relations through the religious leaders of the new subject peoples. Most of the vanquished kept their private estates, while 'Umar confiscated the public lands and those of some selected enemies as property of the *umma* (Islamic community). People in the conquered lands, as well as Muslims, paid taxes that provided the new Arab empire with substantial revenues which 'Umar used to meet communal obligations. While this approach did not eliminate plunder by the conquering armies, it greatly reduced it; more importantly, it enabled the professional central authority to retain a social order. The vanquished came to expect fair treatment and lower taxes than

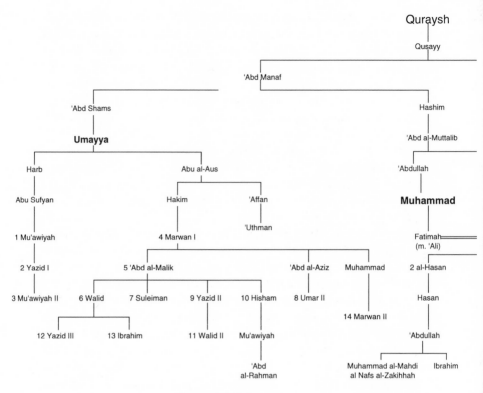

Umayyad Caliphs

Umayyad Caliphs		Twelver Imams		Abbasids	
1. Mu'awiyah	661–680	1. 'Ali	d. 661	1. Abu al-Abbas al-Saffah	749–754
2. Yazid I	680–683	2. al-Hasan	d. 669	2. Abu Ja'far al-Mansur	754–775
3. Mu'awiyah II	683–684	3. al-Husayn	d. 680	3. Muhammad al-Mahdi	775–785
4. Marwan I	684–685	4. 'Ali Zayn al-Abidin	d. 712	4. Muhammad al-Hadi	785–786
5. 'Abd al-Malik	685–705	5. Muhammad al-Baqir	d. 731	5. Harun al-Rashid	786–809
6. Walid	705–715	6. Ja'far al-Sadiq	d. 765	6. Muhammad al-Amin	809–813
7. Suleiman	715–717	7. Musa al-Kazim	d. 799	7. 'Abdullah al-Mamun	813–833
8. 'Umar II	717–720	8. 'Ali al-Rida	d. 818	8. Abu Ishaq al-Mutasim	833–842
9. Yazid II	720–724	9. Muhammad al-Jawad	d. 835	9. al-Wathiq	842–847
10. Hisham	724–743	10. 'Ali al-Hadi	d. 868	10. al-Mutawakkil	847–861
11. Walid II	743–744	11. Hasan al-Askari	d. 874	11. al-Muntasir	861–862
12. Yazid III	744	12. Muhammad al-Muntazar	d. 878	12. al-Mustain	862–866
13. Ibrahim	744			13. al-Mutazz	866–869
14. Marwan II	744–750			14. al-Muhtadi	869–870
				15. al-Mutamid	870–892

» CHART I «

Genealogy of the Early Islamic Leaders

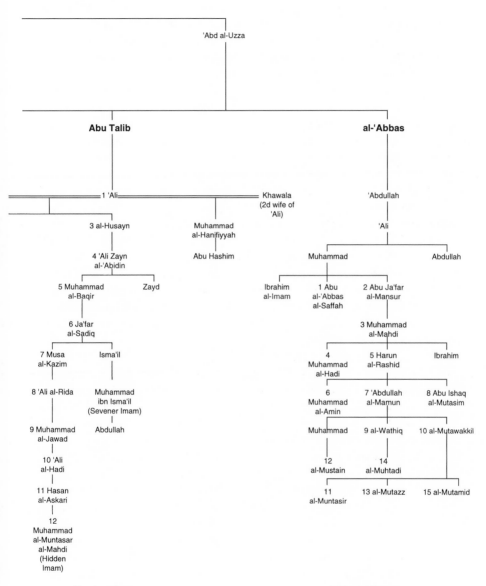

Twelver Imams **Abbasid Caliphs**

before, while the victors learned that authorities in Medina would provide them with rewards.

Wise policies of the Arab leaders transformed the diverse and expansive conquered lands into an empire. Under instructions from Medina, the Arab armies often remained removed from the established population centers. This policy and the lenient approach to land confiscation and religion reduced conflict and animosity between conqueror and vanquished.[4] 'Umar's development of a system of pensions for leading Muslims and military personnel helped restrain the wide-ranging and triumphant Muslims from extracting mercenary reward at the time of conquest. The vast revenues of the early conquests made such disbursements possible, but they would soon become a heavy burden for the central government as revenues declined.

'Uthman ibn 'Affan became caliph in 644 after a Persian slave assassinated 'Umar. Members of the committee of Quraysh, which again bypassed 'Ali, apparently believed they could control the empire through 'Uthman, although the latter lacked his predecessor's capacity to instill awe and fear. As the third Quraysh to become caliph, 'Uthman represented the establishment of a precedent that many, especially the Medinans, resented. Also, his father, Abu Sufyan, and the entire Umayyad family had led opposition to Islam until it triumphed over Mecca in 630. Under his caliphate, however, the Umayyads and their fellow merchant-aristocrat friends received high offices, wealth, and prestige as the empire assumed an administrative structure following the rapid expansion during 'Umar's reign.

Many other Arabs belatedly wanted to become involved in the expansion and enrichment. Large numbers who had abstained from earlier campaigns flocked to obtain the rewards associated with success, and soon the demand for rewards exceeded the government's resources. Discontented residents of Medina rose in protest as they observed other Arabs benefiting more than themselves from the success of the movement Medinans had fostered. Medinan discontent developed into riots which others, especially Egyptians, joined, making life unsafe for the caliph and his administrators.

A group of discontented Muslims assassinated 'Uthman in Medina during June 656, but the cleavages in the Islamic and Arab community ran deeper than the causes of 'Uthman's violent death. Medinans resented Meccans, supporters of 'Ali resented the wealthy Quraysh notables, other elements of the Prophet's family disliked 'Ali and his supporters, and strict Muslims deplored policies of the government and its officials, which they believed contradicted religious teachings. In addition, there were extensive personal jealousies among the powerful that could be exploited in order to obtain great fame and fortune.

'Ali finally became caliph in 656. He succeeded in part because 'Uthman's enemies, who conducted the election, wanted to reward 'Ali for his active op-position to 'Uthman's questionable policies. His election especially pleased those who believed that direct descendants of the Prophet should hold the caliphate. While they were not co-conspirators, 'Ali and his supporters were beneficiaries of 'Uthman's assassination.

A significant element of the Islamic community always opposed 'Ali, how-ever, because they sensed that he possessed a different and ill-defined concept of Islamic belief and vision for the Islamic empire. A dissident element rallied around Aishah, the Prophet's favorite wife, and two other cousins, Talha and Zubayr, early allies of Muhammad. They staged their rebellion near the new Arab administrative center of Basra in Iraq. 'Ali triumphed at the Battle of the Camel,[5] but he faced a much greater threat from 'Uthman's nephew, Mu'awi-yah ibn Abi Sufyan, the governor of Syria.

'Ali, who had played such a major role in the early development of Islam and who later would inspire unparalleled devotion, spent his short reign as caliph trying to suppress rebellion. He operated from the new Arab adminis-trative center of Kufa, on the Euphrates River about halfway between Hira and Basra. Mu'awiyah's initial efforts to obtain the right to punish his slain uncle's assassins evolved into open rebellion and a campaign to seize the caliphate from 'Ali. Many supporters of 'Ali, and perhaps the caliph himself, believed that 'Uthman's assassins had simply carried out an unauthorized execution of an abuser of power and a transgressor of Islamic principles. Armed conflict be-tween the two armies at Siffin led to Mu'awiyah's request for arbitration after the battle turned in 'Ali's favor. 'Ali and his closest supporters agreed to arbi-tration because they were confident in their legal position.

Among 'Ali's most fervent supporters were strict, uncompromising adher-ents to Islamic law who, in common with many of his enemies, regarded any deviation from their concept of Islam as apostasy. They staunchly insisted upon full enforcement of every iota of their perceptions of Islamic belief, practice, and law. Consequently, as firm believers in violence toward apostates, they en-dorsed 'Uthman's assassination as a just punishment for his unacceptable poli-cies. They saw Mu'awiyah's disregard for 'Ali's legitimate election and his re-bellion as equally abominable. By their standards, however, 'Ali also became anathema when he agreed to arbitration and compromise with the apostate Mu'awiyah.

These strict constructionists, with their strong belief in the democratic government of the Islamic community, withdrew their support of 'Ali and moved to Nahrawan, where they became known as Kharijites.[6] 'Ali reacted vi-olently to their defection and pursued them to Nahrawan, where his soldiers killed many of them. Elements of the original Kharijites survived to play a

» MAP 2 «

Islam in the Middle East

provocative role in Islam, and individuals and groups with Kharijite-like views down through the ages have served as a conscience for all who have deviated from full, uncompromising adherence to Islamic doctrine.

'Ali's situation deteriorated further; the defection of the Kharijites, 'Ali's treatment of them, and his unwillingness to accept the decision of a respectable arbitration process that favored Mu'awiyah depleted 'Ali's forces below the capacity to confront Mu'awiyah militarily. Many no longer regarded 'Ali as caliph after these developments, but efforts to agree upon a replacement failed. As a result 'Ali remained caliph, but Mu'awiyah was the unquestioned ruler over Syria and Egypt, the two areas which Amir ibn al-As, his ally in the conflict with 'Ali, had conquered for the Islamic empire.

Islam entered a new era when, in 661, a Kharijite assassinated 'Ali, the last of the "Rightly Guided Caliphs."[7] 'Ali's eldest son, Hasan, accepted a payment from Mu'awiyah in return for renouncing any claim to the caliphate. While Hasan's bargain allowed Mu'awiyah to become caliph, 'Ali's second son, Husayn, and the Shi'i retained the belief that only a Hashimite could lead Islam.

A complex belief system and theology that included a separate *sunna* developed to support this view. The Shi'i also adopted a martyred and dissident posture that has persisted. Three major forms of Shi'ism developed,[8] all based upon the legitimacy of the Hashimites. The Shi'i movements tended to attract the dissatisfied, the non-Arab, and the financially deprived elements of the huge Islamic civilization. Usually the Shi'i were a minority, but for significant periods they obtained control over large Islamic areas.

Concomitantly, Mu'awiyah retained the mainstream Arab areas where Arabic became the dominant language. Adherence to the Holy Qur'an, the *sunna (hadith)* of the Prophet, and belief that Muhammad was the seal of prophecy established them as Sunni, the keepers of the traditions. Given their emphasis on retaining tradition and their limited resources for guiding change or innovation, the Sunni were less flexible and inclined to change than the Shi'i, whose imams[9] and their interpreters provided a constant forum for improvisation to meet changing circumstances.

Religious issues remained prominent in the Arab empire in which Islam fairly quickly became dominant, but family and political concerns, as well as the totally new political forces that emerged, would shape most future events and adapt religion to suit their needs.

THE UMAYYADS

The Umayyad period of Islamic development was illustrious, even though few of that dynasty demonstrated laudable leadership or character. While 'Uthman was from the Umayyad clan, he is classified as one of the Four Rightly Guided Caliphs, rather than as an Umayyad. All fourteen Umayyad caliphs were descendants of Umayya, the first cousin of Muhammad's grandfather, 'Abd al-Muttalib. All Umayyad caliphs descended from Umayya's two sons, Harb and Abu al-As, and caliphs 'Uthman and Mu'awiyah were both great-grandsons of Umayya. Some scholars refer to the first three Umayyad caliphs, Mu'awiyah, his son Yazid, and grandson Mu'awiyah II, as Sufyanids after Abu Sufyan, Mu'awiyah's father. Similarly, all other Umayyad caliphs are called Marwanids, after Marwan I, Abu al-As's grandson, who was the first of that lineage to become caliph.

The period of the Umayyad dynasty (661–750) was rife with religious dissent and open rebellion. The Shi'i, the Kharijites, and traditional Muslims from the lineage of the Companions and Helpers, under the leadership of the son of Zubayr, distrusted the sincerity of Umayyad belief in Islam. The personal behavior of the Umayyads and their approach to government did nothing to dispel belief that the Umayyads were opportunistic unbelievers who used Islam as a tool for their aggrandizement. There is some irony in the fact that the Umayyads, who defined the *sunna,* were constantly under attack during their era and later for deviating from traditional belief and for transgressing acceptable means of providing governmental structure.

Despite these problems, the Arab-dominated Islamic empire not only endured, but expanded and realized some of Islam's important architectural and intellectual triumphs. The Islamic empire spread westward all the way across Africa, throughout the Iberian peninsula, and into the Frankish empire.[10] Forays across the Oxus and Indus rivers expanded Islam east of Persia. Islam was dynamic enough, and its neighbors weak enough, that Islam could expand even while experiencing divisive internal struggles.

Mu'awiyah, as the first Umayyad caliph (661–680), made Damascus his capital. Demonstrating strength and judgment that did not hint of his close kinship to the weaker 'Uthman, he set standards in a wide spectrum of matters during his nineteen-year reign that few of his lineage would match in any respect. Strong and capable governors who were loyal to him maintained internal peace and expanded the empire across Africa and beyond the eastern limits of the Persian Empire. The expansion employed additional numbers of Arabs and diverted their energies away from intrigue and rebellion. Mu'awiyah developed largely non-Arab Syrian military units that could deal with Arab uprisings free from the concerns and consequences of Arab-on-Arab conflict. In fact, Syrian *mawali* (non-Arab Muslims) generally fared well under the Umayyads, who relied heavily upon them, and even upon Christian *dhimmi,* to fill high posts. While he acquired force, which he never hesitated to use, Mu'awiyah is more renowned for placating rivals and enemies, such as Hasan, with gifts. Such softness could never please the Kharijite hard-liners, however, and devotees of 'Ali could never forgive him, regardless of the lands and riches he acquired for Islam, because they believed he tainted everything with his deviant Islam. Strong in his governors, Mu'awiyah could safely pursue lenient policies, since all knew he was capable of and willing to use force.

Neither fear nor respect accompanied the reigns of Mu'awiyah's son, Yazid I, and his grandson, Mu'awiyah II, which spanned only four years. All the troubling issues that had emerged since the Prophet's death inspired uprisings in Mecca, Medina, and Iraq. Destructive as the conflicts in Mecca and Medina were, the most important events occurred near Kufa in Iraq. Like his father 'Ali, Husayn used Kufa as a base to oppose the Damascus-based Umayyads. An army of Yazid I, the second Umayyad caliph, destroyed Husayn's small force in 680 at Karbala north of Kufa and killed the Prophet's grandson. Husayn's death became more notable because Yazid's commander, 'Ubayd Allah, sent Husayn's head to Damascus as a trophy. This unusual barbarity outraged the Shi'i, who elevated Husayn to parity with his martyred father, 'Ali, as a source of revealed religious truth. No grounds for cooperation remained between the clans of Umayya and Hashim after the fateful events at Karbala, as the theme of martyrdom became etched deeper into the Shi'i psyche.

It was difficult for the government in Damascus to maintain control over the vast empire even in these seminal years of Arab and Islamic expansion. The Arabian peninsula was an ideal crucible for dissent. While Yazid I subdued Medina after great bloodshed, Mecca, which also suffered massive destruction,[11] remained under the control of Zubayr, who held most of the Arabian peninsula, as well as much of Iraq, and regarded himself as caliph. Kharijite uprisings in southern Arabia and Kharijite and Shi'i uprisings in Iraq freed those areas from central control from either Mecca or Damascus. Pronounced conflicts among the northern and southern Arab tribes provided additional challenges to any attempt to establish order. Marwan I, who had been 'Uthman's principal administrator, was caliph just long enough to give his name to his Umayyad successors.

His son and successor, 'Abd al-Malik (685–705), with his military commander al-Hajjaj, restored order, killed Zubayr, and prepared the circumstances for his son, al-Walid (705–715), to expand the Islamic empire. Islamic armies pushed beyond Persia in the northeast and crossed the Oxus River, while expansion past the Indus River in the southeast signaled Islamic penetration of India. Muslim military efforts were also necessary to reconquer areas of North Africa from the Byzantines, who had resumed control while the Muslims were engaging in their internal conflicts. With North Africa back under control by 705, the Muslims were prepared to move north of the Mediterranean into the Iberian peninsula. The Muslim Berber leader Tariq crossed from Africa to the rocky peninsula on the western shore of the Mediterranean in 711.[12] Over the next decade, the dynamic Islamic forces established control over the entire Iberian peninsula to provide Islam its most substantial platform for transmitting Islamic culture to western Europe. Exploratory Muslim raids north of the Pyrenees over the next fourteen years apprised Europeans of Islam's westward expansion.[13]

By the battle of Tours/Poitiers, a full century had passed since the Prophet's death. The Islamic empire, and in some respects Islam itself, was unrecognizable. Vast new lands and divergent new peoples owed allegiance—often unwillingly—to Arab leaders, and many non-Arabs had embraced the Islamic religion. Umayyad administrators governed loyal Arabs and loyal Muslims, disloyal Arabs and disloyal Muslims, and loyal and disloyal non-Arabs and non-Muslims. Over the years the significant problems with the Arabs over religious issues and political spoils eventually resulted in Umayyad victories in all cases. As years passed, however, the non-Arab elements of the empire, which constituted a preponderant majority, played an increased role and provided cause for concern. While the *dhimmi* (Christians and Jews) had little basis upon which to make a case for better treatment, since they existed at the sufferance of the tolerant Muslim power structure, the case of the *mawali* (converts to Islam) was quite different. The circumstances of their conversions and their attitudes and understanding of Islam varied immensely. Consequently, various attitudes prevailed among converts regarding their place and role within the Islamic *umma*. While many felt blessed to become part of the new religious community of the conquering Arabs, others considered themselves equal to all fellow Muslims and resisted Arab claims of privilege or Islamic superiority. This latter element became involved in the internecine struggles and gradually grew in size, brashness, and influence to a point where they could decide issues which formerly were determined exclusively by Arabs. All the major traditional factions, including the Umayyads, found it necessary to court their favor by the time of the Marwanids. Even the Kharijites recognized that *mawali* discontent was valid for those who embraced the strict letter of Islamic belief and practice. Kharijite acceptance of the *mawali* right to full participation also conformed to the Kharijite belief that all Muslims were not only equal but eligible to become caliph. Shi'ism's tradition of persecution at the hands of the Quraysh merchant elite attracted many who resented their heavier taxes and limited futures under Umayyad governance. Descendants of the Companions and Helpers, who cherished the simple Islam of the Prophet, had an even easier symbiotic rapport with the disgruntled *mawali,* who regarded the need for any compulsory period of religious apprenticeship and tutelage as long since past.

The persistence of dissent was stronger than the Umayyad capacity and will to suppress it. The emergence of still another form of Shi'ism in the reign of Hisham (734–743), the tenth Umayyad caliph, illustrated this problem. 'Ali's great-grandson, Zayd, staged an unsuccessful rebellion in Kufa, but his innovative views survived to guide Zaydi (Fiver) Shi'ism[14] in its stronghold in Yemen. Unrest was rampant in the lower Mesopotamian region and Persia, but dissidents could usually escape Umayyad authorities and find refuge in the Arabian peninsula. Umayyad survival became more difficult under simultaneous attacks by several opponents. Challenges from the two major branches of the Prophet's family, the Alids and the Abbasids, were especially effective, since the only justification for Umayyad leadership rested upon Mu'awiyah's military success and the renunciation of leadership he extracted from Hasan.

THE ABBASIDS

Claims that the caliphate should remain in the Prophet's family discredited the Umayyads and justified the use of force to establish a legitimate caliphate. An uprising which began in northeastern Persia and spread to Mesopotamia resulted in a series of Umayyad military defeats and the flight of Marwan II, the last Umayyad caliph. Systematic annihilation of Umayyads, except in Spain, eliminated any possibility they would participate in future Islamic affairs. Without any direct effort on his part, Abu al-'Abbas al-Saffah, the great-great-grandson of Muhammad's paternal uncle 'Abbas, became caliph in 750 and established a caliphal dynasty which lasted five centuries. We will see that the Abbasid caliphate continued long after it ceased to provide executive leadership. Abbasid claims of legitimacy from the earliest days of Islam helped sustain them in office long after they became powerless.

The Arab city of Medina had been the capital of the Rightly Guided Caliphs, and Damascus, with its adjacent Ghassanid Arab population, had served as the Umayyad capital. But the Abbasids favored the eastern portion of the Islamic empire, with its predominantly Persian population. Al-Mansur, the second Abbasid caliph, emphasized the altered focus of the Islamic empire when he constructed the new city of Baghdad on the Tigris River, which was ready for occupation in 762. Beginning with Abu Ishaq al-Mu'tasim (833–842),[15] however, some Abbasids eschewed Baghdad and built private cities which became administrative centers and auxiliary capitals.

Abbasid success meant Alid defeat. The kinship of these two branches of the Hashimite family might have obligated them to ally against common family enemies, but instead it was the closeness of their kinship that made them the direst of enemies in the struggle for the caliphate, which was the family's patrimony. Only 'Ali's close association with Muhammad differentiated the claims of the two clans, who had descended from two brothers of 'Abdullah, the Prophet's father.

Shi'i uprisings in behalf of the Alids challenged the new Abbasid caliphs, as did a movement *(zandaqa)*[16] to prevent Persian cultural extinction. Bloody conflicts among the Abbasids themselves, especially between the offspring of Harun al-Rashid (786–809)[17] during the sixth Abbasid decade, indicate the magnitude of the stakes which the caliphate represented. Even the most sincere efforts to eliminate the question of succession to the caliphate through compromise only intensified conflicts. As in earlier times, force and the willingness to use it continued to determine caliphal leadership.

In the best of times the Islamic empire, like other such diverse and rambling entities, suffered foreign occupation of some regions, and various portions became autonomous under dissident individuals or groups. Regions sometimes remained unresponsive to central authority for lengthy periods. Such was the nature of empire. Only when too many similar developments occurred simultaneously, as at the end of the Umayyad period, did the whole structure change. The key to imperial survival was to maintain enough talent, loyalty, authority, and force at the center to reassert control when conditions improved.

Abu al-'Abbas al-Saffah established the precedent that the caliphate passed from father to son. That practice generally prevailed, but at times it passed from brother to brother. At other times sheer might and mere convenience triumphed. Uncertainty of the line of succession, succession by heirs of immature age, and occasional weakness in candidates allowed strong *vizirs,*[18] military commanders, or governors to exercise their will upon the choice of caliph. Frequent disorderly and turbulent successions to power became normal in a volatile empire, surrounded by expansionist and fearful neighbors, where so much was at stake.

Uprisings and invasions were secondary considerations to Abbasid caliphs, who gave their closest attention to their personal safety and retaining their thrones. As early as Harun al-Rashid (c. 800), the caliph began to rely on Turkish slave soldiers and body servants to increase personal safety. Thirty years later, Caliph al-Mu'tasim first entrusted his personal safety entirely to Turkish units and then created an army almost exclusively composed of Turkish slaves. Just as the Umayyads had employed *mawali* of largely Christian origin, the Abbasids came to rely on Turks, who enjoyed privilege solely on the basis of their personal relationship with the caliph. It was not, therefore, a big step when Caliph al-Mutawakkil (847–861) began to entrust the highest administrative positions to Turks. Rapidly, Turks, who had emerged because of their lack of involvement in political and religious conflicts among the Arabs and Persians, became the most concerned parties in affairs at the pinnacle of Abbasid power.

Turks determined the course of succession by assassination of reigning caliphs four times in rapid succession. While interesting in itself, this strong reliance on Turks also indicates a high level of Turkish acculturation into Islamic society long before any large Turkish invasions occurred.

Shi'i unrest of every description was an ongoing problem for the Abbasids. That none of the Shi'i factions was able to prevail during this period in no way mitigated the chronic threat they posed to political stability. The Alid element remained a clear menace to Abbasid power until the last direct descendant of 'Ali, the Twelfth Imam, Muhammad al-Muntazar, mysteriously disappeared in 874. The obscurity of his condition and location shaped the entire future of Twelver Shi'i Islam. While insurrections could no longer occur in behalf of an imam related to 'Ali, the belief soon developed that the Twelfth Imam would emerge from occultation.[19] The absence of the Imam, with the promise of his return to lead the faithful, gave reason for the Twelver Shi'i to exist and remain organized. Oddly, while the main body of believers frequently suffered persecution and restrictions upon their activities, some of their leaders held high positions in the Abbasid government.

Flux and change, rather than stability or continuity, characterized most of the Abbasid period. Frequently, violent change at the highest levels virtually ensured adventurism at lower echelons. For instance, after the central government moved from Damascus to Baghdad, Egypt became less important and more difficult to control. The Abbasid governor, Ahmad ibn Tulun, who went to Egypt in 868, not only established personal control of Egypt, but added Syria to his holdings in 878. The Tulunids and their successors contributed little to the Abbasid caliph's revenues, but they guarded the western region and kept it loyal to Sunni Islam. Indeed, the Egyptian-Syrian region prospered under the strong central Tulunid authority, with its army composed largely of Turks, Greeks, and black Africans. This union was reminiscent of the earlier affiliation during the conflict between 'Ali and Mu'awiyah.

Baghdad authorities looked back on the Tulunid period as favorable once the Fatimids had conquered Egypt from their Tunisian base in 969. The Fatimids were militant Isma'ili Shi'i who—as supporters of Muhammad ibn Isma'il as the Hidden Imam—rejected the basic premise of the Abbasid caliphate. They unabashedly proclaimed their goal of overthrowing the Abbasids and establishing the Isma'ili approach to Islam throughout the world. Toward this end, the Fatimids simultaneously constructed the new city of Cairo and the al-Azhar center for Islamic studies in 969. The Fatimid rulers assumed the title of caliph and exercised absolute power as infallible imams.

Building upon the basic prosperity of Egypt, the Fatimids established an empire that included Syria, Palestine, the Hejaz, both shores of the Red Sea, Yemen, North Africa, and Sicily. The Fatimids adopted a religious policy that was as aggressive as their military and commercial policies were. Missionaries went throughout the Abbasid areas to spread the unique Isma'ili version of Islam with its penchant for Qur'anic interpretation that gave particular groups, and the Isma'ili in general, a sense both of superiority and of persecution which often inspired fanatical activity. It placed considerable emphasis upon class differences and interpreted most human activity as a struggle of "have-nots" against "haves." Some elements of the Isma'ili abrogated large portions of more traditional Islamic belief and practice.

Increasingly, the Abbasid Sunni caliphate came to exist in name only. The Buyids began to emerge in 930 and established a series of loosely connected political entities in western Persia. Although they were Shi'i, when they seized Baghdad in 945 they allowed the Abbasid Sunni caliph to function, under their close control. Thus, once the Fatimids had conquered Egypt in 969 and proceeded to expand across North Africa into the Arabian peninsula to Yemen and along the African coast of the Red Sea, as well as into Palestine and Syria, most of the Islamic world was under the domination of some form of Shi'ism.

Ironically, the Abbasid caliphate and Sunni Islam revived following a new wave of invasion from the northeast. The Seljuk Turks, who had converted to Sunni Islam when they still dwelled in the steppes northeast of Persia, began to enter Persia in 1025. They steadily expanded westward until they captured Baghdad in 1055 and restored the Abbasid caliph to full authority. The Seljuks dealt particularly severely with Isma'ili Shi'ism, and eventually it remained only in remote, virtually impenetrable areas and as a clandestine movement in Seljuk-controlled areas. Prolonged famine and economic decline in Fatimid Egypt, accompanied by conflicts among the military units, invited Seljuk expansion even further westward. Military strongmen, often of non-Isma'ili conviction, controlled even the Fatimid caliph by the late 1060s. Seljuk units expanded into Syria in 1064 and gained control of most of Syria and Palestine over the next fifteen years. As ardent Sunni, the Seljuks insisted that Muslims practice Sunni Islam in the areas of their expansion. Their approach was less tolerant than most previous patrons of Islam. Experiences with the crusaders led to an unprecedented level of persecution of Christians, who had always been protected before Seljuk authorities began to suspect them as allies of the invaders.

Despite their losses to the Seljuks, the Fatimids retained Jerusalem until 1099, when the first crusaders captured the Holy City and proceeded to establish control over extensive lands in Palestine and Syria. The crusader invasion surprised the Seljuks, who maintained only enough military resources to hold regions against internal uprisings, while the main bands moved on to further conquests. The Seljuks began a serious campaign to expel the crusaders in

1127 and were able to push the crusaders out of most of Palestine and Syria by 1154, when they regained control of Damascus.

Fatimid internal problems led some Egyptians to request assistance from the Seljuk Turks. This appeal accounts for the arrival of Salah ad-Din ibn Ayyub—better known in the West as Saladin—in Egypt in 1163. Over the next few years he obtained command over the Seljuk forces which his kinsmen had led. This Kurdish commander led an army composed largely of Seljuk Turks but including men from various Sunni peoples. Saladin first played a prominent role in 1170, when he defended Egypt against a crusader invasion. Following the death of the Fatimid caliph in 1171, Saladin did not allow a replacement but returned Egypt to Sunni Islam and restored its affiliation with the Abbasid caliphate. In all these activities in Egypt, Saladin functioned as a subordinate to the Abbasid caliph and Nur al-Din, the Seljuk ruler of Syria.

In keeping with widespread practice of the times, Saladin became increasingly independent, taking advantage of the confusion and lack of a clear order of command following Nur al-Din's death in 1174 to extend his control beyond Egypt into Syria. Once he had secured control of the Seljuk areas, he moved against the remaining crusader strongholds. Saladin captured Jerusalem in 1187 and defended his lands against the Third Crusade in 1192.

Saladin has justifiably attracted attention because he made important lasting changes during his comparatively long period of eminence. He replaced Fatimid Isma'ili domination of Egypt and Syria with Sunni Islam under the Abbasid caliph of Baghdad. He expelled the crusaders from the Holy Land, except for Acre and a small adjacent region. He even established civilized rules for continued relations with the Christians.

While Saladin gained a reputation for civility and wisdom, his success depended upon his development and leadership of a formidable army. He used Egyptians and Syrians, but only as auxiliaries to his Turkish and Kurdish cavalry. In this respect, as well, he left his mark on the region. His kin, who succeeded him in power after his death in 1193, used soldiers of Turkish, Kurdish, and Circassian origin even more extensively. Known as the Ayyubids, his relatives provided effective leadership for Syria and Egypt over two full generations. Typically, Syria soon lost the unity Saladin had imposed, although Ayyubids ruled the various parts.

In Egypt, primarily, the Ayyubids adopted the practice of buying boys, usually of Christian origin, in the Black Sea and Caucasus regions and training them in military and administrative skills while converting them to Islam. They received their freedom upon completion of their training, but their first loyalty remained to their former owners and masters. These Mamluks ('owned ones') remained the dominant class in Egypt until Muhammad 'Ali destroyed them early in the nineteenth century. While the practice of various Mamluk commanders of developing their own armies caused frequent change in the Egyptian sultanate, it provided Egypt with military strength to meet all external challenges.

By 1250 the Mamluks no longer bothered to confer the sultanate upon an Ayyubid and instead chose one of their own as sultan. Succession to power was often disorderly due to the constant intrigue and manipulation among various Mamluk elements attempting to seize power either from the reigning sultan or upon his death.

THE MONGOLS

All of Islam was imperiled when the Mongols under the leadership of Hulegu swept into Persia in 1256. Unlike previous invaders from the steppes, they were not Muslims, although some were Christian and demonstrated favoritism toward Christians. In general, most Mongols did not respect Islam, except for an element that demonstrated a proclivity toward Twelver Islam. Mongols conquered Baghdad in 1258 and executed the Abbasid caliph. This was an abrupt and bloody end to the Baghdad caliphal dynasty that had begun in 750.

There seemed to be no force capable of thwarting the Mongols, even in their reduced numbers, as they moved westward into Syria and Palestine. But an Egyptian Mamluk army defeated the Mongols in northern Palestine at 'Ayn Jalut in 1260. Authorities generally agree that Mamluk familiarity with the military thinking and practices of the steppes helps account for the success of the cavalry-based Egyptian force. In anticipation of further attacks, the Egyptians retained control of most of Syria to protect their heartland from invasion. In fact, the Mamluks extended their influence over much of western Islam, including the Hejaz. In view of the demise of the Baghdad caliphate and their new preeminent status in Islam, the Mamluks conferred the caliphate upon a member of the Abbasid family in Cairo in 1261. The Cairo-based Abbasid caliphate lasted until the Ottomans defeated the Mamluks in 1517.

Egyptian Mamluks prevailed politically, militarily, commercially, and in religious leadership in the lands west of the Mongol-held territories. An attack upon Acre in 1291 established Muslim control over the last crusader stronghold in the Holy Land. Some additional effort removed the last crusaders from other areas they had repopulated following the death of Saladin. As in Fatimid times, Egypt extended its control over Palestine, Syria, the Hejaz, both coasts of the Red Sea, and Yemen.

Fortunately for Islam, the Mongol leader, Ghazan Khan, embraced Sunni Islam in 1295. Islam had remained strong in the Mesopotamian–Persian region during the nearly forty years when it lacked governmental support. The Mongols had not singled out believers or their places of worship for unusual brutality, nor had they been unduly active in converting Muslims to the Buddhism some of the Mongols professed.

A second and more terrible wave of Mongol destruction began in 1379 under Timur. While he professed to be a Sunni Muslim, he showed little regard for Muslims of any persuasion as his army swept all before it across southwest Asia. Christian areas suffered even greater destruction. Mamluk forces had to abandon Syria in the face of this Mongol onslaught.

No construction followed in the wake of Timur's destruction, which reached from India to Turkey. The plethora of offspring who fought over his conquests following his death in 1405 varied so much in ability and outlook that it is difficult to give a general history of the Islamic lands of southwest Asia during this period. Slowly, however, regions began to mend, and characteristics emerged that reflected both the good and the traumatic in their past. There was little indication that larger states might emerge from the fragmented Islamic world. Many complications had occurred in Islam since the days when a few Arab factions fought to define belief and practice and for the right to govern. It was, in fact, quite clear that the preeminence of North Africans, Persians, Turks, and Mongols augured against Arabs' ever regaining a leadership role in Islam. Arab control of Mecca and Medina offered the best possibility for Arabs to assert themselves and move to the forefront of the religion they had initiated.

THE OTTOMANS

Even the most casual student of the Middle East knows that until very modern times most invasions of the region came from the east. But a new force which would dominate Islam for centuries began to emerge in western Anatolia at the beginning of the fourteenth century. The Ottomans were among the many Turkish tribes that had moved westward from the steppes in previous decades. They had settled and thrived in northwestern Anatolia. These Ottoman (Osmanli) Turks benefited from a combination of capable leadership and the decline of the Byzantine Empire. Like most of the other Turks, they adopted Sunni Islam; but unlike the others, the Ottomans assumed that they had a special duty to expand the pure Islam. They prided themselves as *ghazis*,[20] whose duty it was to lead the entire world to Sunni Islam. Moving out from the region around Bursa, the Ottomans conquered the Balkans up to the Hungarian border and then moved south and east into the former heartland of the Seljuks. Their success, like that of other Turkish peoples, depended upon a system of loyal slave soldiers and administrators. Despite their aggressive *jihad* missionary approach to spreading Islam, the Ottomans were usually benevolent conquerors. Christians and Jews normally found the Ottomans tolerant. Non-Sunni Muslims, however, learned it was wise to keep their deviation from Sunni Islam either silent or low key. Much of the Ottoman expansion occurred at the expense of the Byzantine Empire, which suffered from internal decay and wars with Turks, Mongols, and crusaders and other Latin Catholics.

Constantinople, the last remnant of the illustrious Byzantine Empire, fell to the forces of Mehmed II, the Conqueror, at the end of May 1453. This was a momentous development in both the Christian and Muslim worlds. Its fall could hardly have been a surprise, since the superior Ottoman forces had systematically acquired most of the territory in the city's immediate environs. The Byzantine capital had already suffered prolonged isolation and duress as the Ottomans gradually usurped the economic base which had supported it. The Ottoman decision to administer the coup de grâce to the Byzantine Empire indicated a willingness to assume control of the entire region. Although some might think it strange, the end of the Byzantine Empire clarified a significant matter of principle, if not of law. The Ottomans did not believe they could legitimately replace the authority of the Byzantine emperor as long as he existed. Later, they demonstrated a similar attitude toward the Mamluk Abbasid caliphate. In short, total conquest and extermination cleared the books and allowed the Ottomans to establish a new legitimacy.

Ottoman benevolence toward conquered peoples prevailed as long as there was no resistance to their domination. Areas in the path of conquest usually learned from advance delegations the kind of treatment they could expect if they accepted the superiority of the Ottomans and submitted. The Ottomans pillaged Constantinople because it resisted their siege for fifty-five days. Unlike more brutal marauders, the Ottomans gave careful attention to the ongoing economic production of the lands they conquered. Most regions, whether Byzantine, Turkish, or Mongol, benefited from the easier and clearer tax system of the Ottomans. The Ottomans appreciated the various skills of the diverse populations in their vast lands. Like most other major regimes of the region, the Ottomans moved large numbers of people to places where they and the government could benefit most from higher production. Instead of making Constantinople into a Muslim city, the Ottomans did not hesitate to repopulate the devastated city with an assortment of different peoples, including Christians and Jews from faraway places. Ottoman militancy never regarded all Christians as enemies. From the earliest stages of their expansion the Ottomans appreciated the need for economic intercourse with the Christian West. By the fifteenth century the Ottomans had become a major factor in

Mediterranean affairs, where they entered into alliances with and against Christian states.

As suggested earlier, Muslim areas that deviated from Sunni Islam or refused to accept its superiority in religious leadership had more to fear from the Ottomans than the Christians did. It was predictable that the bold and confident Ottomans would eventually clash with the aggressive new force of Safavid Shi'i Islam, whose emergence in Persia paralleled the Ottoman ascendancy. A struggle between them of any magnitude might very likely require decisive action from the Egypt-based Mamluks, whose Asian territories adjoined those of both the expanding Ottomans and the Safavids.

THE SAFAVIDS

The Safavid dynasty, which would endure into the eighteenth century and shape the entire outlook of Persia continuing into the future, developed on the foundation Safi al-Din established in the thirteenth century. Safi al-Din joined the Zahidiyyah Sufi order, which took his name after he became its leader. From its center in Ardabil in the southwest region of the Caspian Sea, the movement spread throughout Persia and beyond. Its spread into eastern Anatolia would in time cause conflict with the Ottomans. The emphasis upon mysticism, spiritualism, and miracles strongly appealed to Turkoman and Mongol tribes, who were ill-prepared to comprehend the legalistic and moral foundations of mainstream Islam. The movement was unusually well organized to send missionaries among the tribes and establish a deep, solid grassroots support. By the fifteenth century, the movement had decreased its emphasis upon mysticism and had evolved into full adoption of Twelver Shi'ism.

Having adopted a Twelver Shi'i approach to Islam, the Safavids decided to utilize their broad popular base to establish a Shi'i state in Persia to replace the dominant Sunni practice. In the tradition of Shi'ism, the first three Safavid leaders who attempted to establish a Shi'i state suffered martyrdom. But in 1501, from his base in eastern Anatolia, the Safavid leader Esma'il won a decisive battle at Sharur that gave him control of Azerbaijan. He assumed the title of Shah, proclaimed Shi'ism the official religion, and made Tabriz the capital of the new state. Where persuasion failed, Esma'il used force to convert Persians to his religious practice. Within the next decade he added the remainder of Persia to his realm and pushed westward to Baghdad. The Safavid push westward into eastern Anatolia posed a threat to both the Ottomans and the Mamluks.

OTTOMAN TRIUMPH

Shah Esma'il's success in uniting Persia and spreading Shi'ism into eastern Anatolia required a strong Ottoman response. Inhabitants of that region, which the Ottomans regarded as part of their empire, had been imbued with the Safavid belief long before Shah Esma'il obtained power. The Ottoman sultan, Selim I, killed 40,000 suspected Safavid supporters within his own borders before he launched his attack against the Persians. A decisive Ottoman victory over Safavid forces on August 23, 1514, at Chaldiran in northern Azerbaijan determined Ottoman suzerainty over eastern Anatolia, although Persians continued periodically to challenge the Ottoman conquests. The superiority of their army, especially their muskets and artillery, demonstrated that the Ottomans were the dominant Muslim military force. This shocked many supporters of Shah Esma'il, who believed that God favored him and his mission to spread Shi'i Islam, and did nothing to dampen the belief of the Ottomans that they were the true *ghazis*. Ottoman forces seized Tabriz but internal concerns and belief that Mamluk Egypt required immediate attention prevented the Ottomans from attempting to eradicate Safavid Shi'ism, which they regarded as anathema.

The Egyptian-Syrian Mamluk regime was quite aware of the emergence of the Ottomans' military power, which had become refined through conflict with the Christian West and the adoption of the most modern weaponry. Also, in keeping with their posture as the protectors of Islam, the Ottomans had made overtures to obtain the support of Arab officials in the Hejaz. These efforts threatened Mamluk domination over the Holy Places and the annual Pilgrimage. Moreover, Ottoman forces had treated Mamluk territory as their own in the campaign against Persia in 1514. The Mamluk decision to contest Ottoman supremacy led to the battle of Marj Dabik near Aleppo in August 1516. The presence of the Mamluk sultan, Kansu al-Gauri, and the Mamluk Abbasid caliph, al-Mutawakkil, attests to the importance of the confrontation in northern Syria. The outdated Mamluk equipment and tactics were of no avail against the Ottomans, who proved beyond doubt that they were the dominant Muslim power. The Mamluk sultan died of shock, and the Mamluk caliph was captured.

Mamluk leaders in Egypt refused to believe their regime of more than 250 years could end with a battle in Syria. Ottoman forces proceeded south into Palestine and implored the Egyptian Mamluks to surrender. The campaign concluded with a military invasion of Egypt and a forceful entry into Cairo in January 1517. The Mamluk dynasty ended,[21] and Egypt and Syria became provinces of the expanded Ottoman Empire. The Abbasid caliph went to Istanbul, where the Ottomans claim that he transferred his authority to the Ottoman sultan. This provided the kind of legal authenticity the Ottomans had always desired to justify their break with previous practice. The devastation of both the Persians and the Mamluks within a two-year period left no viable force to contest any claims Selim chose to make. The Hejaz also fell under Ottoman control, and in the subsequent reign of Suleiman the Magnificent, the sharif of Mecca acknowledged the Ottoman sultan as caliph.

The might of the Ottoman Empire, which soon pushed the Persian border to east of the Tigris River, ensured the ascendancy of the Sunni approach throughout western Islam. Ottoman control of the Hejaz and most of the Arabic-speaking portion of the Islamic world added to Ottoman authenticity as the protector of traditional Islam. No Muslim state could challenge Ottoman dominance. No new wave of marauding Oriental tribesmen appeared to destroy civilization. The Byzantine Empire was dead, and the Ottoman Empire was built upon the ground on which the former had thrived for more than a millennium. The Christian West, except for Spain, was a collection of small, semifeudal kingdoms who squabbled among themselves over petty matters in Europe and increasingly directed their energies toward exploiting the New World or the new routes to the Far East. Under these circumstances, the Ottoman Empire had little reason to fear invasion, and it maintained adequate control of all internal elements.

The overpowering dominance of the Ottomans probably enhanced the Persians' sense of their own uniqueness, which Twelver Shi'ism exemplified. Their choice seemed to be either to persist in their peculiar Islamic practice or to become like the Arabs and Turks to the west and south. Although there is no question as to the sincerity of the Persians' belief in Twelver Shi'ism, their persistent practice of it also provided a means of defining and preserving a Persian identity. Twelver Shi'ism became an integral part of the Persian character that continued to develop over the years, providing spiritual and political strength to the Persian Empire and giving Persians both an additional source of pride and a special sense of mission.

The incorporation of so much of Middle Eastern and North African Islam into the Ottoman and Persian empires early in the sixteenth century provided unusual stability. Conflict among warring fragments of western Islam had prevailed since the first Mongol invasion in the mid-thirteenth century. None of the Islamic regimes from that time had developed an orderly means of transferring executive power. Consequently, societies suffered from frequent military coups and frequent changes in policies. The Safavids and Ottomans at times used brutal tactics of fratricide, blinding, and imprisonment. Also, harems and slave-servants occasionally gained control of imperial affairs. But Safavid and

Ottoman approaches to transferring power within their respective royal families provided a method which normally allowed stability and continuity at the pinnacle of power.

IN PERSPECTIVE

Islam had spread rapidly beyond the Arabian peninsula, in large part because the neighboring Byzantine and Persian regimes were declining. Islam spread throughout North Africa, southwest Asia, parts of southeast Asia, and even parts of southern Europe. Islam defeated the crusaders and converted the Turks and Mongols who attempted to conquer its territories. In the course of those centuries, the nature of Islamic society changed considerably. Arabs receded into the background as Turks, Persians, and other later converts assumed leadership. Seldom unified, the factions of the Islamic world directed their greatest hostilities toward each other. In such conflicts Islam in general could not lose, since all contestants were Muslims. For instance, for the prolonged period of the Fatimids, Isma'ili and other forms of Shi'i Islam seemed likely to dominate Islam. The Seljuk invaders revived Sunni Islam in the eleventh century, but its survival was never secure in the tumult of later years. By the sixteenth century Sunni Islam and various forms of Shi'ism had acquired havens in which to practice their beliefs. Border conflicts between Persians and Ottomans occurred periodically, but usually resulted in continuation of something close to the status quo. The Persians generally were not strong enough to initiate aggression toward the Ottomans, and the Ottomans concentrated on their affairs with the Christian West.

The achievement of greater stability in the Islamic world by the sixteenth century was fortuitous, because Christian Europe was beginning a transformation that would provide it with unprecedented knowledge and wealth. Such developments would likely influence the Islamic Middle East, whether the Westerners decided to reenter the affairs of the region as crusaders or as merchants. The Islamic world had met all previous challenges. Islamic culture, including its science and technology, was an interesting combination of everything it had ever had the opportunity to learn and its own creative ingenuity. Western creativity would challenge the Islamic world's capacity and willingness to assimilate beneficial developments in the human quest for domination over other humans and Nature. The universalist outlook of Islam had thrived on such behavior in the past to produce an exciting, rich culture that others envied and attempted to emulate.

FOUR

SHI'I ISLAM

Shi'i, or partisans of 'Ali, believed that 'Ali and his direct descendants should provide caliphal leadership of Islam. In addition, Shi'i regarded 'Ali and some of his direct descendants as imams who had a special relationship with God to acquire divine insight into the true meaning of existing religious revelations and into proper religious practice.[1] Adherence to this concept began immediately upon the death of the Prophet Muhammad. Strong Shi'i traditions, in fact, insist that the issue arose even earlier and that the Prophet died assuming that Muslims understood his intentions for Islamic leadership to remain among 'Ali's descendants.

Shi'i claims that the Prophet Muhammad intended 'Ali to lead the Islamic movement make sense in several respects in addition to the evidence Shi'i used to prove their claim. 'Ali was a blood relative who had been like a son to the Prophet. 'Ali had been the most capable soldier of the Islamic movement. He was loyal and obedient, and he had performed tasks for the Prophet that ranged from the mundane to the extraordinarily dangerous. He was married to Fatimah, the Prophet's only surviving offspring, and was the father of the Prophet's grandchildren, Hasan and Husayn. 'Ali apparently had a reputation beyond dispute. In addition, there was no reason to believe that Abu Bakr and 'Umar, who were possible candidates, would outlive the Prophet, since their ages were similar to that of the Prophet, who generally enjoyed good health.

Elements in the Islamic community who felt excluded from power and rewards, along with other dissidents, helped constitute the mass of early Shi'i development. Movement of the capital to Damascus relegated Medina, Mecca, and all of Mesopotamia to the periphery. The Abbasids initially joined with 'Ali and his family in asserting the claim that the caliphate should reside in the Hashim clan.[2] Large numbers of Arabs who participated in expanding Islam into the Persian empire were particularly disappointed when friends of the first three caliphs, especially 'Uthman, reaped rewards they believed should have been theirs. Understandably, therefore, the Arab garrison towns of Kufa and Basra became the primary centers for the early Shi'i movement, which was almost exclusively among Arabs during the first half-century of Islam.

A nonhereditary approach to determining the succession prevailed, however, and not only did 'Ali have to wait to become the fourth caliph, but no direct descendant of his ever attained that position. The status of the Shi'i element within the Islamic world varied widely at different times and places. They continued to exist much like disinherited members of a family, never invited but allowed to attend family gatherings. Periodic attempts to exterminate them failed. Shi'i even occasionally became dominant in large areas and attempted to impose their will upon Islam. While deviation from the mainstream and a predictable level of persecution accounted for some of Shi'ism's hardship, it also resulted from fragmentation. Shi'ism remained only loosely defined. Loyalty to 'Ali attracted many different types of followers, who varied widely in their knowledge, beliefs, motives, backgrounds, and sense of direction.

Most Shi'i probably acknowledged that certain male descendants of 'Ali shared in his precocious understanding of God and his extraordinary gifts for interceding with God in behalf of believers. Belief that the religious leader was devoid of normal human needs and foibles and directly connected to God validated believers' religious choice and sanctified efforts in their leader's behalf. At a more mundane level, individuals and groups who lost favor, or could never achieve favor, in the Sunni mainstream gravitated to Shi'ism in search of meaning and effectiveness.

Shi'ism was a source of discontent and ferment for decades before it evolved into distinctive approaches and became generally more effective—although in some respects its early lack of definition gave it greater vigor. On balance, Shi'ism evolved in response to specific experiences of the partisans of 'Ali . Almost nothing besides belief in the imams remained constant among different groups of Shi'i. The imams differed dramatically in age, ability, knowledge, background, relations with the Sunni establishment, and freedom to communicate with their followers. Quite obviously, Shi'ism was very different during the first 142 years, when its imams lived, than it could be at any time afterward.

The main branches of Shi'ism obtained their character and names from their concept of the nature of the imamate and their belief as to which of 'Ali's descendants shared his special attributes. Twelver Shi'i acknowledged the validity of twelve imams, beginning with 'Ali and progressing through his male offspring over ten generations, until the line expired in 874.[3] Sevener Shi'i agreed with the Twelvers on the first six imams, but differed among themselves on the proper holder and function of the imamate. Fiver Shi'i accepted the first four imams of the other two branches, but regarded Zayd ibn 'Ali ibn Husayn (Imam Husayn's grandson), yet another descendant of 'Ali, as the Fifth Imam, who understood and defined Islam in its proper form and practice.[4]

THE IMAMS

Shi'i regarded 'Ali and certain of his direct descendants as God's representatives on earth, despite the unwillingness of Sunni to allow them to obtain the title of caliph. In their view, appointments made in Heaven did not require earthly approval. 'Ali or one of his male descendants was, therefore, imam in each era, regardless of age or capacity to commune with believers.

The twelve men who constitute the Twelver Imamate attained the status of imam during the period from the Prophet's death in 632 until the line failed to produce an offspring in 874. All faced hardships during their lives, and all but the last died as martyrs. 'Ali died at the hands of an assassin, Husayn was executed and beheaded, and the others were supposedly poisoned, except for the twelfth and last imam, whose mysterious fate required voluminous explanation and led to a decisive definition of Twelver Islam. Some imams openly led their followers with the establishment's approval, some operated clandestinely and under duress, and others hardly acted at all. 'Ali and Husayn, the First and Third Imams, were blatantly political and lived and died violently in the political arena. Imams Two, Four, Five, Six, Seven, and Nine lived all or most of their lives in Medina, which remained a spiritual and intellectual center of Islam after first Damascus and then Baghdad became the center of politics, wealth, and war. The Eighth Imam enjoyed a short stint in public when the ruler of the Persian portion of the Abbasid empire made an effort to reconcile Shi'i and Sunni Islam. Imams Ten, Eleven, and Twelve experienced the ignominy of incarceration at the new Abbasid capital of Samarra. Their seclusion grew increasingly severe, to the point that it became impossible to establish the exact birthdate and time of disappearance of the Twelfth Imam. The Twelve Imams differed in almost every possible way except for their kinship with 'Ali.

'Ali, who played no role of significance during the reign of the first three caliphs, became caliph after the death of Abu Bakr, following two years in office, and the assassinations of both 'Umar and 'Uthman. Dissent and turmoil marked his five-year caliphate, during which his enemies held much of the Islamic empire. He used brutal force against former supporters and suffered the indignity of an assassin's blade. His burial at Najaf established that site and his tomb as a holy place for veneration and scholarship. 'Ali's eldest son, Hasan,

Descendants of 'Abdullah (and of Muhammad, The Prophet, 570–632)	Descendants of Abu Talib	Descendants of al-Abbas (Abbasid Dynasty, 750–1258)

1 'Ali
(d. 40/661)

2 al-Hasan
(d. 49/669)
Eldest son of 'Ali and Fatimah, daughter of Muhammad. Some always believed the imamate should remain in al-Hasan line, but he conceded leadership to Mu'awiyah.

Muhammad al-Hanifiyyah
(d. 81/700)
Son of 'Ali and Khawala of the Hanif tribe. Believed by **Karibiyyah** to be in occultation. Expected by **Kaysaniyyah (Mukhtariyyah)** to return as Mahdi. Elements of this movement were closely allied with the Abbasids. **Harbiyyah** broke up into **Riyahiyyah, Janahiyyah,** and **Khurramiyyah.**

3 al-Husayn
(d. 10 Muh. 61/10 Oct. 680)
Son of 'Ali and Fatimah, daughter of Muhammad.

'Abdullah ('of Pure Blood')
(d. 144/762)
Imam for those who insisted the imamate should remain in line of al-Hasan. Husayn was his maternal grandfather. Direct descendant of both Hasan and Husayn. Father of Muhammad ibn 'Abdullah al-Nafs al-Zakiyyah.

4 'Ali Zayn al-Abidin (The Pure One)
(d. 94/712)

Abu Hashim
(d. 98/716)
Son of Muhammad al-Hanifiyyah, who **Hashimiyyah** believe appointed *(nass)* Abu Hashim as successor, in what was perhaps the first use of the *nass* concept. Hashim would return as the Mahdi. Some believers known as **Bayaniyyah,** others as **Rawandiyyah.**

Muhammad ibn 'Abdullah al-Nafs al-Zakiyyah
(d. 144/762)
A Hasanid who was great-grandson of Hasan and grand-nephew of Husayn. His brother, Ibrahim, had an almost equal role in their activities.

5 Muhammad al-Baqir
(d. 113/731)
Expected by **Baqiriyyah** to return as the Mahdi. **Mughiriyyah** Gnostics emphasized symbolism and esoteric knowledge. **Mansuriyyah** believed that the seventh prophet after him would be the Mahdi.

Zayd
(d. 122/740)
Half-brother of Muhammad al-Baqir. Founder of Zaydi or Fiver Shi'ism. Fivers believed anyone in Hashimite family of good character could be imam.

6 Ja'far al-Sadiq
(d. 148/765)
Khattabiyyah were radical followers of Ja'far who introduced some important concepts that Shi'ism later accepted. Endorsed imamate of Isma'il in his lifetime and then that of his son, Muhammad ibn Isma'il. **Mubarakiyyah** were radical followers whom Ja'far rejected; they supported the imamate of Muhammad ibn Muhammad.

Yahya
(d. 125/743)
Son of Zayd. Abu Hashim was his maternal grandfather.

7 Isma'il (ibn Ja'far)
(d. c. 146/754–763)
Son of Ja'far by Fatimah, great-granddaughter of Hasan ibn 'Ali. Died before his father, Ja'far al-Sadiq, between 754 and 763. Because his father had designated him as his successor, questions arose over who should succeed him, leading to a split between Imami (Twelvers) and Isma'ili (Seveners).

7 Musa al-Kazim
(d. 183/799)
Choice of Imami (Twelver) Shi'i. Son of Ja'far al-Sadiq by his concubine Hamida.

7 Muhammad ibn Isma'il
(d. c. 181/796)
Hidden Imam of most Isma'ilis. Probably died in Kuzistan c. 796. The choice of most Shi'i, who rejected Isma'il ibn Ja'far al-Sadiq as Imam on grounds that he died before his father. They believed that he, rather than his uncle, Musa al-Kazim, was the Imam.

8 'Ali al-Rida
(d. 203/818)

9 Muhammad 'al-Jawad
(d. 220/835)

10 'Ali al-Hadi
(d. 254/868)

11 Hasan al-Askari
(d. 260/874)

12 Muhammad al-Muntazar (al-Mahdi)
(d. c. 264/874)

» CHART 2 «

The Twelve Shi'i Imams and Their Rivals for the Imamate

the Second Imam, forsook any claim to the caliphate in the face of the over-whelming military strength of Mu'awiyah, the founder of the Umayyad dynasty. 'Ali's next son, Husayn, accepted leadership of the Shi'i as the Third Imam, but perished at the instructions of Mu'awiyah's son, Yazid, whose soldiers slaughtered Husayn and his followers at Karbala. The dramatic dispatch of his severed head to Damascus entranced Shi'i with the horror of Husayn's martyrdom. He quickly acquired veneration comparable to that reserved for Muhammad and 'Ali. No shrine, including those of Mecca, Medina, and Najaf, has had greater appeal for Shi'i pilgrims than Husayn's tomb at Karbala. The mourning of his death on the tenth day of the Islamic month of Muharram became the most important event of the year for most Twelver Shi'i. Husayn's reputation for virtue and purity, in contrast to his older brother, ennobled the Shi'i cause to the point that even less distinguished descendants of 'Ali attained veneration, and Shi'ism developed beyond the danger of extinction.

One of Husayn's sons, 'Ali, the Pure One, survived Karbala and received adoration as Fourth Imam, although he lived in self-imposed isolation and indicated no interest in Shi'i affairs. The more than thirty years of his imamate represented a considerable period of drift, which supporters of Muhammad ibn al-Hanifiyyah, a son of 'Ali by a different wife,[5] exploited to extol his claims as his father's successor. Al-Hanifiyyah's twenty years of active political and religious activities allowed this offspring of 'Ali to increase the hold he had on many supporters. His associates introduced the concept of *al-Mahdi* ('savior')[6] into Islam and contended that after al-Hanifiyyah died in 700, he was only in occultation[7] and would return in the future to fulfill his role. While most Shi'i later rejected this contention, it foreshadowed the direction Shi'ism would take. The numerous groups which grew out of the imamate claims for al-Hanifiyyah provided many of the often-radical ideas that subsequent Shi'i groups have held, in various combinations.

The son of the Pure One, Muhammad al-Baqir, who was almost as retiring as his father, became the Fifth Imam. His half-brother Zayd also claimed the extraordinary right to lead Islam; and, although Zayd's activities created considerable turmoil in his lifetime, it was he who had the longer-range importance as founder of Fiver (Zaydi) Shi'ism.

Al-Baqir's son Ja'far al-Sadiq, the Sixth Imam and probably the most important of those who sought to fulfill this role, provided direction for the entirety of Islam. His fame as a teacher derived from his embrace of generally mainstream Islamic principles rather than those associated with Shi'ism. Two future giants of Sunni Islamic law, Abu Hanifa and Malik ibn Anas, studied with him. It is instructive to remember that he, like his father and grandfather before him, had no way of knowing the kind of role he was playing in developing a separate belief. These imams possessed no administrative structure or

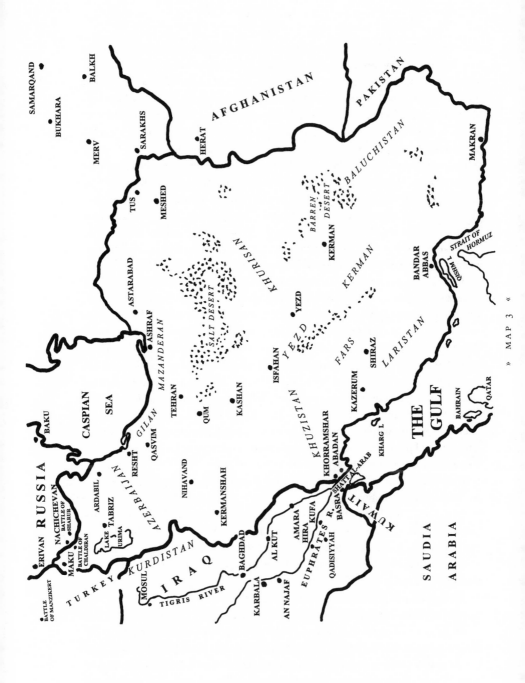

MAP 3

army to enable them to profit from the veneration of their adherents. With rival claimants emerging throughout this period, the future direction of Shi'i Islam remained very uncertain.

The Seventh Imam, Musa al-Kazim, suffered from the persecution and confusion which surrounded his long but inactive imamate. Some Shi'i pledged their loyalty to Musa's nephew, Muhammad ibn Isma'il, who was the heir of Musa's older brother, Isma'il ibn Ja'far. The latter had been designated as the Imam before his premature death, giving rise to the Isma'ili Shi'i[8] branch, whose assertive claims and actions attracted unusually harsh persecution for Musa and other Shi'i from Harun al-Rashid. The indignities Musa suffered inspired Esma'il, the first Twelver Shah of Persia, to construct a remarkable shrine to him north of Baghdad at Kazimayn.

'Ali al-Rida, the Eighth Imam, moved to Merv in northeastern Persia to participate in Caliph al-Mamun's abortive effort to reconcile Sunni and Shi'i elements of Islam. He even enjoyed the title of heir to the Abbasid throne for a while before opponents of the experiment poisoned him. The town of Qum inadvertently benefited from 'Ali al-Radi's unusual adventure in Persia. After the Imam's sister, Fatimah, died in Qum en route to visit her brother, Shah Esma'il's daughter sponsored the construction of a magnificent shrine there to commemorate Fatimah's death. The shrine developed into one of Shi'i Islam's foremost intellectual centers.[9]

The Ninth Imam, Muhammad al-Jawad, spent some time in Baghdad as the guest of the optimistic Caliph al-Ma'mun. He barely provided a successor, 'Ali al-Hadi, before his death at a young age. This Tenth Imam spent his entire adult life under the watchful eye of the Abbasid government in the new administrative center of Samarra, north of Baghdad. A similar fate awaited 'Ali al-Hadi's son, Hasan, the Eleventh Imam. His short life and his isolation raised serious questions about whether he even had a son. But his mysterious child, Muhammad al-Muntazar, became the Twelfth Imam. While the seclusion and isolation of the last three imams might well have terminated Shi'i Islam, it in fact had the opposite effect. The mystery provided an aura and a rationale for which there was sufficient precedent to allow the Imam to become whatever the faithful desired. Whatever the reality of the last Imam's fate, both informed and imaginative believers defined a role for him in Shi'i belief that at least rivaled those of 'Ali and Husayn.

By most accounts Muhammad al-Muntazar, *al-Mahdi* ("the Messiah"), went into occultation at Samarra in 874 at an age of no more than ten. The Imam's youth was no obstacle to fulfillment of his functions, since his special attributes came from God, rather than from earthly experience. Also, his total disappearance initially was not much different from the circumstances of his two predecessors, who had been secluded for a total of twenty-five years. Their secretary, 'Uthman al-Amri, who had communicated the comments of the Tenth and Eleventh Imams to Shi'i representatives, continued to serve that function. Al-Amri called himself the Bab ("door") to the Hidden Imam. Three other individuals served as the Mahdi's Bab until the last one died in 941. The existence of other claimants, the imamate's prolonged removal, and numerous important developments of the time minimized any realization that something of great magnitude regarding the imamate was occurring.

THE APPEAL OF THE IMAMATE CONCEPT

Questions arise regarding how the simple message of Muhammad could lead some Muslims to believe in something close to continued revelation and the intercession of imams between believers and God. But Islam spread rapidly from the Arabian peninsula into the Persian and Byzantine empires, which abounded with religious diversity. Gods of all kinds were in the heavens and on the earth, as were messiah concepts and beliefs in salvation on this earth and in the heavens. Islam could not escape influence from existing religions. It is understandable that some parts of existing belief offered more comfort than Islam, which, however universal in outlook, derived from an Arab ethos.

From the earliest days, some who found Islam attractive were not content with an invisible God of spirit, so far removed as to seem hypothetical, and a prophet who died. Such people often generated robust movements to deify Muhammad, 'Ali, Husayn, and their descendants. Muhammad, 'Ali, and the eleven direct descendants from 'Ali and the Prophet's daughter, Fatimah, all inspired a veneration that was questionable, given Muhammad's insistence that he was merely a mortal with a heavenly message. Interestingly, more deification occurred in behalf of 'Ali and his offspring than in behalf of the Prophet himself. A feeling that 'Ali had to wait unjustly to become caliph apparently initiated more unusual feeling for him than for Muhammad. Strong animosity toward the first two caliphs, Abu Bakr and 'Umar, who the Shi'i believe misguided Islam after the Prophet's death, accompanied veneration of 'Ali and his offspring.[10] There is no way to establish how much of this sentiment was religious and how much political. The record shows, however, that the closest associates of these first two caliphs, as well as those of the third caliph, 'Uthman, did receive preference in the distribution of offices, wealth, and power.

Advocacy of the deity of 'Ali and his offspring was the best possible argument for his right to both the caliphate and the imamate. People who wished to establish their primacy among 'Ali's supporters professed the highest possible claims for his powers. Some supporters refused to claim anything less than divinity for all the Alid imams. 'Ali and some of his successors even felt compelled to implement severe punishment for those who made the strongest claims of Alid divinity. The level of deification corresponded roughly to the degree of the suffering of the different imams. In this regard, even 'Ali could not match Husayn. After each Alid imam died, some of his supporters began a movement based on the claim that he had been the last imam. They further claimed that the infallible, suffering leader was not dead, but merely in occultation, from which he would arise as the Mahdi.

The most active Shi'i movements arose in behalf of individuals whom the mainstream of Shi'i Islam did not venerate as imams. These movements caused considerable ferment, since groups acted fervently in behalf of their imams. Meanwhile the majority of Shi'i believers rather matter-of-factly accepted their own imams, who had little visible power and led esoterically, according to the peculiar circumstances of their times. Thus, the mainstream was drifting toward an uncertain future, while the heterodox elements actively tried to seize the moment to shape that future. Support for 'Ali's son Muhammad ibn al-Hanifiyyah, which cropped up early and persisted for several generations, could have become Shi'ism. The Fifth Imam's brother, Zayd, acquired a vibrant following that has controlled parts of the Islamic world even to the present. Contention over the transfer of the imamate at the choice of the Seventh Imam resulted in several significant Sevener Isma'ili sects which destroyed tranquillity at the time of their origin and lasted in varied forms to the present.

In short, it was virtually impossible for supporters of the Twelfth Imam to make claims which the Shi'i had not already heard. However, Shi'i at all levels of knowledge, understanding, and belief required a fuller explanation of the imamate after the 67-year hiatus between the Imam's disappearance and the death of the last Bab in 941. A large proportion of the Shi'i accepted that the last Alid, Muhammad al-Muntazar, was the Twelfth Imam. Acknowledgment that he was in occultation and would only reappear at the instruction of God soon followed to provide the basic outline of Twelver Shi'ism. When and why the Imam would reappear as the Mahdi, how he would guide the faithful until his return, and the nature and role of his agents on earth remained undefined. The dominance of non-Shi'i elements throughout Islam eliminated any urgency to answer these questions among the Shi'i, who themselves generally remained clandestine. Their constant jeopardy, in fact, inspired the 'ulama's acceptance of the practice of dissimulation, by which Shi'i, contrary to the exigencies of mainstream Islam, could deny their religious affiliation if it served the cause of their religion.[11]

The travail of Shi'i lessened throughout the tenth and part of the eleventh centuries. Fatimid Isma'ilis controlled Egypt, most of Syria, and the Hejaz; the Buyids[12] controlled most of Persia and Iraq; the Hamdanids controlled northern Syria; Zaydi controlled Daylam and Tabaristan[13] along the southern rim of the Caspian Sea; and Zaydi or Qarmati controlled Yemen and eastern Arabia. Despite the rule of Shi'i regimes, however, it seems that Sunni practice remained dominant in the Arab and Persian heartland. Peripheral areas such as Bahrain, Lebanon, Daylam, Tabaristan, Tunisia, and Yemen were more ardently Shi'i. The aggressive nature of the mostly Isma'ili Shi'ism in these regions generated considerable Sunni retribution once the latter regained control. Most of the less ardent Shi'i who survived the backlash forsook the radical approaches to Shi'ism which had produced numerous *mahdis* and imams in occultation.

ISMA'ILI SHI'ISM

The often tumultuous relations among Shi'i clarified toward the end of the imamate of Ja'far al-Sadiq, the Sixth Imam, but while the future divisions were fewer, they were decisive. The Hasanid and Hanifid branches descended from 'Ali had died out, leaving all subsequent competition for the hereditary imamate among the Husaynids. Ja'far, who founded the Shi'i school of religious law, was the last imam to be held in common by both main branches of Shi'ism—Twelver and Isma'ili. He solidified the concepts of infallibility of the imams, the necessity for imams to designate a successor *(nass)*, and the permissibility for Shi'i to deny their religious belief[14] in order to avoid persecution. While the two major Shi'i branches that emerged after his death differed on who the imams should be, they generally agreed that Ja'far's claim was above contention. They were also in accord that the imamate should pass from father to son in the Alid-Fatimid line; that the imams were necessary to explain the hidden, deeper, esoteric meaning of the Holy Qur'an and religious law; and that if only two people existed on earth, one of them must be the Imam. Ja'far vehemently rejected claims of divinity which some made in behalf of him and the other imams. While Ja'far denied that imams possessed powers of divinity or prophecy, he insisted that they had the extraordinary role of explaining the meaning of religion to believers. Most subsequent Shi'i views conformed to these rulings of Shi'i Islam's foremost jurist. While Shi'i imams generally did not cite *isnad*—the chain of transmission—to validate *hadith* (on the grounds that they needed no explanation for their conclusions), neither did they acknowledge the validity of any *hadith* al-Ja'far did not recognize.

Wise and respected as he was, however, Ja'far could not control the circumstances following his death in 765. Ja'far's apparent failure to designate a successor after his son Isma'il died sowed genuine confusion and allowed various personal agendas to unfold. The Imamis, who became the Twelvers, recognized Ja'far's son by a concubine, Musa al-Kazim, as the Imam. He generally enjoyed the protection of the Hashimite family and friends in Medina. Some Shi'i, on the other hand, refused to accept Isma'il's death and regarded him as the Mahdi, while most Shi'i outside Medina accepted Isma'il's son, Muhammad ibn Isma'il, as the new Imam. By most standards, except for the possible absence of designation *(nass)* from his father, he was the right choice, since his father was dead and acceptance of Musa, his uncle, violated the prevailing principle of primogeniture.

The number seven and the Seventh Imam became a strong theme in Isma'ili Shi'ism, in part because of the influence of some renowned gnostics and numerologists such as Abu al-Khattab. Different Shi'i elements, sects, or subsects developed their own arcane ways of calculating the list and the sequence of imams, and some assigned titles higher than Imam *(al-Mahdi* and *al-Qa'im)* to their favorite luminaries in order to accommodate their entire preferred list and still keep the magic number of imams at seven. Significantly, most Isma'ili movements, some of which developed into enduring sects, emphasized a major role for Jesus in God's continuum of revealed truth, on a teleological course which would end with the Mahdi. One must remember, of course, that considerable disagreement prevailed about the identity of the Mahdi. The fact that people closely associated with the imamate often had to deny their true identities for self-protection adds to the confusion about sequence of ancestry and succession to the imamate or some lesser version of authentic religious leadership. The three generations following Muhammad ibn Isma'il's seclusion presented the greatest confusion because of the uncertainty about his progeny and their location.

Being unable to operate openly in the shadow of his uncle in Medina, Muhammad ibn Isma'il moved to Khuzistan in southwestern Persia, where he disappeared from public view and became widely known as the Hidden Imam. Considerable confusion developed among Isma'ili about whether he was in occultation and whether he or his representative would appear as the Mahdi. While the term "Hidden Imam" usually conveys the concept of the imam who is in occultation to return as a harbinger of Judgment Day, Isma'ili often use the term to describe imams of every generation who had to conceal their identities to avoid death or imprisonment. Muhammad ibn Isma'il's total disappearance or death seems to have occurred about 796. The question of the location and condition of the Imam and his six sons produced additional mystery and confusion about his intentions, whether he had dispensed his power, and—if so—to whom.

'Abd Allah, a son of Muhammad ibn Isma'il, moved to Salamiyyah, about twenty miles southeast of Hama in Syria, which became the Isma'ili headquarters for three generations before it moved to North Africa. An active missionary program targeted the dissident Arabs and *mawali* in southern Iraq, which remained the most fertile ground for Shi'i growth. About the time that the Twelfth Imam of the Imami (Twelvers) went into occultation in 874, the emergence of an unusually effective missionary named Hamdan Qarmat provided vigor and direction for supporters of Muhammad ibn Isma'il. While the Imami were willing to remain passive until the return of their Imam, supporters of Muhammad ibn Isma'il adopted an offensive approach of missionary and military activity. Partisans of Muhammad ibn Isma'il as the Mahdi soon became known as Qarmatians, or Isma'ilis.[15]

For more than a century, beginning in approximately 900, Qarmatians posed a major problem for all other entities in the region. Salamiyyah remained the hub from which all activities radiated. The Qarmatians soon spread eastward into Persia and beyond, but were strongest in southern Iraq, the al-Hasa/Bahrain region on the Gulf coast,[16] Yemen, and North Africa. Qarmatian activities based at al-Hasa engendered the greatest concern and gained the most attention, although it was not the center of their more enduring influence. No contemporaries could inspire the fear and terror that Qarmatians spread from the Gulf to the Mediterranean Sea. Muslims with contrary views were almost always the object of their fury. Huge payments designed to avoid their wrath seemed at best to lengthen the intervals between their raids, which often seemed more venal than ideological. Not the least of their appeal, however, was their advocacy and partial implementation of a society that limited and redistributed wealth while permitting a modicum of participatory government. Some part of the Qarmatians' success from the base in al-Hasa/Bahrain also undoubtedly derived from their location so far from the Abbasid heartland.

Qarmatian/Isma'ili Shi'ism was bifurcated because it spread cautiously to a carefully selected and slowly initiated stratum of elite intellectuals, while it garnered mass appeal by promising to replace rule by the privileged few with social justice for everyone. Bedouin and peasants from the rural areas constituted the majority of the rank and file, while a variety of literate urbanites joined as initiates to embrace Isma'ili scholarship, which varied from gnosticism to rationalism.

FATIMID DEVELOPMENT

A major cleavage occurred in 899 when Muhammad ibn Isma'il's great-great-grandson 'Ubayd Allah, who coordinated Isma'ili activities in Salamiyyah, overtly claimed, as he had hinted for a few years, that he was the Imam. According to him, designated members of the 'Ali-Fatimah (Fatimid) line were always the imams rather than just their spokesmen. His entire lineage over the four previous generations had consisted of the "Hidden Imams," each of whom had taken the name of Muhammad ibn Isma'il and perpetuated the ruse that the original was being in occultation until his return as the Mahdi. They had been "hidden" because it had been unsafe for them to lead the faithful openly. In keeping with this new interpretation he referred to himself as 'Ubayd Allah al-Mahdi and renamed his son "al-Qa'im," which was an even more exalted title for the provider of wisdom and justice on earth. Fatimids were prepared to accept their role as leaders of the faithful in the fullest spectrum of human activities, among themselves and with their God.

This was a perfectly feasible explanation for many Isma'ilis, in view of the persecution Shi'i had suffered at every level. Their support of the Fatimids' right to rule made them willing subjects where the Fatimids seized power, and they served as agents for Fatimid expansion throughout the Islamic world. For these Fatimid Isma'ilis, Muhammad ibn Isma'il represented a very important link to the earliest generations of Islam and the entire monotheistic development. But, in light of the new interpretation, his return as "The" Mahdi was no longer necessary or acceptable. Fatimids, however, were never unified on exactly who had been imams and where the future would lead. Fatimid claims of infallibility proved a burden at times, since even the most faithful observed that their leaders made untrue predictions and engaged in errant behavior. The non-Fatimid Isma'ili were even more riddled with "false" imams too numerous to discuss, although some caused considerable stir, both in their own times and later.

While claims to the imamate occurred quite frequently, 'Ubayd Allah was too prominent to ignore. He fled from Salamiyyah in 902 to escape the Qarmatian and Abbasid forces which descended on the town to punish or kill him. He enjoyed some support from various parts of the far-flung Isma'ili network, which explains Abbasid efforts to obstruct his activities. 'Ubayd Allah moved to Palestine and progressed westward across North Africa before he found haven and widespread support among the Kutama Berber tribe and others in the region that has become modern Algeria. He suffered a short period of imprisonment in 909 before his supporters obtained control of the entire region and declared him caliph in January 910. With his capital in the old Islamic center at Qayrawan in Ifriqiyyah (modern Tunisia), he had a base far enough removed from the heart of Abbasid power to implement the ambitious intentions of the Fatimids to impose their authority and approach to Islam upon the entire Islamic world. Much of North Africa and Sicily fell under Fatimid control, but their initial attempts to wrest Egypt from the Abbasids failed.

The removal of the Fatimid leadership from Salamiyyah left the Qarmatians a freer hand among the Shi'i in southwest Asia, especially after 903, when they destroyed the remaining Fatimid family and facilities and the missionary network which had been so effective. A strong Qarmatian element remained in Kufa, but the establishment of a Qarmatian state in al-Hasa/Bahrain altered its role in the region. Located a great distance from the center of Abbasid power, the Qarmatians could conduct lightning-fast campaigns out of the desert and return to safety with little fear of retaliation.

This aggressive movement was more than a nuisance, as it became particularly active in 923 under the leadership of Abu Tahir Sulayman, in anticipation of the predicted return of the Mahdi, Muhammad ibn Isma'il. The Qarmatians had no respect for traditional belief and practice since they believed that the Mahdi would abrogate prevailing worship and law with his gift of perfect wisdom and justice. Pilgrim caravans became favorite targets for Qarmatian aggression in an effort to increase both their wealth and their influence. They devastated Mecca in 930 and added insult to injury by carrying away the Black Stone. Once they had absorbed Oman in 931, they controlled the entire Arabian peninsula. Kufa fell under their control, but they failed to conquer Baghdad. Qarmatian Shi'ism spread by more peaceful means to the Caspian Sea areas of Daylam, Tabaristan, and Gurgan, as well as to the area southwest of the Caspian around Rayy. The Qarmatians ceased their raids on pilgrims in 939, but retained the Black Stone until 951. These concessions resulted from generous Abbasid payments rather than a change in Qarmatian attitudes.

The Fatimids obtained control of Egypt in 969, after the reigning Abbasid regime had declined to a mere shadow. They constructed the new city of Cairo to serve as the center of their new empire,[17] which they extended by negotiation to the Hejaz within a year. Abbasid and Qarmatian resistance delayed the establishment of Fatimid control over Syria, but only until 976. The Fatimids also constructed al-Azhar—by some calculations the first university in the world. It trained the Isma'ili scholars who conducted missionary work throughout the Islamic world. Much of their activity had to be clandestine to avoid their eradication. Like most successful organizations of later times,[18] the Isma'ili missionaries concentrated their activities upon carefully selected individuals, whom they trained extensively. They relied upon a less well-informed mass following to provide the numbers they needed to establish greater influence and prepare for Fatimid domination.

Whether out of conviction or to expand Fatimid influence, Caliph al-Mu'izz (952–975) altered the Fatimid views that 'Ubayd Allah had initiated at the turn of the century. Al-Mu'izz accepted the mainstream Isma'ili concept that Muhammad ibn Isma'il was the awaited Mahdi. He insisted, however, that the Fatimid caliphs served as the Mahdi's infallible imams until his return. Large Isma'ili areas soon responded favorably to the new Fatimid interpretation, which returned them to the Isma'ili mainstream. Areas as far away as

India and places in between acknowledged the validity of the Egypt-based Fatimid caliphate. The change in doctrine enabled al-Mu'izz's successor, al-Aziz (975–996), to obtain the allegiance of the al-Hasa/Bahrain Qarmatians, but only after paying them a large annual tribute. Fatimid success spelled the end of the Qarmatian movement. Abbasid allies gained control of the large island of Uwal in 1058, and al-Hasa came under Abbasid authority in 1077 to close a major chapter in Isma'ili influence. In effect, al-Mu'izz's acceptance of Muhammad ibn Isma'il as the Mahdi a century earlier had eliminated the doctrinal reasons for Qarmatians to remain a separate element of the Isma'il movement.

The demise of the Qarmatians corresponded to a rise in Abbasid power and signaled the impending fate of the Fatimids. Seljuk Turks, who were firm believers in Sunni Islam, had overthrown the Buyids in Baghdad in 1055 and restored the Abbasid caliphate to its full religious authority. Seljuks captured most of Syria and Palestine from the Fatimids by 1065 and restored the Hejaz, with its holy cities, to Abbasid control in 1070. Famine and general economic deprivation in Egypt at this time caused the Fatimid caliph, al-Mustansir, to rely first upon an Armenian general and then upon Turks to retain his power and continue the Fatimid dynasty. The crusader invasion of Syria-Palestine in 1099 added another alien force the Fatimids could not successfully combat or expel. Vital assistance from Turkish officer/administrators[19] and their foreign troops kept Fatimid caliphs nominally in power in Egypt until 1171, when Saladin did not allow the selection of another caliph after al-Adid died. Egypt at that time, like most of the Islamic world, returned to Sunni Islam.

CONCLUSION

Isma'ili Shi'ism in its various forms had burst upon the Islamic world in the eighth century. It had demonstrated inordinate vigor because of its strong sense of direction in behalf of heartfelt beliefs, combined with a strong sense of being misunderstood and maligned. Its two principal rivals did relatively little to counter the Isma'ili challenge. Imami (Twelver) Shi'ism remained fairly docile in an apparent acceptance of failure, despite adherents' conviction that they embodied correct belief and practice. Sunni Islam successfully squelched the small Shi'i outbreaks with such regularity that it seemed to regard Shi'ism as simply a chronic condition which was not life-threatening.

The Shi'i, however, had a strong message. The connection with the family of the Prophet appealed to Arabs of various persuasions, and Shi'i emphasis upon social justice appealed to most *mawali*. Individuals with a strong commitment to Isma'ili Shi'ism took sword and pen in hand to advance their cause, while the Imami slowly and silently evolved into a form which would not become clear until generations later. In essence, first the Seljuk and then the Ottoman Turks asserted their strength in behalf of Sunni Islam, and the Safavids moved with similar swiftness in behalf of Twelver Shi'ism, to relegate Isma'ili Shi'ism to the periphery of Middle Eastern Islam. Sunni Islam became dominant. Twelver Shi'ism, in fact, seemed to survive mostly because of Persians' determination to remain distinctly different from Arabs and Turks.

Shi'ism had, however, transformed Islam and the region in the time of its zenith, and the changes would reach far into the future.

DRUZE

Within a generation after al-Mu'izz reduced the imamate claims of the Fatimids, a movement began that ascribed divine power to al-Muslimun al-Hakim (996–1021), the sixth Fatimid caliph. In truth, al-Hakim's behavior had been unusual in several respects. This new leader of a family with a strong tradition of tolerance[20] ordered severe treatment of Christians and Jews and their holy properties in the early years of his reign. Later he rescinded some of his harsh orders and adopted an ascetic approach to life, which apparently stimulated esteem and veneration from some of his contemporaries.

An Isma'ili clergyman named al-Hasan ibn Haydara al-Akhram proclaimed him the personification of God in 1017. A Persian in Cairo named Hamza ibn 'Ali endorsed al-Akhram's conclusion, but the namesake of an emerging new religion was a Turk named Muhammad al-Darazi.

Even though the new Druze religion was so different that it falls beyond the broadest possible definition of Islam, it deserves attention because it grew out of the Isma'ili Shi'i tradition of expecting a Mahdi to provide pure wisdom and justice on earth. Also, in the Shi'i tradition, al-Darazi disappeared in 1019 and al-Hakim disappeared in 1021 at the age of 36. Hamza went into hiding for self preservation and communicated with Baha al-Din al-Muqtana,[21] who actively propagated his message. Hamza assumed the role of the Imam, who conveyed the views of al-Hakim, God's presence on earth.

The supporters of al-Hakim referred to their faith as *al-Tawhid* and themselves as *muwahhidun*[22] to emphasize their monotheism and the unity of everything under God. This essentially Platonic concept of God, with al-Hakim as the earthly emanation, attracted converts as far east as India despite severe persecution. The active proselytizing benefited from dissident elements of the Fatimid missionary network who believed in al-Hakim. The period of outreach was very short, however, ending in 1043, when al-Muqtana issued his last message from Hamza. At that time the ranks of Druze closed; from then on, converts were not accepted and Druze who left their religion were not allowed to retain their place in society.

Knowledge of the Druze religion was closely guarded among a handful of carefully selected, initiated, and educated *shaykhs*. These *'uqqal* had access to the sacred scriptures composed of the writings of the founders of the religion, compiled in six tomes entitled *The Books of Wisdom (Rasa'il al-Hikma)*. Like other believers in a Mahdi, the Druze saw no need for the mundane books or practice of preexisting, errant religions. They expected al-Hakim to return and implement justice and wisdom. The uninitiated, which constitute the majority of Druze, are required to follow the leadership of the *shaykhs* until al-Hakim's return. They know enough to believe that they must have faith. The challenge to live a virtually blemishless life deters the average believer from seeking admission into the higher echelons, who learn the mysteries of the religion and have the responsibility to prepare the way for al-Hakim's return.

Expectation of al-Hakim's reappearance helps explain the Druze belief that souls remain on earth and pass into new bodies. Stories of Druze who encounter souls they knew from the past in new bodies are legend. Such unique experiences and beliefs provide Druze a strong sense of unity, although most do not understand anything beyond the most rudimentary elements of their religion. The dispersal of Druze all over the world in the twentieth century has destroyed much of their traditional means of keeping in touch and retaining their solidarity. Concerned individuals have convinced some leading *shaykh*s to propagate elementary manuals of their faith in order to guide the Druze scattered beyond Syria and Lebanon, who usually have no clergy living among them. Widespread though al-Tawhid has been, persecution—punctuated by major massacres of their leadership—confined continued practice to the protective fastness of Syrian and Lebanese mountains.

TWELVER SHI'ISM

The decline or demise of more radical forms of Shi'ism left the mainstream, which was becoming Twelver Shi'ism, as the most viable choice for supporters of Alid claims. As support for Twelver Shi'ism increased in the eleventh century, it moved closer to the course it would follow in the future.

The central role of reason in Shi'i jurisprudence required a method of producing responsible interpreters. This approach also generated a large number of trained clergy among the Shi'i, while by comparison Sunni Islam required very few. The need arose before any method existed to guide Shi'i legal procedures and interpretation. But from the earliest days, venerable scholars emerged who transmitted their views to posterity. Most generations produced scholars of renown who sometimes wrote treatises and books, but also relied upon their students to preserve their views. While in most cases neither the scholars nor their followers claimed that their rulings replaced those of the Hidden Imam, they obviously served that purpose. Individual Shi'i scholars practiced *ijtihad*,[23] meaning they gave their opinions on specific cases and about specific real and hypothetical questions which arose. These scholars, who in time became known as *mujtahids*,[24] cited the Holy Qur'an, *hadith,* and former decisions that related to all or parts of the questions under consideration. Like other aspects of Twelver Shi'ism, this approach evolved and probably attained something close to maturity only in the late eighteenth century.

The possibility always existed that a *mujtahid* or the entire group, which collectively constitute the Shi'i *'ulama,* at any time represented the exact will of the Mahdi. Most believed, however, that believers could not know the will of the Mahdi most of the time, if ever. A method evolved to address this uncertainty. All but a tiny few of the Shi'i Muslims acknowledged the supremacy and followed the leadership of someone more knowledgeable than themselves in matters of law and theology. Laymen followed clergymen, who in turn followed the guidance of one or more clergymen whose training and credentials exceeded their own. At most times only a handful of *mujtahids* possessed the credentials to be totally independent from consultation with a superior before rendering incontrovertible decisions.[25]

This emphasis on expertise in Twelver Shi'ism generated extensive scholarly activities. Young men entered religious training and progressed through the religious college *(madrasa)* in pursuit of a religious career. Students who terminated their studies at the lower levels usually performed religious functions commensurate with their training and were called *mulla,* while others could continue and aspire to the apex of Shi'i scholarship. Acquisition of a certificate from a *mujtahid* to practice *ijtihad* usually required several years beyond normal college training. The process resembled the modern Western procedure for postgraduate education in both religious and secular fields.

While proper certification was necessary to advance in Shi'i scholarship, recognition as a *mujtahid* required acquisition of a substantial following of clergymen. The adherence of a large number of lay followers to the deferential clergymen was also necessary to provide the formidable numbers and reputation appropriate for *mujtahid* rank. Frequently a clergyman's own followers would initiate his elevation from ordinary *mulla* by referring to him as "Mujtahid." But the status only became valid when established *mujtahids* addressed or treated an aspirant as their peer. Since most *mujtahids* deferred to at least one other clergyman of *mujtahid* rank, a discernible hierarchy of deference and respect developed. These highest-echelon clergymen, who might choose to consult each other but did not need to defer to others, constituted the Shi'i *'ulama*. A decision from any member of this elite was valid and did not require any measure of consensus. Differences of opinion, expressed or not expressed, did not detract from the validity of each *mujtahid*'s view.

The circumstances which accompanied the change of dynasties in Persia at the end of the eighteenth century helped provide direction for the evolving role of the *'ulama* in Twelver society. While the Safavids had claimed sacerdotal powers based on a lineage—however spurious—from the Seventh Imam, the new Qajar dynasty of Turkoman origin could make no such claim. Persia, which had become inseparably associated with Twelver Shi'ism since the Safavids ascended to power in 1501, needed religious guidance that the Qajars could not claim to provide. The elite Shi'i clergy who comprised the *'ulama* increased in power, wealth, and prestige as they provided this service.

If a single *mujtahid* emerged as unquestionably the most worthy clergyman of his time, he enjoyed the status of *marji i-taqlid* ('source of emulation'). More frequently, a few renowned scholars were similarly ranked in piety and scholarly erudition, but clearly superior to all other contemporaries. The inability and/or awkwardness of having a group which almost never sat together serve as a *marji* spawned the term *ayatollah* ('sign of God') to differentiate these particularly august clergymen from other *mujtahids*. The development of the terms *mujtahid* and *ayatollah,* as well as the functions their holders served, reflected more the increased stature of Twelver Islam clergy in society than any significant change in the religion or its structure.

CONFRONTATION WITH THE MODERN STATE

The significantly larger role of the clergy, particularly in relation to education, inheritance, endowment management, and other major areas of law, created an intrinsic conflict with any government which aspired to establish control over its population and assets. Fairly early in the nineteenth century, Persia faced challenges which demanded the fullest use of its comparatively marginal resources to combat aggression from new enemies much stronger than the traditional foes of Afghanistan and the Ottoman Empire. The vastly stronger Russian and British empires coveted land and concessions in Persia and were willing to use their superior force against Persia and each other to achieve their goals. The need for the Qajar, and later the Pahlavi governments, to modernize or perish ensured a clash between the government and the Shi'i religious structure that permeated Persian society.

Qajar shahs of the nineteenth century initiated significant changes to mod-

ernize Persia and avoid conquest by Russia or Britain. The monarchs extended
financial and trade concessions to foreigners and borrowed heavily abroad to
acquire the funds to pay for modernization. They also built secular schools and
sent students abroad to acquire the knowledge and skills necessary to construct
a modern society. These changes disturbed numerous elements of Persian society for financial or political reasons, but also offended the national pride of
most Persians.

Shi'i clergy assumed the leadership in resisting Western cultural and economic imperialism, beginning with the ramifications of the tobacco monop-
oly the Persian government extended to a British company in 1890. Prominent Persian *mujtahids* and the leading Pan-Islamic activist Jamal al-Din
al-Afghani took the lead. They also obtained a ruling against the concession
from the foremost Shi'i divine of the time, Ayatollah Shirazi of Karbala in Iraq.
The dramatic movement in 1891, which involved much of Persia's population,
was clearly a nationalist rather than a religious concern, but it demonstrated
the kinds of influence Shi'i clergy could exercise.

Persia's clergy became deeply involved in the even more dramatic and prolonged developments of the Constitutional Movement in the first decade of
the twentieth century. Qajar changes to meet the challenge of modernization
threatened the traditional role of the Shi'i religious establishment. Governmental regulation of clerical activities (especially those related to education) in
the later Qajar period presaged restrictions usually associated with the later
Pahlavi period. Throughout the world, a significant role for an independent
religious establishment seemed incompatible with modern statehood. Large
numbers of dissidents seeking to *bast* (obtain sanctuary)[26] on Shi'i religious
property helped draw clergymen into conflicts, sometimes against their will.

Most clergy who took part in the constitutional struggle supported the establishment of constitutionalism in behalf of a limited franchise, the sanctity of
private property, and the continued domination of Islamic law. The constitu-
tionalists made concessions to obtain clerical support and to counter clerical
fears that representative government would divert power from the monarch
and clergy to the masses. Article One of the new constitution established
Imami (Twelver) Shi'ism as the religion of the state, and Article Two created
a panel of five clergymen to approve all legislation.

Reza Khan's seizure of power in February 1921 proved to be the greatest
challenge to the Shi'i clergy since the time of the Mongols. Within three years
this military commander of the Cossack Brigade extended his control over
much of Persia and sent the shah on "vacation." Fear arose in religious circles
of Persia that Reza intended to establish a secular republic similar to the one
Ataturk, another military leader, was implementing in neighboring Turkey.

Reza reassured the clergy with overt acts of apparent piety, and in return he received the blessings of most Persian clergymen and the 'ulama at Najaf in 1924. The following year the clergy approved his termination of the Qajar dynasty and his declaration of himself as monarch.

Once Reza was strong enough to withstand the clergy's resistance, however, he implemented numerous laws which relegated the clergy to minor status in society. The state, rather than religious authorities, established the standards for determining which teachers and students had religious status and deserved the traditional privileges accorded. The state established a dress law that greatly reduced the number of Persians who could wear clerical clothing. The state assumed jurisdiction over large areas of law which religious courts had formerly adjudicated and required court officials to train in Western-style law schools. The state also assumed the right to record documents and property, which formerly had been in the purview of religious authorities. Government control over the *waqfs,* or religious endowments,[27] in 1934 was a clear indication that the Shi'i religious establishment had been stripped of any independence of action in all but spiritual matters. In one decade Reza had dismantled the role of Shi'i clergy in Persian society which had prevailed for the more than four hundred years since the first Safavid shah, Esma'il, established Twelver Shi'ism as the official religion in 1501.

Like many other modern states, Reza's Iran[28] allowed no major role for religion. Shi'i religious authorities receded into the background and concentrated on spiritual matters, much as they had in earlier centuries when they lived among a Sunni majority. Highly respected *mujtahids,* and even some of the imams, had always maintained that clerical participation in politics and other secular activities adversely affected the clergy and religion.

The posture of *mujtahid* noninterference in public affairs generally prevailed after the iron rule of Reza ended in 1941 and his son, Mohammad Reza, assumed authority in an initially weakened condition. The fate of religion and the 'ulama seemed of little concern in the struggles among the Great Powers which occupied Iran during World War II. Shi'i religious leaders did not become heavily involved in the dramatic events after the USSR withdrew, and the Communist Tudeh party nearly triumphed in Iran. Ayatollah Kashani, whom the British had exiled from Iraq, was an exception then as later as he involved his following of lower clergy and laymen in overtly violent acts in opposition to the Shah's increased dependence upon support from Britain and the United States. An attempt to assassinate Shah Mohammad Reza in 1949 was pivotal in several respects. The Shah exiled Kashani to Beirut,[29] sentiment both for and against the Shah increased, and the *marji-i-taqlid,* Ayatollah Burujirdi, threatened expulsion from the religious hierarchy of any *mujtahid* who broke his recent vow to abjure participation in politics. Many lower clergy who had neither family nor academic reputations to protect found it difficult to remain aloof from politics during this period which was shaping Iran's future.

Abstention from politics seemed nearly impossible by 1950, when Iran was electrically charged with nationalist concern centered on the widespread desire to nationalize Great Britain's concession on Iranian oil, the nation's main financial asset. Prime Minister 'Ali Razmara opposed nationalization because he believed Iran was unprepared to manage its petroleum industry. Razmara's assassination on March 7, 1951, at the hands of Kashani's *fidayeen al-Islam* ignited an unprecedented level of legislation and violence in support of nationalization. The religiously and economically conventional nationalist leader Muhammad Mossadegh welcomed support from all sectors, including Kashani and the Tudeh. Kashani returned from Lebanon to lead his particular religious elements, in concert with other activists, in massive demonstrations. The resulting hostility forced the parliament to nationalize the oil and expel the British, and it forced the Shah into exile. The world-shaking events in Iran lasted until August 1953, when Mossadegh lost support, the Tudeh melted away, the Shah returned, and Kashani passed into obscurity.

The Shah and clergy enjoyed good relations during most of the 1950s, due largely to their mutual fear of communism. This fear justified Iran's alliance with Western and regional nations in the Baghdad Pact. Indeed, concern about communism and Iran's dependence upon the petroleum industry dictated extensive relations with Great Britain and the United States. The Shah's reliance upon American financial, military, and diplomatic support created strain in relationships with the clergy. For instance, the monarch's concern about Western reaction prevented him from destroying the Baha'i religious movement, which the clergy (including the nonpolitical Ayatollah Burujirdi) demanded. The West, particularly the United States, could tolerate general repression of Iran's population, but would condemn persecution of any particular religious or ethnic group.

The Shah's ambition, Iran's technological backwardness, the presence of a large Tudeh following, and Iran's proximity to the Soviet Union made the Shah susceptible to American pressure. Because the Shah desired to obtain large quantities of advanced American military equipment, he met American demands that he improve his nation domestically and leave defense of the region to the United States. First the Eisenhower and then the Kennedy administration tied military aid to changes in the quality of life of Iran's population.

Land redistribution would have to be a part of such an undertaking, since most Iranians still lived on the land. Most owned no land but farmed as sharecroppers for the Shah and a small number of other landowners. The clergy were among the greatest landholders, usually as custodians of the extensive *waqfs* which supported mosques, shrines, schools, and the clergy. The issue was vital enough to the clergy that the normally quiescent Ayatollah Burujirdi expressed his opposition when the Shah proposed his first major land redistribution plan in 1959.[30]

Significant changes in the 1960s reduced the clergy's political role and the government's concern for their reaction. The creation of the Organization of Petroleum Exporting Companies (OPEC) in 1960 signaled the acquisition of unfathomable revenues for the government. The Kennedy administration relentlessly demanded change in return for the extensive armaments the government could afford to buy with its increased income. Burujirdi died in March 1961 and the Shah announced the changes which would become his White Revolution in November. The activities of Gamal Abdel Nasser in Egypt aroused the entire region against Western influence and the dictator of Iraq, 'Abd al-Karim al-Qassim, stirred both Iraq and communism against Iran.

The White Revolution, which the Shah announced in January 1963, conformed to the United States' demands on the Shah, but it also provided him the opportunity to transform Iran into a modern, technologically sophisticated, and militarily dominant nation. This revolution from the top included extensive land redistribution with monetary compensation for the landowners, with the understanding that they could invest their remuneration in industrialization. It provided for extensive government involvement in educating the new peasant landowner class about modern farming and marketing techniques through government-sponsored schools and consultation with experts. A Health Corps and a Literacy Corps were central to improving the health and knowledge of Iran, which the Shah planned to transform into one of the world's foremost industrialized nations. Full implementation of this program would have centralized almost everything in Iran under control of the government, which possessed the assets and inclination to abolish the nation's uniqueness. While the White Revolution touched everything in Iran—and, therefore, everything related to the clergy—the Literacy Corps probably presented the greatest concern. Such massive government involvement in education, down to the village level in the countryside, threatened to divest the clergy of their last vestige of control over primary education.

Many Iranians could visualize personal benefits from the Shah's plan, since Iranians had increased experience with the role of education and money in modern society. The promise of land and education reduced concern about changes that might be greater than most Iranians could imagine. The government's willingness and ability to punish detractors[31] almost guaranteed the absence of extensive resistance from those who thought otherwise. The Shah's dismissal of the parliament before issuing his program created some opponents, who claimed the higher goal of obstructing totalitarianism but in reality objected mainly for provincial or selfish reasons. But the most likely political leaders for the opposition were abroad in voluntary or involuntary exile, and the clergy were in disarray following a long period of inactivity and Burujirdi's death.

Ayatollah Ruhollah Khomeini asserted himself to resist changes in Iranian society which he feared would make the country a carbon copy of the decadent and irreligious West. Khomeini was not considered to be among the highest echelon of Iran's scholarly clergy, although he had a considerable political following. Indicative of his inclination to appeal to the masses was his venting of his views in public speeches from his teaching forum in Qum, the center of Iranian religious scholarship. His virulent speeches voiced the concerns that Iran's more conventional clergy refrained from expressing, either orally or in writing. His comments against the White Revolution, the Shah, the West, and the subservient clergy contained most of the concepts and much of the language people associate with his later activities. He did not, however, express support for popular revolution and mass participation in public affairs in 1962 and 1963. His activities nevertheless led to his arrest on June 15, 1963. In keeping with the Shah's general treatment of major dissidents, Khomeini was neither killed nor imprisoned but sent into exile. Iranian authorities sent him to Turkey, where he remained until October 1965, when the internal affairs of Iraq made it appealing for him to move to Najaf, the center of Twelver Shi'i worship and scholarship. The Iraqi government allowed the Ayatollah just enough freedom to be an irritant to the Shah without attracting any significant following in Iraq, where the government closely monitored most religious activities, especially among the Shi'i, who constituted a majority of Iraq's population. Iraq's deportation of Khomeini to France in the fall of 1978 tremendously increased his effectiveness in both Iraqi and Iranian affairs. He flew from Paris to Tehran in February 1979 to repeat many of the comments he had made in 1963.

FIVE

CONFRONTATION WITH MODERN SECULARISM

Extensive innovations in the Christian West beginning in the fifteenth century, created a cultural chasm greater than the differences between Islam and Christianity. Building upon mathematical and scientific knowledge nurtured in the Islamic world from its largely Greek foundation, the Europeans created the dominant methodologies, institutions, knowledge, and technology of the modern world.

As modern nations with modern tax systems, military preparedness, administrative apparatus, and complicated economies replaced the medieval monarchies and their stagnant economies, each stage of the metamorphosis to modernity shook traditional beliefs, practices, behavior, and values in the West. Relatively small modern European nations obtained immense wealth and extensive power which surpassed the accomplishments of the greatest empires of the past. The Western world mastered the capacity to transform raw materials into unimagined power for its states and wealth for its citizens.

Western nations were dominant globally by the eighteenth century through a combination of growth in their strength and a failure to grow on the part of most of the other "nations"[1] of the world. Islamic areas of the globe were no exception. No Islamic state or society participated in forging the future during this crucial era. Indeed, modernity emerged before any major Islamic society became sufficiently aware of the disparity of strength between the West and the Islamic world. Eventual awareness sometimes led to a shrug and a self-satisfied observation that traditional ways, often believed to be "God's way," were superior. In most cases a more astute reaction could not have led to a better solution.

Mighty and grand as the Ottoman and Persian empires had been, they were little better equipped than any other part of the Islamic world to withstand Western capacity to render them harmless. The leadership in both formerly great empires concluded that imitation of Western ways was necessary to combat Western strength. This conclusion led inexorably to the conviction that extensive secular education was the foundation of modern Western strength. Islamic leaders also saw the need for a much stronger central government to increase economic production and generate greater revenues. Efforts to emulate the West required time, economic investment, and a major deviation from traditional education and cultural orientation. Even with a full commitment to modernization, establishing a rudimentary educational foundation would require decades. In the meantime, Western influence over resources and policies became a factor in internal politics, while Western cultural characteristics eroded traditional practices.

The Middle East fell steadily under Western influence throughout the nineteenth century. Rivalry between Russia and Britain to control or influence Persia (later Iran) drove the Persian empire into debt, prevented the development of either economic or administrative integrity, and left it divided between British and Russian spheres of influence at the beginning of the twentieth century. Muhammad 'Ali unabashedly patterned almost everything in Egypt on Western models after he attained power in 1805. His military and economic success beyond that of all regional opponents, including the Ottoman Empire to which Egypt belonged, vindicated his approach. The Ottoman Empire learned early in the nineteenth century that it could not survive Russian aggression without European support. Western pressure on the Ottoman Empire spawned the adoption of Western-style laws and practices for which there was little or no preparation, and the predictably confusing results pleased almost no one. The Ottoman Empire was basically under European receivership after 1881. Outright British control of Egypt from 1882 on indicated the inability of Muslim regions to endure once Europeans decided to assert their superiority in almost every measurable form of human activity.

Submission to the dictates of a foreign culture met with considerable resistance in the Ottoman and Persian empires. The innovations which had shaken Europe as they evolved piecemeal over centuries descended upon the Middle East over a very brief period. Adherence to a foreign culture was in itself undesirable to traditional societies, but adoption of foreign ways was also an admission that foreign (Christian) culture was superior. Opponents of change found influential support among most of the clergy, some administrators, and much of the military. For all it mattered, the masses almost instinctively opted to retain traditional ways. The time-honored belief that traditional ways were "God's way" ensured that reaction to the challenge of modernity would become a major issue for religious leaders.

Western imperial expansion in every form accompanied and fostered the phenomenon of modern nationalism. The trend for each linguistic and cultural group to establish a separate nation was antithetical to the universalist out-look of Islam. In theory, all Muslims were brothers who should work together for their common good and for the good of Islam. Large amorphous entities such as the Ottoman and Persian empires suited Islam as they compelled vari-ous ethnic, linguistic, and religious groups to live together in relative peace. While there had been different Islamic states—even warring Islamic states—from early in the religion's history, such divisions contradicted religious theory.

ADVOCATES FOR CHANGE

The most active Muslim leaders, who saw the danger of total subjugation of the Islamic world, endorsed nationalism to combat Western imperialism. They also generally embraced modern knowledge, which they recognized as having been born or nurtured in the earlier glorious eras of Islamic civilization. These foremost religious leaders blamed restricted interpretations of Islam for the in-ability of the Islamic world to capitalize upon existing knowledge. They in-sisted that an accurate understanding of Islam could arm Muslims with the freedom to comprehend and enjoy everything God had created.

Before proceeding with the linear development of this story of modern Is-lamists,[2] it will be useful to survey briefly the Wahhabi movement of a century earlier in the Arabian peninsula. The connection rests in the similar conclu-sions these two very different movements reached in their efforts to solve the problems of Islam in very different times and locales. Treating them adjacently emphasizes that, as late as the eighteenth century, Muhammad ibn 'Abd al-Wahhab could confine his concerns to the problems within Islam without concern for their ramifications in dealings with the non-Islamic world.

The Wahhabi and the more modern Islamists also merit juxtaposed treat-ment because, different as they are, they are all *salafiyyah*s. This simply means they looked to the past, to those who preceded them, for guidance.[3] They be-lieved the basics of the Qur'an, the *hadith,* and the experiences of the first three generations of Muslims should serve as the guide for all later Islamic practice. For eighteenth-century and modern *salafiyyah*s alike, deviation from those ways was unacceptable and the cause for Islam's loss of validity, identity, and vitality.

Al-Wahhab, who was a trained Islamic scholar, disapproved of the changes in Islam which would have made it unrecognizable to its founders. In his view, God had spoken in the Holy Qur'an and in the life of the Prophet Muham-mad. The earliest Muslims had shown how to adjust to life in ways compatible with the Prophet's teachings and the Holy Qur'an. Al-Wahhab taught that any additions to Islam which fell beyond these limitations were innovations *(bidah)* and, therefore, the result of unacceptable *ijtihad,* or personal interpretation. Sufism, especially, was in all its forms anathema to the Wahhabi, as was veneration of Muhammad or any other Islamic leader. Most Shi'i practice, therefore, was considered deviant Islamic practice. Wahhabi taught that believers should direct all praise, prayer, and adoration to God. For them, dead prophets and dead ancestors alike should be buried in unmarked graves to prevent behavior approximating worship of any entity but God. The Qur'an, the *hadith,* *ijma',* and *ijtihad* in the literal interpretive tradition of Ahmad ibn Hanbal (one of the preeminent jurists of the Islamic third century) constituted the perimeters of Islamic definition. Like the Kharijites of early Islam, the Wahhabi felt compelled to destroy edifices and people who failed to live by their strict interpretation of Islam.

For several reasons, the most important Islamist to define the problems of the Muslim world in the second half of the nineteenth century was Jamal al-Din al-Afghani. He was the first significant figure to take up the challenge he encountered in his native Persia and in Egypt, where he spent his most productive years. In addition, he charted a basic course which guided others for the next few decades. Fear that Europe would obtain total control of the Islamic world moved this Persian clergyman to action. He blamed Islamic weakness, rather than European strength, for the plight of the Islamic world. According to him, the Europeans had explored the potential of the human mind and faculties to establish better harmony and control over nature. He attributed Islamic weakness to the leadership of ignorant clergymen who rejected innovation in areas totally unrelated to religious concerns. In his view it was natural and even imperative for Muslims to acquire scientific and philosophical knowledge. Strong as his feelings were against foreign occupiers, economic exploiters, and their co-conspirators in the Islamic world, his harshest words were for the Islamic teachers whose restrictive interpretations of Islam prevented Muslims from being competitive in the modern world. He and his followers lamented that a lack of understanding of Islam prevented Muslims from comprehending Islam as a liberating rather than a limiting religion.

His fiery oratory attracted a political and religious following. In the 1870s he helped organize Egyptian resistance to the Egyptian Debt Commission, which was composed of foreigners who controlled Egypt's finances and governmental policies. One of his disciples assassinated Shah Nasir al-Din of Persia in 1896. Some supported his efforts to reestablish Islamic cultural integrity and independence, although they did not fully understand his reasoning. His best disciples believed as he did that modern knowledge was compatible with Islamic principles. Furthermore, they aspired to implement modern knowledge and techniques to expel foreign domination and guarantee an Islamic future. Because of al-Afghani's itinerant life, he failed to attain rank or office to enhance his stature. He also wrote very little. Still, discussion of Islam's efforts to adjust to modern challenges and cope with threats of annihilation must begin with al-Afghani, because he basically defined Islam's best response.

Muhammad 'Abduh, an Egyptian associate of al-Afghani, held similar views. His stronger standing in Egyptian society and his deeper familiarity with Western knowledge provided him a greater influence and credibility. While he worked closely with al-Afghani and leading Egyptian nationalists 'Urabi Pasha and Mustafa Kamil on Egyptian nationalist matters, and even experienced a period of exile, he enjoyed something close to establishment status. He advocated acquiring knowledge, on the assumption that nothing true contradicts God's will. In his view, Muslims should employ their capacity to reason as a means of determining and explaining truth. He concentrated upon educating Egyptians and even distrusted anti-British activities which capitalized upon the ignorance of the Egyptian masses. His faith in the truth of unfettered Islam gave him the confidence to destroy the myths which surrounded much of traditional practice. His roles in Egypt as mufti and member of the Legislative Council provided him with opportunities to implement his ideas officially.

A Syrian Muslim from Tripoli named Muhammad Rashid Rida journeyed to Egypt to work with al-Afghani and 'Abduh. Although his entire education had been confined to traditional Islamic scholarship, Rida seemed compelled to incorporate Western learning into the Islamic world to avoid cultural and religious extinction. He also blamed ignorant religious leaders for emphasizing trivial and wrong religious policies while ignoring the essence and truth of Islamic foundations. His new approach entailed concentrating on the earliest Islam, which he regarded as pure, open, and strong. According to Rida, Arabs needed to regain primacy in Islamic leadership. He thought that non-Arabs had introduced inappropriate practices and had failed to comprehend the simplicity and value of earliest Islam. While he tried to avoid offending the Ottoman sultan-caliph, he openly advocated returning the caliphate to an Arab as a means of regaining Islamic purity. His 1923 book, entitled *The Caliphate or the Supreme Imam,* addressed the entire spectrum of possibilities that could follow the establishment of an Arab caliphate, with assistance through consultation *(shura)* and interpretation *(ijtihad),* to adapt Islam to modern times in a healthy way that retained Islam's identity. He transmitted his influential concepts of Islam and society in his magazine *al-Manar* ('The Lighthouse'), which began as a weekly in 1898 and later became a monthly. Rida edited it until his death in 1935, when others continued its publication.

By the end of the nineteenth century the issues of religion had become more closely entwined with politics. While Islam had always insisted on their inseparability, the Islamist activists had previously attempted to avoid criticism of Ottoman officialdom. Increasingly, however, knowledge of Western affairs and institutions led to the widespread appeal of Western constitutionalism as both liberating for individuals and at least partly responsible for the West's modern success. Activists of the Young Ottoman and then the Young Turk movements touted constitutionalism and increasingly levied accusations of Ottoman tyranny. The Islamists embraced the call for some level of participatory government and the accountability of public officials. This political milieu, which moved Rida toward Arab nationalism to escape Turkish restraints, led his contemporary 'Abd al-Rahman al-Kawakibi to a more stridently anti-Turkish posture.

Also Syrian, al-Kawakibi joined his countryman in Egypt in 1898. Within a year he published *Mecca: Mother of Cities,* and soon thereafter he published *Attributes of Tyranny* before dying in 1902 at the age of forty-eight. The first book is an account of a hypothetical conference in Mecca at which the members defined the problems of Islam. They concluded that deviation from the basic initial principles and practices of Islam had caused these problems. Furthermore, they concluded that Turkish ignorance, along with educational and moral decay, had added to their problems. The second book revisited the same themes but offered the solution of electing, for a three-year renewable term, an Arab caliph who would conduct religious affairs in conjunction with an elected assembly. This approach, which advocated a strict Sunni base, provided a very modern way for the Sunni system to incorporate *ijma'*.

Egyptians soon realized that, however accurate the anti-Ottoman observations of Rashid Rida and al-Kawakibi might be, criticism of the Ottomans was detrimental to Egyptian nationalist aspirations. Rida's role in creating the Ottoman Decentralization Society as a partial answer to Arab nationalism indicates that he realized Egypt's need to remain affiliated with the Ottoman Empire. Simply put, in his estimation, national problems surpassed religious problems, and problems with Great Britain surpassed those with the Ottoman Empire. Ottoman titular ownership of Egypt and Ottoman titular friendly relations with Great Britain provided Egypt with the only hope of escaping outright annexation to the British Empire. Islamists in Egypt began to direct most of their efforts toward expelling the British, just as Algerian Islamists under the leadership of 'Abd al-Hamid ibn Badis labored to expel the French.

THE MUSLIM BROTHERHOOD

Hasan al-Banna, who was one of the most influential figures in modern Egyptian and Islamic history, invigorated adherence to *salafiyyah* Islam and led the nationalist effort to expel British influence from Egypt. There was a direct connection between al-Banna and the earlier *salafiyyah* pioneers in Egypt. He was educated and then taught in the schools Rashid Rida had established. He edited Rida's magazine, *al-Manar,* from 1939 to 1941. With a grounding in both Islamic and Western knowledge, he became a primary school teacher in 1927 in Isma'iliyyah on the Suez Canal. His continued relations with associates in Cairo, however, ensured that he would not become an isolated and obscure provincial.

There was nothing remarkable about his establishing, with six others, a chapter of the Hasafiyyah Sufi brotherhood in Isma'iliyyah in 1928, because al-Banna had been a member of that Sufi order as a teenager. The small group, which originated to rectify the problems of Islam in their locality, very quickly evolved into the Muslim Brotherhood (Jamiyyat al-Ikhwan al-Muslimun), the most important political-religious organization in modern Egypt. New chapters developed, and al-Banna moved the headquarters to Cairo in 1933. The simplicity and honesty of the Muslim Brotherhood attracted a large membership and stimulated the rapid creation of new chapters. Reliable estimates place its membership at half a million in two thousand chapters by the time of al-Banna's death in 1949. Even this figure is not an accurate measure of its influence, however, since many who avoided the risk of membership in the Brotherhood supported its activities.

The expulsion of Great Britain from Egypt dominated al-Banna's activities. The presence of the British was a religious as well as a political problem, however, since the weakness of Egypt's Islamic society made British occupation possible. The Muslim Brotherhood adopted a policy of education, political activism, and social welfare to meet the immediate needs of its members. A wide spectrum of Egyptians soon regarded the Brotherhood not only as the best means of expelling the British, but also the best source for spiritual and physical security.

In the *salafiyyah* tradition, al-Banna said, "The Qur'an is our constitution." This theme and his insistence that traditional Islam was the only legitimate foundation for a viable Islamic society could lead to the misconception of al-Banna as a cultural xenophobe. While he only accepted sources of Islamic law in the Sunni tradition, he openly acknowledged the acceptability of non-Islamic knowledge and practice in certain areas. The British presence in Egypt was the only thing which upset al-Banna more than the widespread belief among his countrymen that Westerners alone had the answers to modern problems. His message urged Egyptians and other Muslims to familiarize themselves with the heart of their religion and use its rich and comprehensive approach to human needs as the guide for creating a strong, modern society built upon an Islamic foundation. He maintained that Islamic teachings encompassed almost everything any society needed in any age. His confidence in Islam led him to assert that Islamic societies could selectively adopt non-Islamic answers when a thorough investigation proved that no Islamic answer existed. There was the additional stipulation that Islamic societies should reject anything which directly conflicted with Islamic principles.

The Muslim Brotherhood evolved as a secret underground organization into a political force that most other politicians, including the monarchy, courted. Its formidable publications and its role in strikes, demonstrations, and even assassinations appealed to many, as did the provision of education, religious guidance, food, medicine, housing, and a meaning for life. While some militant elements engaged in activities al-Banna did not accept, he exercised a level of political control that belied his spiritual title of "Supreme Guide." He proved to be an accomplished politician who allied at one time or another with almost every Egyptian party or group. Branches of the Brotherhood emerged in Syria, Iraq, Sudan, and Palestine in an era dominated by secularism. Its strong emphasis on social justice appealed to many who could not embrace the secular, even atheistic, solutions other groups proposed.

As the Muslim Brotherhood moved underground, it perfected the use of the small cells which early Arab nationalist movements had found effective. The small units had the principal virtue of limiting damage, because authorities could only learn the identities of the five or six people any member might divulge under torture or other pressure. Initially, members came from among lower-level government workers, junior military officers, small merchants, teachers, and artisans, but urban working-class membership provided the formidable numbers it enjoyed after 1945. From its earliest days it opened schools and mosques, but it soon acquired clinics, factories, and businesses. In essence, it constructed a largely self-sufficient society parallel to the Egyptian society which the government administered.

While it was not a political party, it engaged in widespread political activities. Al-Banna would advise the leadership of the Free Officers' Society on organizational matters, having shared political objectives with them while the Society was still a clandestine movement. Increased anti-British sentiment in Egypt after 1945 gave the Brotherhood and other groups hope of expelling the British. The Brotherhood's armed element proved relentless and effective in the Palestine war of 1948 and never acquiesced to the truce Egypt and other Arab governments accepted. The government finally outlawed the Brotherhood on December 6, 1948, for its intensified role in demonstrations and strikes and its general political effectiveness in collusion with a spectrum of other groups, from communists to fascists. A Muslim Brother's assassination of the Egyptian prime minister three weeks later led to the secret-police assassination of al-Banna on February 12, 1949. The Brotherhood's strong organization and important role in society, however, minimized the effects of al-Banna's assassination and the organization's legal dissolution. The Brotherhood would play an increased role as opposition increased against both the government of King Farouk and a continued British presence.

The Free Officers' coup of July 23, 1952, initially appeared favorable to the Brotherhood. Calling themselves the Revolutionary Command Council (RCC) after King Farouk went into exile, the officers' group seemed to respect the importance and popular appeal of the Brotherhood. Although they cavalierly abolished the Wafd and other political parties in 1953, they did not dare infringe upon Brotherhood activities. The RCC, who were a group of unknowns, had no popular support because their intentions were unclear. The apparent leadership of General Muhammad Neguib, whom the Brotherhood trusted, was their best hope of retaining their position; however, the RCC's secular approach to altering society soon became apparent to the Brotherhood, who also disapproved of the terms of the treaty the RCC negotiated with Great Britain in 1954. General Neguib's replacement by Gamal Abdel Nasser as leader of the RCC alienated the Brotherhood. A Brotherhood member's attempt on Nasser's life on October 26, 1954, signaled the end to an uneasy relationship with the RCC. Six Muslim Brothers died on the gallows, and a government again outlawed the Brotherhood, which returned underground in Egypt and moved its headquarters to Damascus.

By the summer of 1955, Nasser's popularity had begun to soar in Egypt and the Arab world. His unique form of Arab nationalism and Arab socialism soon swept the region. Secular Nasserism rendered minuscule every other possible answer to Arab problems. The RCC even co-opted Islam as an issue through creation of the International Islamic Congress (IIC) in January 1955. The RCC was not willing to say that Islam was unimportant or irrelevant to modern problems but made it clear that Islam would serve the regime. As the IIC framed revolutionary Egypt's relations with the international Islamic world, Islamic institutions within Egypt, including al-Azhar University, became instruments of the secular government. Attention paid to Islamic laws, issues, or principles amounted to little more than occasional lip service. The exhilaration which accompanied Nasserism in the 1950s and 1960s hypnotized a region which had not experienced triumph for centuries. Even defeats such as that of the 1956 Suez Canal war seemed like victories to people who had previously been unable even to compete. In the zeitgeist of the era,[4] adoption of this approach did not require a rejection of Islam. Secular Nasserism seemed so obviously right. Compelled to reject most of the past, it propelled the region into the future. Muslim and Christian Arabs alike envisioned full liberation and fulfillment of their national destiny under Nasser's leadership. They were as inimical to Arab regimes, especially the monarchies, as they were toward the West. New and modern socialism seemed the hope for the downtrodden underdeveloped nations, while Islam suffered almost inadvertently, since it was not only old, but also identified with the "reactionary" regimes which were allied to the West.

Although their differences had not been apparent when they cooperated on the margins in opposition to Farouk's regime, the juxtaposition of the Muslim Brotherhood and the RCC in Egypt had been innately explosive, since the first could accept nothing less than Islamic ways, and the latter required total agreement with its means and goals. The groups' rivalry would eventually destroy two of the preeminent figures of their time: Anwar Sadat was one of the RCC's main links with the Brotherhood, while Sayyid Qutb, an Islamic author/philosopher, was a member of the Brotherhood who had ties with the RCC. The RCC hanged Qutb in 1966, and Brotherhood members killed Sadat in 1981.

While a succession of others, principally Hasan al-Hudaybi, served as Supreme Guide following al-Banna's death, Sayyid Qutb became the Brotherhood's principal theoretician. This educator and author possessed nationalist views similar to those of other Egyptians of his era. He became the editor of the Brotherhood's weekly newspaper, *Jamiyyat al-Ikhwan al-Muslimun,* and served in other important roles soon after he joined the organization in 1953. Indicative of his status, Qutb also directed the newly established Liberation Rally, which the RCC created to replace all political parties and bind the entire nation to RCC methods and objectives. In little more than a year, however, Qutb was in prison, where he suffered torture as a prominent leader of the Brotherhood. A Brother's attempt on Nasser's life on October 26, 1954, reduced the likelihood of Qutb's release. Qutb remained in prison until 1964, when he enjoyed freedom for fourteen months before being reincarcerated in August 1965.

Qutb's short but influential book *Milestones* called for true Muslims to fulfill their duty to wipe out governments which supported *jahiliyyah,* or ignorance of Islam. In his view, all existing societies did so: "Islam cannot accept or agree to a situation which is half-Islam and half-*jahiliyyah.*"[5] Qutb's uncompromising attack upon non-Islamic society provided grounds for his conviction and execution on August 29, 1966.

Qutb's views became the standard by which Brotherhood members and foreign sympathizers judged themselves and everything else. His stark and simple view of Islam went little beyond its definition in the Qur'an. According to Qutb, God's words in the holy book left little space for interpretation. Deviation from the Qur'an was willful disobedience which deserved no mercy.

Qutb merits special attention both for his embodiment of the tradition of Islamic activism, dating back to al-Afghani, and for his influence over the most important activists of his own time and the future. In *Milestones,* Qutb outlined his concept of the journey Islam must take. He described a world, including the Islamic regions, where European-based secularism, materialism, and ignorance *(jahiliyyah)* prevailed. He condemned capitalism, imperialism, and communism as equally demeaning, debilitating, and misleading. Evil governments and religious organizations alike deprived humans of liberty, dignity, and spiritual development. Qutb contended that Islam, which was the only genuine civilization, must reemerge in its total potential to "conserve the benefits of modern science and technology and fulfill the basic human needs."[6]

While portions of Qutb's work disparage nationalism, he asserted that Islam's journey to destroy *jahiliyyah* must begin with obtaining control over a country.[7] One nation must become the model for all others and provide a demonstration that Islam is a "practical religion" and "not a theory." He implored travelers upon the path to Islamic fulfillment to be as bold as the earliest Muslims had been, forsaking families and careers to embrace the Prophet's teachings. Such dedication, he observed, explained why early Islam was pure and successful. The original Muslims had realized it was impossible to combine Islam and *jahiliyyah*. God's will and civilization were only possible when a body of believers dominated an entire nation to serve as an example for others. Islamists must "abolish the existing system . . . and come into the battlefield as an organized movement and viable group."[8]

Qutb disagreed with apologists who believed that *jihad,* or holy war, was only justified to defend the faith. This followed from his basic belief that Islam was the only valid religion because it alone stressed the primacy of God and doing His will. He maintained that people were free to accept or reject Islam, but should anyone reject it, Muslims should "fight him until either he is killed or until he declares his submission."[9] Qutb's commitment to God's glorification and human liberation inspired him to observe that "freedom does not mean that they can make their desires their gods, or that they can choose to remain in the servitude of other human beings, making some men lords over others."[10] He deemed preaching about Islam inadequate, because some people and groups would require the use of force to change their errant ways. In Qutb's view, Muslims must accept the responsibility for using force in those cases.

Again, Qutb firmly accompanied his militant *salafiyyah* approach to Islam with an appeal for Muslims to obtain the blessings of modern Europe's "industrial culture," which he said originated in the Islamic world. In fact, Qutb connected the technical and political backwardness of Islamic regions to their deviation from Islam. He observed that "the Muslim world gradually drifted away from Islam, as a consequence of which the scientific movement (of Islamic civilization) first became inert and later ended completely."[11]

Qutb acknowledged that since the Islamic world was unprepared to educate itself, it would have to obtain its initial training in modern technical knowledge from the West. He specifically approved obtaining technical, scientific, military, and administrative knowledge from non-Muslims. Qutb cautioned, however, that education in all matters dealing with society, including such subjects as the origin of the universe and life, must remain in the hands of properly prepared Muslims. He particularly warned against association with people tainted with Darwinism, pointing out that cooperation with nonbelievers in acquiring scientific knowledge was risky, because in general the scientific community was "against all religion."[12] The diligence of the faithful would have to guard against allowing nonbelieving scientists to exert influence beyond the strictest confines of their disciplines.

ISLAMIST EXPANSION

The influence of Egypt and its role as the educational and communications center of the Middle East ensured that strong movements there spread into the surrounding countries. The Muslim Brotherhood was no exception; some form of it spread to all the Muslim countries where secularism seemed dominant. The Brotherhood obtained varying levels of influence in Syria, Sudan, Jordan, Algeria, Tunisia, Turkey, Palestine, and Morocco. Meanwhile, Tunisia and—until the 1990s—Algeria vehemently pursued secular policies which pointedly opposed anything more than modest Islamic expression. Turkey had adopted a virulent anti-Islamic posture from the beginning of the Ataturk republic, but deep-seated Islamic belief found increased expression from the early 1980s. Countries in the Arabian peninsula remained strongly traditional and were also generally hesitant to accept religious leadership from outside of Islam's heartland. Mu'ammar Gadhafi of Libya had adopted an Islamist stance soon after seizing control in 1969, but the esoteric Libyan experiment proved premature and unappealing, while Nasserism and Arab nationalism remained fashionable and viable. Islamist movements in Iran, Iraq, and Lebanon responded more to Shi'i stimulation; however, al-Banna and Qutb struck responsive chords with some Shi'i on some subjects.

The Muslim Brotherhood's greatest influence outside of Egypt was probably in Syria, where it generated immense activity but never came close to replacing the government. Brotherhood-type organizations inspired by al-Banna's activities developed in Syria in the 1930s. By the late 1940s a fully developed Brotherhood organization was strong enough to battle the Baath, Communist, and Syrian Social Nationalist parties, which were the other dynamic forces in Syria with strong organization and ideological agendas. The other parties had no place for Islam in their proposals for society, despite the strong lip service Baath ideology gave to the Prophet Muhammad. As years passed, the Baathist party, which seized control in 1963, became the only formidable foe of the Brotherhood.

The Brotherhood in Syria directed most of its activities against the totally secular orientation and policies of the Baathist party. There was no need to address the question of imperialism, since France had withdrawn from Syria before the Brotherhood became significant there. The Brotherhood was strongly nationalist, however, in behalf of both Syria and Arabism, to the extent that it endorsed Syria's close affiliation with the Soviet Union in the 1950s as a means of obtaining the modern technology and weapons necessary to prosper in the modern world. Their willingness to acquire knowledge and material from foreign atheists in no way prepared them to acquiesce to Baathist domestic policies. Baathist theory was intrinsically secular, totalitarian, and exclusive in its effort to control every aspect of Syrian life. Its inability to exercise such total control did not prevent it from trying. The Baath could and did refuse to leave any significant role for other organizations. The predominance of 'Alawi (a Shi'i sect)[13] in the Baath leadership was an additional source of conflict between the party and the Muslim Brotherhood, which was Sunni, like more than 80 percent of the nation. From the Brotherhood's perspective, the regime's 'Alawi and Baath identification constituted two major reasons to oppose it.

The direction the Baathists intended for Syria became quite clear soon after they seized power in March 1963 in conjunction with Nasserists. The Baath quickly eliminated the Nasserists and began to implement large-scale socialism in the agricultural and business sectors. These changes frightened the entire spectrum of landowners and businessmen. In addition, professionals of all kinds, merchants, educators, and many ordinary workers disliked the underlying goal of a highly centralized secular society in the control of 'Alawi military officers.

The Brotherhood had the best organization for coordinating the nationwide uprising that occurred in April 1964. Rioting, demonstrations, and violent confrontations occurred in most larger population centers, but the heaviest fighting and greatest bloodshed occurred in the city of Hama, where the Brotherhood was strongest. The conventional military forces of the Baathist government quickly prevailed, after substantial destruction of lives and property. While the Brotherhood failed to lead the opposition to victory, it took its stance to remain in constant challenge to a regime which embodied the characteristics of *jahiliyyah* it had originated to combat.

Supporters of traditional values and Islamic practice remained numerous after the failure to defeat secularism in 1964, but they lacked the forum or opportunity to assert themselves. Such views contradicted the times. Nasserist sentiment prevailed, and Pan-Arabism dominated the late 1960s, even as the Arab countries engaged in near-war among themselves to emphasize their various "Arab" credentials. The 1967 war, Nasser's death, the war of 1973, and the outbreak of civil war in Lebanon in 1975 all diverted attention, consumed energy, and failed to stimulate belief that Islam or Islamists had answers. Oil wealth helped minimize recognition of Arab weakness and fed the appetite for additional material development and contentment in the generally higher standard of living in the region.

Islamists had the additional dilemma of facing overpowering Arab governments which were either leftist allies of the Eastern Bloc or monarchies allied with shamelessly materialistic Western nations. The Islamists could not ally with either, nor could they defeat either combination. That the sheer numbers of those who did not share, or did not want to share, in the prevailing feast of mammon constituted a natural force of great potential was not self-evident; secularism seemed too powerful to confront. As years passed, an entire generation stopped going to the mosques and ceased to consult religious sources for answers.

Oddly, a resurrection of Brotherhood appeal and activity occurred following the Islamic Revolution of the Iranian Shi'i in 1979. Muslims in Syria and other Sunni regions became aware of the viability of Islam to right old wrongs and shape the future. The remarkable success after 1975 of the formerly powerless Shi'i in Lebanon offered additional proof that a new generation of young people would embrace Islam, since the secular answers of their parents and grandparents had failed. The Arabs were still weak after at least two generations of secular pursuit of Arab nationalist goals. Israel still existed as a reminder that Westerners had shaped the modern Middle East. After all the blood, words, and efforts, Palestine was still under foreign control. Israel's continued ability to defeat all the Arab states had become the best measure of Arab weakness. By 1979 the near-religious appeal of Arab nationalism was exhausted. No leader had emerged after Nasser died in 1970. Regimes had learned how to govern. The formerly revolutionary Arab governments had been in power for ten years or, in the case of Egypt, for more than a quarter of the century. Arab borders, while they remained the artificial work of Europeans, had existed for about sixty years. In short, most Arabs finally identified with their country of residence and preferred peace to further violence in pursuit of Arab unity. There was, however, considerable discomfort with the loss of cultural identity as Arabs increasingly looked and behaved like Westerners.

The rapid and total success of the Muslim activists in Iran struck a responsive chord throughout Middle Eastern Islam. From all appearances, hoards of ordinary young Muslims under the leadership of an obscure old man who had been in exile for sixteen years had toppled the most powerful and wealthiest regime in the region. The close relationship between the Shah and the United States, which was Israel's guarantor, sweetened the victory. Arab youths, for the most part, knew little and cared less about the traditional differences between Arabs and Iranians or Sunni and Shi'i. A new reality and relationship emerged as Arab youths marveled that people similar to themselves had toppled one of the world's six mightiest military regimes and humbled the United States, the mightiest nation on earth. Unified young Iranian Muslims had accomplished more in six months than the older Arab generations had accomplished in six decades.

Iran's Islamic Revolution activated a generation which lacked importance in their society. As Malthus had predicted, approximately one-fourth of the Middle-Eastern population was now twenty-five years of age or younger. Nearly as many were fifteen to thirty years of age, which is a volatile age group in most societies. They had several things in common. Most lacked a major stake in society. Modern life was becoming expensive, and wealth was necessary to become important. In the vibrant new times, life on the farm or in small villages had become intolerable. Residence in a large city, preferably the capital, was essential to receive the blessings of modern life. More young men went to cities than the cities could properly employ or house. Bad jobs or no jobs, and bad housing or no housing, awaited a large percentage of the uneducated members of this age group. In spite of their higher expectations, educated youth experienced similar fates. Leadership usually emerged among these youth who had acquired some college education at home or abroad. Needless to say, some older clergy seized the opportunity to affiliate with the unexpectedly large numbers who sought advice and guidance to reshape society.

Young dissidents who had studied abroad often proved to be the most volatile leaders. Many, like Qutb before them, were appalled at the moral decay and family disintegration they had observed in the West. They perceived that their region was fast succumbing to Western ways and mores, as well as Western dress and popular culture. These young people, who had often not fitted into the Western societies where they studied, also did not find appropriate positions when they returned home after their education. They could, however, find meaning and leadership roles in resurrecting a more traditional society, which their elders had rejected and which fascinated the dissatisfied youth.

The situation was ideal for a *salafiyyah* revival. Commitment to the simplest approach to Islam did not require prolonged study or deep understanding. Stark Islam, based upon selected portions of the Qur'an and a literal conformity to the Five Pillars, established the necessary Islamic credentials. The adoption of traditional clothing, including veils for women, completed the transformation from infidel to believer.

Tolerance was usually the first victim of this religious fervor. New believers followed Qutb's command and rejected everything and everyone involved in *jahiliyyah*. They tended to sever peaceful relations with those who attempted to be partially Islamic and partially *jahil*. In contradiction of Islam's long tradition of religious toleration, the new *salifs* (proponents of *salafiyyah*) often adopted militant postures toward adherents of such religions as Judaism and Christianity, which Islam had traditionally regarded as kindred faiths. Muslims who failed to fulfill all Islamic obligations became targets of abuse and derision.

Beginning in 1979, a rapid transformation swept the Middle East as mosques began to fill and religious leaders assumed more importance than they had enjoyed for generations. Western dress, which had become widespread, declined and almost disappeared in some areas of the Middle East. While the Qur'an and the *hadith* had only implored women to behave and dress modestly, the new fervor defined "Islamic dress." Emphasis upon clothing became important because—like a great deal about this movement—it was an outward manifestation of Islamic commitment. More than in the recent past, outward appearance provided a quick indication of an individual's loyalties.

Within a fairly short period, there was no denying that many people in the Middle East no longer looked like people in the West. Pride in being Muslim soon acquired a status reminiscent of earlier days when commitment to Arab unity was the litmus test for personal worth. The speed of this transformation should not be regarded as an indication of insincerity of belief or shallowness of intentions. It emerged so quickly because it was so totally appropriate. A kind of cultural schizophrenia had existed in the region, as people had been aware for generations that adoption of modernity brought success and praise. But as individuals became "modern" and "strong," they also came to look and behave like Westerners. Islamic resurgence invited Middle Easterners to embrace their cultural and religious traditions and, in the process, to enhance their status in society.

The Syrian Muslim Brotherhood, which had maintained a strong underground organization, increased its resistance to the Baathist regime in 1977. Assassinations of unprotected officials, military officers, educators, and others closely associated with the Baath party created apprehension and reminded opponents and supporters alike that the Brotherhood still cared about the traditional values that Baathist-controlled schools and other institutions had tried to destroy.

Limited and sporadic acts of violence perpetrated by the Brotherhood intensified with their attack upon the Aleppo Artillery School on June 16, 1979. Between thirty and eighty-five cadets perished, and many others suffered wounds. Shortly after this incident, violence against the regime erupted all over the country, but Aleppo and Hama experienced the greatest number of incidents. An urban war ensued between the government and the Brotherhood in the ancient, narrow streets of these cities. The Brotherhood began by assassinating selected targets, but expanded their activities to include strikes and demonstrations, which reached most major population centers. Membership in the Brotherhood became grounds for execution. Hundreds of Brothers in custody were summarily shot, even those who had been incarcerated before the new trouble began. President Hafiz al-Assad's appointment of his brother Rifat to confront the Brotherhood militarily ensured a full response. The President's brother commanded the best forces in Syria, and he had all the resources of the state to accompany his ruthless character. Arms distribution to citizens the regime trusted soon left the Brotherhood hopelessly outgunned. Ten thousand troops with heavy tank support killed approximately two thousand in the process of subduing Aleppo in 1980.

In Damascus the regime's good relations with religious officials and the city's broad streets inhibited the guerrilla activities that had worked for the Brotherhood in Aleppo and Hama. Still, dramatic bombings and shootings in the capital during 1981 dictated a life of limited activity and pervasive security precautions. Appealing proposals for a freer life under a Brotherhood government never convinced tens of thousands to fill the streets, however, as had happened in Tehran. A major difference between the two countries was, of course, that there was no doubt that Rifat al-Assad and his fellow 'Alawi officers would use the entire military capacity of the state against the Sunni Brotherhood.

The outbreak of violence in Hama on February 3, 1982, was too massive to have occurred without premeditation. Assassination or capture of Baath officials paralyzed the regime's local governments. The scale of the outbreak, just four months after Brotherhood members had killed Sadat in Egypt, demanded an unusual response. It became clear that a showdown was inevitable between the government and Hama, where the Brotherhood enjoyed its greatest support. More than 10,000 troops with artillery, tank, and aerial support battled the Brotherhood for a month. The government pursued systematic destruction of Brotherhood members and those suspected to be Brotherhood members, along with their property, in an effort to exterminate the movement. Most informed sources outside the regime place the number killed above ten thousand, while estimates of thirty thousand are not uncommon. Given the challenge to the regime and Rifat's outlook, it is safe to assume they did not stop until they were sure their efforts had broken the Brotherhood in Hama.

The Syrian regime had attributed much of the Brotherhood's success to support from foreign countries, particularly Jordan. This was a well-founded accusation, as Syria's enemies employed many tactics to disrupt Syria domestically as a means of reducing its regional influence. Jordan, which was always vulnerable to Syrian provocations, had seized the opportunity to assist and encourage Brotherhood activities in Baathist Syria. The Jordanian government's long, cordial relationship with the Brotherhood had reduced earlier fears that the organization's initial success in Syria might jeopardize Jordan. After the Brotherhood registered as a religious and charitable organization in the 1940s, it proceeded to become an integral part of Jordanian life, with a steady prolif-eration of schools, clinics, hospitals, religious centers, and mosques. Brother-hood participation in politics in Jordan has always been in conjunction with legitimate political parties. It remains a significant force in Jordanian society and has even provided some cabinet ministers. While they could not produce a majority, Brotherhood members constituted the largest group in the 1993 legislature. Growth in public support for the Brotherhood and other Islamist groups creates the possibility that they could dominate Jordan's recently re-stored constitutional process in the near future.

Sudan, which has long been a center of activist Sufi Islam, experienced dra-matic change when President Ja'far Nemeiri suddenly imposed a harsh *salafiy-yah* approach on the law in 1983. The recent spread of Islamist appeal through-out the region helps explain the abrupt detour from a secularist orientation. It is widely assumed that Nemeiri acted under the influence of Hasan al-Turabi, the longtime leader of Sudan's Muslim Brotherhood. Turabi had earlier served briefly as attorney general, but he exerted his greatest influence while out of office. The Brotherhood's influence grew steadily and surpassed that of all other groups in shaping policies and institutions in Sudan. Its role in influenc-ing nearby African countries from its Sudanese base adds to its importance.

Most observers believe that when President Hafiz al-Assad's fragile health collapses, except for a struggle among the Baathist factions, the Muslim Broth-erhood will be the principal claimant of control in Syria. Brotherhood attach-ment to Islamist beliefs and the Sunni majority's frustration with 'Alawi dom-ination support that prediction.

HAMAS

The emergence of a major Islamist movement among Palestinians was the most surprising Islamic development after the Iranian revolution. From the begin-ning, Palestinian resistance had been nationalist, even when related to such re-ligious questions as changes at the Wailing Wall in the 1920s. Even under the leadership of Haj Amin al-Husayni, the grand mufti of Jerusalem, Palestinian resistance to the British mandate and Zionism had always been heavily secu-lar. Active militant leftist groups like the Popular Front to Liberate Palestine, the Popular Democratic Front to Liberate Palestine, and Saiqa in the Palestine Liberation Organization (PLO) had advocated a level of social revolution which forced Fatah, the largest PLO group, away from its early affiliation with the Muslim Brotherhood. Yasser Arafat, who had joined the Muslim Brother-hood in his youth, personally commanded Fatah, and became secretary gen-eral of the PLO, needed to placate the contentious leftists, who had grown increasingly Marxist. The Palestinians' fate as the foremost participants in the Arab/Israeli confrontation inspired a call to arms rather than a call to worship. The existence of the PLO and the lack of an Islamist sentiment help explain why the Muslim Brotherhood, whose counterparts had led struggles in Egypt and Syria, and most other Palestinian Muslims were not in the forefront of early Palestinian resistance.

Although the United Nations assembly and almost all the nations in the world recognized the PLO as the spokesmen for the Palestinians by the mid-1980s, there was no indication that Palestinians would regain their land or control over their affairs. After great effort, significant bloodshed, much disruption, and considerable monetary expense, the PLO had reaped marginal results and appeared to have lost its revolutionary zeal. Many believed that Arafat was willing to accept a settlement which fell far short of the goal of liberating Palestine. His capacity to retain his leadership seemed in jeopardy as leftists from the village grassroots to the Palestine National Council challenged Fatah.

In face of Israel's overwhelming power, Palestinian resistance increasingly became theater after the first several years of PLO guerrilla warfare proved fruitless. Large amounts of money and increased diplomatic recognition prompted the PLO to behave more like a state. It needed world attention to achieve its goals by this new approach. Unfortunately for the PLO and other Palestinians, first the quagmire of the Lebanese civil war, which began in 1975, and then the Iran-Iraq war, which began in 1980, occupied the world stage.

While it was interesting, virtually no one understood the significance when large numbers of Palestinian youths zealously embraced Islam soon after the Iranian revolution. Their uncompromising ardor in living Islamic lives began to transform the behavior of their families and their neighbors. But strong Israeli security precautions kept resistance activity low. The Israelis filled the jails and prisons, and finally placed thousands more Palestinian youths in large prison camps. These measures and the collective punishment of relatives and friends of suspected activists minimized manifestations of Palestinian distress. Again, most activities related to Palestine emerged in Lebanon, where the conventional elements of the PLO centered their efforts.

Unexpectedly the entire Palestinian question acquired a new character early in December 1987, following a traffic accident in Gaza. Palestinian bereavement following the four deaths and seven injuries quickly generated large demonstrations, which normal Israeli tactics failed to quell. Remarkably young Palestinian children grabbed the world's attention as they boldly faced Israeli soldiers. These stone-throwing children defiantly displayed a near-total disregard of Israeli firepower and tear gas. The bravery of the boys, many of whom were under thirteen years of age, captured the imagination of a large worldwide audience. Sympathy for the youths increased when the public soon realized that the "plastic" bullets Israel used to counter public criticism were really steel bullets encased in a thin layer of Teflon. Provocative photographs and videos of armed soldiers shooting and beating children weakened the Israeli public relations claims of a moral high ground. The often deliberately staged Palestinian confrontations excluded anyone old enough to shave. Frequently, world viewers could also see the unathletic, traditionally attired Palestinian women hurling their symbolic stone curses at their oppressors. In the David and Goliath analogy previously used by Israel to illustrate its predicament vis-à-vis the Arab world, Israel suddenly became Goliath.

This phenomenon of Palestinian youths' using the rocky land itself as a weapon to regain their birthright became a symbol of the Palestinian struggle, and their sustained efforts soon became known as the *Intifada,* or "The Uprising." Although the Palestinian-Israeli conflict had passed through many phases since 1919, the events of 1987 and thereafter may well have been the uprising of the century, since such a large proportion of the indigenous population of Palestine had revolted with their bare hands to expel the occupier. Because the British and the Israelis had used repressive actions to prevent sustained Palestinian guerrilla activities, any successes the PLO had realized had occurred outside of Israel-Palestine and from bases outside of Israel-Palestine. For forty years Israel had held the portion of Palestine which formed the Israeli state, and for twenty years Israel had occupied the portion the United Nations had allotted to the Palestinians. And, after all of this time and so many stymied efforts, it was the children who had assumed the burden of liberation.

Adults—especially the PLO—almost immediately recognized the public relations value of the phenomenon and attempted to gain control of it. Adults living in Palestine benefited as they organized various support activities for the public displays of the boys and women. Prolonged strikes, which seemed to hurt Palestinians more than Israelis, became a standard tactic. Israeli attempts to deny vital supplies to the Palestinians from Israel or abroad inspired many small Palestinian manufacturing enterprises. When educational institutions at all levels closed, teachers and students continued to meet and sustain educational efforts. Unions, clinics, workshops, bartering alliances, and other vital organizations sprang up in a participatory grassroots self-government. Age and gender were no deterrents to advancement in a society newly open to talent. Gender, in particular, was of less importance in the acquisition of position than it had ever been in recorded Arab history. Women filled vital positions that made the entire undertaking successful.

Groups with different visions for Palestine sparred among themselves for domination while they simultaneously struggled against Israel. Some Islamist activists, who called themselves Islamic Jihad, emerged under the leadership of Shaykh 'Abd al-Aziz Awdah shortly before the Intifada began. Patterned after the amorphous groups in Lebanon which used the same name, the Palestinian *jihad* Islamists engaged in acts of violence that the Palestinian Muslim Brotherhood had opposed. Despite their name and source of inspiration, they apparently were Brotherhood members who had refused to remain uninvolved while leftist elements of the PLO seized control of Palestinian resistance. As *jihad* adherents, they planned to enact Sayyid Qutb's militant commands.

Israeli officials have admitted that they helped the Muslim Brotherhood develop a movement called Hamas (Movement of Islamic Resistance) under Brotherhood control to oppose PLO leftist elements and the Islamic Jihad. The rapid march of events in 1987 probably convinced the Muslim Brotherhood mainstream to become active in the Intifada. The aggressive role of the leftist elements of the PLO gained them significant influence. It is equally plausible that the Brotherhood had to become involved or lose leadership of traditional Palestinians to the Islamic Jihad.

Hamas apparently originated in January 1988 and immediately became involved in the Intifada, but it did not publish its covenant until August. While Islamic Jihad operated almost exclusively in the Gaza Strip, Hamas spread from Gaza throughout the West Bank within the basic framework of the Muslim Brotherhood. Like Islamic Jihad, Hamas was most effective in Gaza, under the direct leadership of Shaykh Ahmed Yassin. The vile conditions under which so many Palestinian refugees lived in Gaza provided a nurturing environment for the kind of social philosophy Hamas wanted to prevent.

Although it was a religious organization, Hamas could only gain a following by offering the Palestinians hope of achieving their national goals. Hamas declared Palestine an "Islamic *waqf*,"[14] which the organization and all Muslims were obligated to save from partition. This key position signaled that Hamas would not compromise on Palestine's territorial integrity and informed Muslims all over the world of their obligation to help liberate Palestine. The covenant proceeded to condemn the "Communist East" and the "Crusading West" as equally bad and unacceptable sources of assistance or emulation. The document also charged that almost every major mischief of the modern world was directly attributable to Jewish planning and execution. Clearly, none of these enemies of Islam and of Palestinians was worthy of trust or honorable behavior. Hamas acknowledged the goal it shared with the PLO to liberate Palestine, but it forthrightly insisted that cooperation with the PLO was only possible if it shared Hamas's commitment to create an Islamic society.

Few people initially regarded Hamas as a major new player in the old Palestinian game. The early underestimation of Hamas was reminiscent of the virtual disdain which accompanied the entry of Lebanon's downtrodden Shi'i organization, called AMAL (Movement of the Disinherited Militia), into the Lebanese civil war. Longtime supporters of the PLO and the concept of a multiethnic, multireligious democracy in all of Palestine shrugged off Hamas activities as inconsequential. Belief prevailed among knowledgeable Palestinians and scholarly observers that most Palestinian residents had lived too long with religious accommodation and toleration, as well as with the vices and mischief of modern life, to embrace "Khomeini" puritanism. The Palestinian situation was well established, and most assumed that whatever Palestinians and others believed initially, they would all eventually recognize that the PLO would preside over Palestinian affairs. It also seemed clear that the Intifada would soon gravitate, like all else Palestinian, beneath the PLO umbrella.

But Hamas soon became a relentless force which changed life among Palestinians. Many who originally seemed embarrassed by Hamas's attempts to enforce "old ways" soon began to attend mosques, perform their required prayers, alter their clothing, forsake minor vices, and enroll their children in religious classes. Shopowners learned it was better to cease playing secular music and selling alcohol than to have their businesses burned. Alcohol and music at weddings could result in destruction of the family's automobiles, which were very expensive and difficult to acquire. The Hamas emphasis upon abolishing all practices inconsistent with their religious revolution paralleled the insistence of their bitterest leftist enemies on abolishing all practices inconsistent with their goal of socialist revolution.

The methods Hamas used to discipline errant Muslims indicated the greater severity it might employ against the Israeli enemy. Israel made a large mistake if it assisted Hamas on the assumption that the organization would confine its activities to fostering exemplary Islamic practice. Hamas's entry into the fray against Israel provided genuine religious zeal to the Palestinian cause, which had already for some time been something like a religion. Palestinians in Jordan and the Gulf region who had disliked the PLO involvement with other leftist movements willingly contributed financial and moral support to Hamas, which served as a major conduit for aid to relieve the embattled Palestinian population. The Gulf countries, especially Kuwait, provided additional vital medical assistance and other supplies in their more comfortable relationship with genuinely Muslim Palestinians.

The Intifada changed the Palestinians, and it changed their relationship with Israel. Hamas also changed Palestine and the relations of the people living within it. The Gulf War in 1990–1991 ended the Intifada and changed the entire region and its relationship with the world. Hamas, by contrast, changed little. It committed itself to liberate Palestine and called on all Muslims to engage in the level of *jihad* ('struggle') necessary to fulfill that goal. The defeat of Saddam Hussein, who had promised to liberate Palestine, the disgrace and financial collapse of the PLO because of its support for Saddam, and the loss of any pretense of Arab solidarity because the groups supported different sides during the war had nothing to do with Islam and did nothing to alter Hamas's views of its goal.

The Hamas covenant stated that it was the duty of Muslims to liberate Palestine. Defeat in war did not change Palestine's identity as a religious *waqf* or Muslims' obligation to wrest it from Israeli occupation. Hamas deplored the practical, secular politics Arafat was willing to participate in to obtain any kind of concessions as he and those who depended upon the PLO seemed totally friendless and devoid of moral or political leverage in the defeat they shared with Saddam. In the view of Hamas, the PLO's acquiescence to exclusion from the October 30, 1991, Madrid peace conference on the Middle East provided the most egregious evidence of compromise with *jahiliyyah*. Two years later, on September 13, 1993, Arafat shook the hand of Israeli Prime Minister Yitzhak Rabin in Washington, D.C., to symbolize his acceptance of an Israeli state in return for the right to administer the civil affairs of the isolated enclaves of Gaza and Jericho. The promise that Israel *might* allow Arafat similar jurisdiction in other parts of Palestine *sometime* in the future could not dispel the indignity of receiving crumbs when religious duty demanded the full portion.

There were no grounds for belief that the Hamas hard-line stance was posturing or pandering, because it ran contrary to prevailing sentiment. The general elation which accompanied Palestine National Authority control of the two areas of Palestine indicated that popular opinion agreed with Arafat's acceptance of a pittance. Hamas persevered in true *salafiyyah* fashion, however, and emphasized the rewards of martyrdom for those who sacrifice their lives in behalf of God's work.

Certitude that the struggle for Palestine was over, that peace had come to the Middle East, and that *jahil* elements could control the future without resistance ended almost as quickly as it had begun. Hamas engaged in a policy of bombing predominantly easy, civilian Israeli targets, to the dismay of most of the world's population. Failure to understand that Hamas had a religious mission which required political actions prevented observers from understanding the organization's intransigence. Albeit a religious organization, Hamas represented the last vestige of the Palestinian resistance which had insisted upon the sanctity of a unified Palestine under Arab control since 1917. Its faithful guardianship of the Arab Palestinian patrimony guaranteed continued support among the same kinds of people who had responded favorably to the original modern *salafiyyah* calls to action more than a century earlier.

SIX

SHI'I RESPONSE
TO SECULARISM

An effective Shi'i challenge to modern secularism, which profoundly influenced the entire world, occurred later than the Sunni *salafiyyah* movements. The outburst of Shi'i activity was all the more remarkable since the 15 percent of the worldwide Islamic population identified as Shi'i had generally accepted a minor role vis-à-vis majority Sunnism. Over the previous eight centuries, significant Shi'i Islamic influence had been confined to the Persian empire, which officially became Iran in 1935. The approximately 55 percent Shi'i population of modern Iraq and perhaps 25 percent Shi'i population of Lebanon customarily assumed low profiles befitting their subordinate status in society. While Iran's population was overwhelmingly Shi'i, the country's dramatic modernization during the 1960s and 1970s created a level of wealth and strength which usually renders critics helpless or ineffective. The strength of the government's internal security forces, and the even greater importance of the *perception* of their strength, was additional reason to believe that Iran was infertile ground for Islamist activism. The overt, long-standing policy of Iran's clergy to remain aloof from the contaminating influence of politics deprived Islamists of respectable leadership. This posture was crucial among Shi'i, who normally behaved in accordance with revered, scholarly religious leadership.

Despite the general prosperity, however, considerable dissatisfaction existed in Iran. Merchants, intellectuals, members of the professions of law, medicine, and engineering, lower clergy, common urban laborers, lower ranks of the military services, and others had difficulty benefiting from Iran's new social and economic orientation. Those who disagreed with the materialistic nature of their nation's activities bore additional pain and resentment.

A large percentage of the discontented were in the age group of fifteen to thirty, which constituted about one-fifth of Iran's population. Particularly important were the youths who were in school or had recently graduated from the massively expanded educational system. Exposure to education from the lowest levels through technical schools and universities aroused higher expectations for advancement in society than reality could match. Education which overqualified youths for employment in the provinces usually proved inadequate to ensure a career in the large urban areas. The result was a massive conglomeration of unemployed and underemployed youth in Iran's big cities, especially Tehran. Their inability to fulfill their dreams contrasted starkly with the extraordinary success of those fortunate enough to obtain positions among Iran's new global affiliations. Often hoarded closely together in the crowded slums of south Tehran, these young people, with their widespread discontent, frustration, and idleness, were receptive to a vision of a society based upon different assumptions.

But not all the unrest came from these crowded masses. Some who had acquired adequate credentials and even had the contacts to prosper from the Pahlavi prosperity rejected the opportunity for philosophical reasons. Their efforts, which could have enhanced the regime, were usually directed to altering or overthrowing it. Since sustained efforts against the regime were difficult, such people often chose to live abroad rather than suffer frequent or prolonged imprisonment. The limited number who experienced some success within Iran usually couched their criticism in veiled expressions that selected audiences could understand.

Informed observers agreed that numerous groups strongly opposed some or almost all of the Shah's policies. Collectively, these groups, with their adherents in Iran and abroad, constituted a significant level of discontent; however, the lack of unity which characterized so many other areas in Iran prevailed among the opposition groups as well. Consequently, observers generally envisioned no significant problems for the Shah, since his enemies were so diverse and had so little in common except their resentment of him. Iranians, who generally had a strong sense of their unique culture, also had a long history of including diverse and divided groups that operated independently of other groups and of the central authorities. The unlikelihood that the Shah's opponents would ever find common cause and mount a coordinated effort against him seemingly ensured his safety.

Shi'i Islam unexpectedly provided the unifying force for dissidents. In time it became obvious why dissidents in a country which seemed to have forsaken its Islamic foundation coalesced around an Islamic program. The search for a solution to prevent Iran's losing its national and cultural character led to the realization that Shi'i Islam was an integral part, if not the very soul, of Iran.

Once dissident leaders arrived at that determination, it became axiomatic to eliminate non-Shi'i elements, including the Shah. This analysis also indicated that, since Iran had lost identity proportionally to its adoption of Western ways, it could regain its identity with each deletion of Western mores and cultural manifestations. For some, no Western practice, such as wearing a necktie, was too small to eliminate in the quest to salvage the identity and integrity of Shi'i Islam and Iran. Love of Islam, love of Iran, and contempt for the West became a three-point platform which enough people could vigorously embrace to eliminate the Shah and change Iranian society. Iranian Islamists, however, in the tradition of their predecessors in other Islamic regions, openly acknowledged their receptivity to Western science and technology.

Laymen, rather than clergymen, led the resurgence of Iranian Shi'i Islam. Men like Mehdi Bazargan, 'Ali Shari'ati, Jalal al-e Ahmad, and Abu al-Hassan Bani-Sadr were among the most influential laymen who essentially defined a new role for Islam in modern Iran. In addition, they aroused a large portion of the Iranian population, particularly young men, to respond to religious issues and demand the creation of an Islamic society. Their commitment to full implementation of their vision did not allow for a gradual evolution from the existing society into an Islamic society.

Understanding why laymen had to initiate action requires an explanation of the role clergy played in Iranian society by the twentieth century. Long-standing 'ulama policy forbade Shi'i clergy from participating in political and other tainted and tainting activities. Government policies, moreover, had stripped the clergy of most of their duties, influence, and income. The clergy treaded lightly in limiting lay behavior, lest they drive laymen away from religious guidance and willingness to pay religious gratuities, which constituted the clergy's principal remaining source of income. Numerous critics, of varying degrees of sophistication and stature, agreed on the ineffectiveness of the Iranian clergy, whose response to the government's religious retrenchment had been to restrict themselves to monotonous, traditional presentations of the Qur'an and hadith and tiresome explanations of the proper methods for performing personal hygiene and toilet functions. These critics, in fact, emphasized the necessity of full involvement of the clergy in revitalizing Islam and Iran.

Ayatollah Khomeini's vivid public opposition to the White Revolution in 1962–1963 was an anomaly, and his exile warned others with similar intentions that his fate was the least that could happen to them. Even much milder efforts of respected clergymen to address contemporary issues in the Monthly Religious Society in 1960–1961 attracted government recrimination. Authorities forced the termination of the group's public lectures and their subsequent publication. It seemed unnatural, however, for the clergy, which had such a major role in guiding laymen in Shi'i Islam, to remain silent while the government rapidly transformed Iranian society.

Mehdi Bazargan, a respected layman, addressed this issue in a speech to the Second Congress of Islamic Societies in 1962. This prominent veteran of the National Front movement of the 1950s concentrated on the adverse results of religious leaders' abstention from all involvement in politics. He observed that such an approach, however noble in concept, not only abrogated religious and moral duty but left the government in total control of society. The results, he maintained, were quite obvious, as unfettered secular values spread corruption and fostered arbitrary dictatorship. In his view, the clergy should become fully involved and save the nation from suffering indignities which God never intended. The religious leaders, he believed, should participate as advocates in behalf of the people and ensure that government was based on consultation (shura). The clergy should protect the people and, if necessary, coordinate action against injustice. He provocatively proclaimed that Shi'i should not wait passively for the Hidden Imam to provide perfect justice at some time in the future. His observation that believers should share responsibility with the Imam for instituting justice was a vital step for others, who soon insisted that believers must create proper conditions for the Imam's return.

ALI SHARI'ATI'S INFLUENCE

While many individuals played significant roles in revitalizing and redirecting Shi'i Islam, it is difficult to imagine its success and configuration without the activities of 'Ali Shari'ati. He obtained a secular education in Iran, while his father, who was a religious scholar, provided him some private lessons on religious subjects. His doctoral work in sociology at the Sorbonne in Paris in the early 1960s dealt in part with Islamic history and exposed him to a variety of modern philosophical approaches. Existentialism and Marxism impressed him as accurate explanations for Iran's past and as adaptable to shaping a better future for Iran.

Beginning in 1965, Shari'ati immersed himself in intense public discussion of Shi'i Islam without benefit of any significant scholarly training in religion. Ordinarily, such audacity would have occasioned ridicule and trouble in a society which insisted that religious commentators possess certified erudition. Shari'ati's survival and later unmitigated success apparently resulted from the Iranians' hunger for discussion of the relationship of religion to the practices and temptations of modern society. Concerned and marginally competent laymen found eager audiences for their discussion of issues that the qualified but reticent clergy ignored.

Shari'ati did not initiate the *Husayniyyah Irshad,* but he soon became and remained the most popular and important spokesman of this movement, which began in 1965. Gatherings called *husayniyyahs,* in which people could proclaim the virtues of the Imam Husayn, had taken place in most Shi'i communities since at least the tenth century. Their primary use, of course, was to commemorate the Imam's martyrdom on the tenth day of Muharram each year. The Husayniyyah Irshad was quite different. Meetings developed throughout urban areas of Iran following the success of a privately funded, totally modern building in Tehran where laymen and some youthful clergymen met to discuss a wide range of topics related to religion and modern times. Lecturers often used films or audio- or videotapes to enhance their presentations on religious subjects, and these exciting approaches contrasted sharply with the traditional methods of the older, conventional clergy. Sessions for women in some of the facilities broadened the participation of that element of society, which usually played little or no role in defining religious belief and practice.

Shari'ati's ideas, oratory, and passion quickly established his fame as the most popular speaker. Befitting his interest in Jean-Paul Sartre, the Husayniyyah Irshad was allowed to become whatever its participants desired and/or needed. Thoughts, concepts, beliefs, and suggestions that could never meet the traditional Shi'i clergy's standards for formal philosophical or theological argument burst out for consideration. The mix of disciplines among the modernly educated discussants placed unconventional thoughts and possibilities into juxtaposition. For these reasons and others, the Husayniyyah Irshad infused its participants with a vivacious sense of mission which was difficult to keep behind the closed doors of their religious centers.

For all of Shari'ati's emphasis upon religion, it became clear that he primarily desired to improve the quality of life and ensure justice on earth. His orientation was very strongly in behalf of the underdeveloped nations of the world. In most of his lectures, many of which were later published, he explored the need for and means of reducing the wealth and power of the mighty in order to make these earthly accouterments available to more people on a more equitable basis. According to Shari'ati, Western imperialism's insatiable grasping for wealth and cultural expansion was the most obvious enemy that the aroused deprived nations and peoples needed to combat. He blamed Iran's plight upon the ignorance of the upper clergy, who also perpetuated ignorance among the masses. He observed that the educated *'ulama* had an obligation to understand developments at all times and guide people who looked to them for advice. The *'ulama*'s concentration upon some of the most useless aspects of religious learning and practice had resulted in an ignorant society who lacked a sense of their own identity and values, making the young, in particular, easy prey for decadent and immoral Western ways. The 'ulama's refusal to comment upon the important aspects of peoples' lives and their failure to understand the modern world, he said, left control of education and other institutions to the exploitative secular government.

To the delight of his audiences, Shari'ati offended both government officials and the 'ulama. His far-reaching accusations traced the problem to the beginning of the Safavid dynasty in the sixteenth century, when Shi'ism became subservient to the state. He openly praised Jamal al-Din al-Afghani and Muhammad 'Abduh for their realization that Muslims must return to the religious practices of the Imams 'Ali and Husayn.

Useful as the glorification of 'Ali, Husayn, Afghani, and 'Abduh were to Shari'ati in discrediting the malpractice of Islam, his major influence resulted from unifying traditional Shi'i Islam with modern socialist ideologies. Citing Islamic sources, he observed that Islam was intrinsically an egalitarian religion in which believers shared their love of God and love for each other. The domination of mighty, self-glorifying individuals was unnatural and largely responsible for delaying the Imam's return. According to Shari'ati, the dictatorships, injustice, and inequities perpetrated by powerful individuals disrupted the dialectical development necessary before the Imam could appear and bring equality and justice. This, he explained, was why Shi'i were particularly suited to lead the earth's downtrodden to liberation. Shi'i alone expect the Imam. Shi'i alone understand that a life of toil and tribulation for the world's masses is not only immoral but contrary to natural law.

Shari'ati's observations became particularly provocative when he implored Shi'i to take the initiative and create a society appropriate for the Imam. While Shi'i had traditionally waited patiently for the Imam to return and bring justice, Shari'ati insisted that the Imam would not come until Shi'i had created a just society. This invocation struck a responsive chord among the restless youths, who formerly expected nothing but travail in this world. Dr. Shari'ati and others who lacked his erudition infused their audiences with a sense of mission to fulfill their own and God's destiny.

The Husayniyyah Irshad became an important subculture throughout Iran and among expatriate Iranians worldwide. By the 1970s, conversations about the Husayniyyah Irshad and the comments and writings of Dr. Shari'ati and his disciples dominated most Iranian conversations. Groups formed abroad to discuss the new philosophical developments. The widespread familiarity of Shi'i Muslims with the fundamentals of scholarly discourse prepared them particularly well for such argumentative exchange. All but staunch supporters of the

Shah found reformist themes in the new proposals that suited their sociopolitical predilections. The often well-educated, secular Iranians abroad tended to gloss over the Islamic slant Shari'ati and the Husayniyyah Irshad brought to advocacy of social reform. The inextricable association of Shi'i Islam with Iran made it seem natural to incorporate Shi'i moral principles into reform. Many who endorsed implementing fundamental concepts of Islam, such as upright personal behavior and community responsibility for the social welfare, gave no thought to the possibility of returning to ancient practices in dress or female seclusion. Bright, secularly oriented Iranians seemed, however, to find considerable satisfaction in discovering that the old values of their ancestors' religion were relevant to modern philosophy, morality, and ethics.

The government's closure of the Husayniyyah Irshad and arrest of Shari'ati in 1973 had a marginal effect on the movement. Publications of Shari'ati's views continued to circulate, and his arrest added appeal for most, who believed that the Shah's government destroyed everything which was noble and worthwhile. Shari'ati's mysterious death shortly after he went to England in 1977 enhanced his reputation as another Shi'i who suffered martyrdom in the struggle for equality and justice.

AL-E AHMAD'S UNRECOGNIZED EFFORTS

Jalal Al-e Ahmad, a contemporary of Shari'ati, helped prepare the intellectual climate in which the Husayniyyah Irshad movement and later revolutionary concepts thrived. This descendent of a distinguished Shi'i family of clergy lost his faith in the early 1940s. He held office and wrote extensively for the quasi-communist Tudeh party from 1943 to 1947 before he affiliated with the National Front movement. Throughout Al-e Ahmad's political activities he remained a teacher, but he was always primarily a writer. During a historical writing project in 1960, he suddenly realized that the term *gharbzadegi,* which his friend Ahmad Fardid had coined, accurately expressed the massive hold Western culture had obtained on Iran. Through his efforts the word, which translates as "Occidentosis," "Weststruckness," or "Western plague," became inextricably connected with the imperative to terminate Iran's dependence on the West and Western culture.

Al-e Ahmad's forceful admonitions against the "Western plague" combined strong themes of Frantz Fanon and Marx with his personal emotional analysis of the Western domination of Iran. He said that, while Marx had described a world of two social classes of individuals, by the second half of the twentieth century the dichotomy was between rich and poor *nations.* According to him, the nation-producers of machines had wealth and power over the nations which consumed the machines and their products. This categorization rendered capitalist or communist designations irrelevant, instead defining modern nations according to their willingness to lead a revolution against the unequal distribution of wealth, power, and influence.

Al-e Ahmad observed that Islam, although very weak in leadership and practice, prevented Westerners from totally subsuming the culture of southwest Asia and North Africa. This heartland of Islam had not fallen as quickly or as thoroughly as had South America, India, eastern Asia, and non-Islamic Africa. Islam, therefore, provided the best hope of ending the hold of the West on the Middle East. But, he warned, the systematic effort on the part of the West to dismantle the Middle East as a viable culture continued. He cited the publication of the first volume of the *Encyclopedia of Islam* as the newest manifestation of Westerners studying Middle Eastern people in order to control them.

Since rejection of Western influence was in its early stages, few seemed to understand Al-e Ahmad's exhortation that Iranians use a Shi'i foundation for modernization. He pointed out that the Shi'i approach to Islam was the major distinction between the Iranians and the Turks and Arabs who surrounded them. Along with other leaders, he believed that Iranians needed to find a way to graft Western technology onto Iran's cultural base, and he warned that failure to comprehend the scientific and technological principles of the machines would keep Iran in a perpetual state of awe and dependence. Al-e Ahmad's novel emphasis in the early 1960s upon creating a Shi'i-oriented Iranian society had become first a popular and then a dominant theme of Iranian dissidents by the mid-1970s.

BANI-SADR

Iran's massive, although haphazard, educational efforts beginning in the 1950s had produced large numbers of people with credentials to support their posture as intellectuals. The Husayniyyah Irshad in Iran and the active verbal debates, conferences, conversations, and publications of the expatriate communities invited young intellectuals to display their erudition. Those who took particularly bold positions—despite the belief that SAVAK, or internal security agents, were in every gathering—built reputations which permeated the worldwide Iranian dissident community. One such person was Abu al-Hassan Bani-Sadr, who became the first president of the Iranian Islamic Republic, which replaced Shah Mohammad Reza Pahlavi's regime in 1979. His sound religious education and lineage from a distinguished Shi'i clerical family provided him additional credentials for intellectual leadership. From the safety of France in the 1970s, Bani-Sadr had proposed a radical agenda to transform Iran and the world. While claiming to base his beliefs on Shi'i assumptions, he proposed pragmatic means and goals which bore little resemblance to the religion he supposedly espoused.

Bani-Sadr characterized Islam as "a continual cultural revolution" which strove to abolish anything distinctive in individuals or nations. According to him, any different characteristic, trait, or possession leads to claims or capacities for domination. His characterization of God as "pure Justice," rather than the source or provider of justice, signaled a totally earthbound concern and un-compromising egalitarianism. He visualized a universal anarchic society which would obtain its inspiration and guidance from revolutionary Iran.

While Bani-Sadr clearly began with an intellectual system and orientation based squarely upon the beliefs of Shari'ati, he moved to an advocacy of vio-lence and social regimentation that Shari'ati had never suggested. His insis-tence upon the total involvement of the entire population in shaping society was also contrary to most existing concepts. Most Shi'i clergymen, in partic-ular, disliked the adoption of democracy or republicanism, which threatened their traditional right to lead society. In addition to the criticism others directed toward the clergy, Bani-Sadr overtly criticized their failure to instruct believ-ers in the use of weapons. He insisted that the righteous should have weapons, not only to prevent subjugation from the oppressive national army, but to enable the spread of revolution worldwide. Furthermore, his concept of an Islamic society demanded that everyone have the same unostentatious food, clothing, housing, furnishings, and consumer goods; neither individuals nor nations should have power over one another. Fulfillment of this goal required righteous Muslims to engage in armed struggle. This man—who would later flee, first from the Shah and again from the wrath of Ayatollah Khomeini—unmercifully mocked the cowardice of clergy and laymen who failed to of-fer their lives in martyrdom to achieve his concept of a perfect Islamic society.

By the time Bani-Sadr had become a well-known leader in the Islamic rev-olution, many others had adopted a belief in the necessity, if not the moral re-sponsibility, of spreading Islam using violence. Boiled down to slogans in the mass demonstrations in Iran or the Shi'i slums of Lebanon, Bani-Sadr's mili-tant rhetoric lost any ambiguity or possible interpretation as metaphor. The surprisingly rapid success of militant Islam attained a level of appeal which did not require theological justification for proposing violent action to achieve the desirable goal of an Islamic society. The active imaginations of intellectual or-ators and writers found lower clergy and martyr-seeking laymen to implement their injunctions, not only among Shi'i, but also among the Sunni Muslim Brotherhood and Hamas.

LEBANESE SHI'I

Surprisingly, a major manifestation of Shi'i political action and violence occurred in Lebanon. This sudden activity was uncharacteristic for a religious
group whose historical minority status in the region and lack of influence in
the modern state of Lebanon had fostered discreet behavior. The fact that the
Shi'i were the largest religious group in a nation where no religion had a majority was no reason for boldness. Even after Lebanon erupted in tumult, the
thought never arose among other groups that the passive and powerless Shi'i
would become a factor in the outcome of the civil war.

Musa al-Sadr[1] prepared the Lebanese Shi'i for a greater role in society. This
Iranian of Lebanese lineage arrived in 1958 and gradually emerged as the most
revered Shi'i leader in Lebanon. His scholarly erudition and political acumen
garnered him respect and a large following. His establishment of a separate Shi'i
Higher Council in 1969 indicated his dissatisfaction with traditional Shi'i subservience to Lebanese Sunni Muslims, and his Movement of the Disinherited
in 1974 strongly stated the Shi'i demand for full access to Lebanon's political
and economic bounty. The dignity he accorded his fellow Shi'i and his demand that they receive equitable status in Lebanon poised them for the military, diplomatic, and financial assistance, as well as the inspiration, that Ayatollah Khomeini extended them after 1979.

The mysterious disappearance of the Imam Musa al-Sadr in Libya in 1979
fueled rather than diminished the Lebanese Shi'i ardor, much to the amaze-
ment of other Lebanese. These formerly passive Muslims burst with a fury
upon the international scene with kidnappings, hijackings, and assassinations to avenge injustice and fulfill a religious obligation. Their unwillingness
to reestablish the pre−civil war status quo was a major reason the traditional
Lebanese leaders could not end the struggle that racked their nation. Traditional secular Shi'i leaders like Kamal al-Assad could no longer make deals for
themselves and their close friends and expect the larger Shi'i community to as-
sent. Lebanon and, to some degree, the entire world had to find a way to deal
with angry young men in guerrilla groups such as AMAL (Movement of the
Disinherited Militia), Hizbullah (Party of God), and Islamic Jihad, whose very
names epitomized terror for much of the world's population. Few outsiders
were aware of the steady stream of armed revolution which had pulsed through
Shi'i communities for nearly twenty years. The general public did not realize
that the violent manifestations emerged from a prolonged theological and
philosophical process. For the most part, the perpetrators of violence were also
unaware of any ideology other than a few slogans which urged action. In religion, as in other fields, ideas discussed in lecture halls, cafes, and salons assume unexpected dimensions in the streets.

IRAN'S ISLAMIC REVOLUTION

Street politics ultimately dominated the Islamic revolution of Iran in 1979, despite the prominence of Bazargan, Bani-Sadr, and other intellectuals in the early stages of the revolutionary government. (See the end of Chapter 4 on Shi'ism for background on the 1979 revolution.) Iran's unsophisticated masses embraced Khomeini, whose continuing opposition to the Shah reached back to the 1950s. His exile in Iraq from 1963 on had caused no great protest among the higher clergy, who generally did not regard him as a first-rate intellectual. Opposition leaders like Bazargan had some contact with him, but could never influence the Ayatollah to follow the Iran Freedom Movement's[2] political agenda. Expatriate intellectuals afforded him a nod of acknowledgment as a persistent critic of the regime who suffered exile rather than conform. His coterie of lesser clergy in Iran served as liaisons for his several thousand followers there. His location in Baathist-controlled Iraq limited his activities to those helpful to Saddam Hussein's regime. Iraq pursued friendly relations with Iran following their agreement in 1975. By any reckoning, therefore, the Ayatollah Khomeini did not appear to be a significant threat to the Shah of Iran.

Everything changed when Iraq expelled Khomeini in October 1978, in response to Iranian pressure. No regional state would accept him. He had little choice but to accept sanctuary in France, where Bani-Sadr and other Iranian expatriates offered him hospitality. This most traditional of Iran's ayatollahs had spent his entire life in quest of a society long since passed. His limited life experiences and scholarly training had never even encountered the concepts which the intellectuals in the Parisian suburb had cleverly appended to a Shi'i foundation. Anyone who comprehended his position knew that his single-minded concept of an Islamic republic did not countenance any kind of evolutionary stage, including the possibility of a government under the 1906 constitution, which was being discussed around him. His Iranian hosts in France apparently believed that the rigidity and backwardness of Khomeini's views eliminated him as a rival to their own ability to merge the traditional with the latest concepts of social engineering.

As Khomeini sat under a pear tree in the Parisian suburb of Neuphle-le-Château, larger and larger demonstrations were held in Iran every forty days to honor those killed in previous confrontations. Victory in street politics in Iran traditionally went to the bold. The demonstrators became bolder. The government of the indecisive and dying Shah did not meet the challenge with an incremental increase of resistance. As the level of action attracted widespread media coverage, a worldwide audience became involved. Cameras and reporters attracted larger, more vociferous demonstrations, which were responsive to increasingly radical speakers.

A pattern soon developed, in the media blitz which followed, of pairing footage of the newest demonstrations in Iran with pictures and comments of the somber old cleric sitting cross-legged on the ground in France. The men around him were obviously equally at ease with this old man as they were with the Western languages they spoke and Western clothes they wore. The reticent Ayatollah seemed to represent an innocent who wished to combine the wisdom of the past with the agenda of these young advocates of democracy in the overthrow of a despotic, militaristic, and extravagant monarch. His spokesmen quoted the Ayatollah's vehement, terse demands for an end to monarchy and the establishment of an Islamic Republic. People who heard and read these comments interpreted the Ayatollah's remarks in the context of their own knowledge and desires. World opinion became so favorable to the idealist intellectuals and their resident sage that even Western governments seemed unlikely to support the Shah.

Iranians had to act out the drama which the world watched. Foreign governments all over the world and an international audience became participants in the dramatic developments, and a flurry of activity in Iranian expatriate communities manifested their hope that they could arouse enough unrest in Iran and public support abroad to overthrow the Shah. Husayniyyah Irshad supporters in Iran generally shared the same views.

The intense animosity against the Shah and his Western allies appealed to many who knew nothing of modern ideologies. Their dislike of a society increasingly under Western influence, which also offered no chance of success for many of them, activated simultaneous rage and hope. The unsophisticated masses could relate to Khomeini because, contrary to most other *mujtahid*s, he called for the liberation of the masses and their participation in a social revolution. Unlike their Western-educated brethren who managed the Ayatollah's scores of media appearances in Paris, the masses in Iran understood Khomeini's comments because they shared the same limited views. They did not know and did not care about grafting modern social management concepts onto a traditional Shi'i foundation. The lack of knowledge of the masses made it impossible for them to misunderstand Khomeini.

The intellectuals seemed to have won when the Shah fled on September 16, 1978, in response to a general outcry against his rule. Everyone understood that in some remarkable way the multifaceted opposition to the Shah had coalesced around the symbolic leadership of an octogenarian cleric who had been absent from Iran for sixteen years. Shapur Baktihar's government, which the Shah had appointed, presided over a steady decay of the monarchy's institutions. If it was possible, Khomeini's appeal grew as the urban throngs celebrated him as the leader who overthrew the Shah.

But when Khomeini finally returned to Iran on February 1, 1979, he installed a government under the control of remnants of Mossadegh's 1950s National Front and their contemporary fellow believers, despite his earlier intolerance of their ideas. His prime minister was Mehdi Bazargan, an active layman who clearly intended to establish a secular republican government based upon the 1906 constitution. Bazargan confidently asserted that the revolution was over. He assumed that the educated engineers and other professionals in his cabinet would provide Iran the blessings of modern management of public affairs. The new government could utilize the talents of educated men like Bani-Sadr, who served briefly as treasury minister and foreign minister before being elected president. Sadeq Qutbzadeh, Ibrahim Yazdi, Mustapha Chamran, and others of the new intellectual class obtained high office and a high public profile. The presence of such men in the Bazargan government gave the appearance of a minimal disruption in Iran's complicated commercial and monetary affairs with nations and international corporations that expected stability. It also indicated that modern men, rather than an ayatollah, were in charge.

In their preoccupation with conducting normal international relations, the technocrats and social engineers overlooked the fact that the Ayatollah Khomeini's following expected an Islamic Republic. The absence of a definition of an Islamic Republic did not diminish their interest in creating a society based on Islam. Islamic organizations of all types, especially scores of revolutionary committees throughout the country, strove to define the ideal Islamic society and struck out against everything they did not regard as Islamic. Little which was closely associated with the Shah met their test of "Islamic."

Astute Iranians of all persuasions knew that a new Iran would emerge after the destruction of the Pahlavi structure. Iran's rapid transition to fulfill the Shah's vision of a modern industrialized society encouraged the technocrats to believe destiny had chosen them. But they never had a chance to control Iran. In the face of the multiheaded Islamic fervor which allowed assertive individuals and groups to ignore his government and act unilaterally, Bazargan realized the futility of trying to conduct normal domestic or foreign relations. He resigned on November 6, 1979, two days after activists had seized the United States embassy.

For all the radical positions he had professed as an expatriate intellectual, once in office Bani-Sadr realized the need for order. He found that groups and individuals who behaved in the revolutionary ways he had previously espoused prevented the establishment of any kind of centralized government policy. For their part, the Islamic Republic Party, which dominated the parliament, and his own prime minister agreed with most other Islamic revolutionary groups that Bani-Sadr's policies contradicted Islamic goals. These critics strongly opposed his domestic policies, even as they supported him in his role as commander-in-chief of the armed forces in an effort to defeat Iraq after it attacked Iran on September 22, 1980.

Despite his surprising ability to influence Khomeini, Bani-Sadr's presidency was doomed. He never enjoyed a day in office with full executive power. The Islamic Republic Party, the revolutionary committees, the hard-line Islamist clergy, and the masses never considered Bani-Sadr and the other would-be so-cial engineers as their compatriots. Only the National Front and leftist organizations like Mujahedin-e-Khalq and the Fadayan-e-Khalq, along with some urban professionals and bazaar merchants, enjoyed a comfortable relationship with the Western-trained intellectuals. Bani-Sadr spent most of his time and energy as president from January 1980 until his departure in June 1981 in un-successful efforts to obtain some public affirmation and support. Success was unlikely in the face of the sheer domination of Islamist forces. Under the cir-cumstances he enjoyed a longer period of quasi-power than most could believe possible. Bani-Sadr's experience in office is of particular interest, however, be-cause he vacillated between continuing to foment revolution and attempting to create a viable central government. Throughout his presidency he lacked a clear sense of direction and popular support, while the militant Islamists un-swervingly proceeded with overwhelming popular support toward establishing an Islamic society.

An incredulous world, including Iran's modern intellectuals, witnessed the creation of an Islamic state in Iran. Disagreement among the Islamists and the intense resistance they met from leftist elements tore Iran apart, especially be-fore the war with Iraq focused attention on repelling their enemy. A grassroots Islamic movement of this scale had never occurred. Anything of similar mag-nitude which had affected a large segment of Islam had been under the direct supervision of a strong individual or a well-defined small group. Ayatollah Khomeini, who did not hold an official position, never controlled the revolu-tion he inspired. "The Imam," as his supporters called him, appreciated the lack of clarity in Islamic doctrine as it related to many human activities. In many cases he was unsure of the exact Islamic answer to questions in the complex combination of antiquity and modernity presented by Iranian society. For all his apparent rigidity, he did understand the difficulty of instituting Islamic practice in a society which had lived so long in error.

A militant and expansive Iranian Islamic Republic evolved as the Islamists eliminated their opposition. Monarchists disappeared quickly, followed by left-ists, until only the more traditional Muslims under the leadership or inspiration of Ayatollah Shari'atmadari opposed the new Islamists, who merged the dis-tant past with the present. The immediate favorable response among the masses in regional nations encouraged Iranian talk of revolutionary expansion. Chaos in Iran, however, impeded any effort to spread the Islamic revolution. Iran's threats against the Baathist regime in Iraq led to the execution of prominent members of Iraq's two leading religious families, the suppression of Shi'i activities, and Iraq's preemptive invasion of Iran in September 1980. The Islamic militants' unsavory occupation of the Grand Mosque in Mecca in 1979 and Shi'i unrest in the eastern provinces of the Kingdom of Saudi Arabia convinced the Saudis of the danger posed by the Islamic revolution. A stir of revolutionary sentiment among the heavy Iranian population in the other Gulf states and islands raised the apprehension of those governments. In this atmosphere, Iraq obtained full financial support from its neighboring Arab states in pursuing war against Iran. Iraq's willingness to expend blood and resources to save the region from Iran's Islamic revolution sowed most of the seeds which would later develop into the Gulf War of 1990–1991.

While the Iranian revolution had its westernmost manifestation among the large Shi'i population of Lebanon, the Iranian Islamic revolution had global ramifications. The prevalent perception of resurgent Islam associates it with regression to ways of previous centuries. Doubtless, some Islamists believe that a thorough practice of Islam is intrinsically most compatible with preindustrial society. Muslims, like practitioners of other faiths, face the challenge of redefining their religion to accommodate the complexities of modern society. In all likelihood, the universal religion which developed in the barren terrain of Mecca can adapt to a considerably more homogeneous world than existed in the seventh century, when Islam began.

NOTES

CHAPTER 2. ISLAMIC BELIEF AND PRACTICE

1. *Hadith* are authenticated accounts of comments and behavior of the Prophet Muhammad, which serve as the principal supplement to the *Holy Qur'an* as the guide to Islamic law *(shari'a)* and proper behavior for Sunni Muslims.

2. Usually "Prophet," but also translated as "Apostle" or "Messenger."

3. Professing one's belief was necessary even if doing so endangered one's life. Some Shi'i believe, however, that denial of belief is permissible when it serves the good of Islam.

4. One who calls Muslims to pray.

5. A *minaret* is normally a narrow tower attached to a mosque from which *mu'adhdhin* call Muslims to prayer. Openings in the uppermost part of the minaret or an exterior walkway allow the *mu'adhdhin* to call in every direction. Loudspeakers, which sometimes project a taped call, have eliminated the necessity for *mu'adhdhin* to go to the top of minarets in many contemporary mosques.

6. Sura 1.

7. Sura 9:60.

8. Sura 9:79.

9. Sura 57:18.

10. Sura 2:187. Traditionally, specialists in most communities signaled exactly when the fast began and ended by a cannon shot or some other means. In modern times, Islamic centers distribute extensive charts that provide the official time to begin and end the fast for each day.

11. Scores of specially skilled craftsmen create a new *kiswa* annually that weighs about two tons and costs a few million dollars. Authorities cut the used *kiswa* into appropriate portions that serve as special mementos to the recipients.

12. The slaughter of far more animals than are required to feed the pilgrims can result in a tremendous waste of food. Still, *hajj* officials do not believe they should prevent pilgrims from making their personal sacrifices. In recent years Saudi officials have provided massive freezing facilities to preserve the surplus meat for shipment to feed needy people.

13. *Qur'an* means "recite" or "recitation."

14. Suras 17:50; 36:11; 39:69; 45:29–31; 50:4; 78:29.

15. Sura 2:136.

16. Suras 2:219; 5:90.

17. Al Ghazali, *Deliverance from Error,* Cultural Heritage and Contemporary Change Series II-A, Islam (vol. 2), trans. Muhammad Abulaylah (Council for Research in Values and Philosophy, 1995), p. 6.

18. Al-Ghazali, p. 67.

19. Al-Ghazali, p. 47.

CHAPTER 3. ISLAMIC EXPANSION: 570 TO 1517

1. Hashimites are descendants of Hashim, Muhammad's great-grandfather.

2. Raqayyah, who had been married to 'Uthman, predeceased her father, the Prophet Muhammad.

3. *Shi'i* comes from the Arabic phrase meaning "party or supporters of 'Ali."

4. Some Arab camps developed into such cities as Cairo, Basra, and Kufa.

5. The battle was so named because Aishah watched the battle from the back of a camel.

6. *Kharijite* comes from the Arabic word meaning "to secede" or "to leave."

7. They were called "Rightly Guided Caliphs" because they had known the Prophet.

8. The three major forms of Shi'ism are Imami (Twelver), Isma'ili (Sevener), and Zaydi (Fiver). The numbers refer to the number of imams each group acknowledged as having unquestioned revealed religious knowledge. Each will receive additional attention later in this book.

9. Imams were individuals who received direct revelations from God.

10. Later France, the land of the Franks.

11. The Kaaba suffered considerable damage at this time, as well as in 692, when Caliph 'Abd al-Malik's general, al-Hajjaj, bombarded Mecca to subdue Zubayr.

12. Gibraltar, the impressive rock formation that separates the Atlantic Ocean and the Mediterranean Sea, took its name from Tariq: Jabal al-Tariq, the "Mountain of Tariq."

13. The Iberian Muslims made no serious effort to conquer the Frankish empire, but the Franks regarded their victory over the Muslims near Tours and Poitiers in 732 as a great victory for Christianity which saved France and Europe from Islamic domination. Muslims regard it as a border skirmish.

14. A fuller discussion of Zaydi Shi'ism may be found in Chapter 4.

15. The eighth Abbasid caliph built Samarra about sixty miles north of Baghdad.

16. The *zandaqa* was a militant Persian cultural movement that opposed the influx of Islam and the Arab culture which threatened to obliterate established Persian culture.

17. Al-Rashid became famous in the Western world because the gifts he sent to Charlemagne informed the Europeans of the Islamic world's superiority to Europe in culture, knowledge, and wealth. The *Arabian Nights* portrayal of splendor and mystery in his court was probably even more instrumental in enhancing his reputation in the Western world.

18. A vizir is usually a chief or prime minister.

19. *Occultation* refers to a state of being in which the subject has disappeared from view but continues to exist.

20. *Ghazis* are holy warriors who expand Islam and guard it from internal and external threats.

21. The Mamluk system remained intact in Egypt, however, and served the Ottoman governors. Like other elements in such large empires the Mamluks occasionally rebelled and acted independently until Muhammad 'Ali eliminated them early in the nineteenth century.

CHAPTER 4. SHI'I ISLAM

1. Acceptance of the idea that Muhammad was the Seal of the Prophets, meaning the last prophet God would send with revelations for humankind, was central to Sunni belief. Varying interpretations of this issue, with the many implications that follow, constitute a major difference between Sunni and Shi'i. While most Shi'i interpretations did not ascribe prophetic powers to imams, to Sunnis they seemed close to such claims.

2. Shi'i claims in behalf of Alid right to leadership of Islam posed the most consistent internal problem of the Abbasids once they obtained power in 750.

3. The imamate passed from father to son in all cases except for 'Ali's two sons, Hasan and Husayn, each of whom became imam in turn.

4. The Twelve Imams are listed here, with the alternates favored by Fivers and Seveners designated in italics. The dates are those generally agreed-upon for their births and deaths. The imamate of each of the Twelve begins with the death of his predecessor. I. 'Ali (601−661); II. Hasan (625−669); III. Husayn (626−680); IV. 'Ali, The Pure One (658−712); V. Muhammad al-Baqir (676−731) *[or Zayd ibn 'Ali ibn Husayn (713− 740), Imam of the Fivers]*; VI. Ja'far al-Sadiq (699−765); VII. Musa al-Kazim (745−799) *[or Isma'il ibn Ja'far (d. 760), Imam of the Seveners or Isma'ili, who predeceased his father, Ja'far, but whose followers regarded his lineage as the legitimate imamate]*; VIII. 'Ali al-Rida (765− 818); IX. Muhammad al-Jawad (810−835); X. 'Ali al-Hadi (827−868); XI. Hasan al-Askari (846−874); XII. Muhammad al-Muntazar, al-Mahdi (unknown dates of birth and death; disappeared into occultation in 874).

5. Hasan and Husayn were offspring of 'Ali's marriage to Muhammad's daughter Fatimah, who had died six months after the death of the Prophet. 'Ali's third son, Muhammad, was called al-Hanifiyyah because his mother, Khawala, was of the Hanif tribe. He was not, therefore, in a direct bloodline from Muhammad through Fatimah, but only related to him through the Prophet's cousin 'Ali.

6. The *al-Mahdi* is a messiah whom God will send in the future to establish justice on earth and prepare for Judgment Day.

7. See note 19 to Chapter 3.

8. See later section on Isma'ili Shi'ism, the most important early branch of Shi'ism, which had numerous configurations and manifestations.

9. Ayatollah Khomeini centered his activities in Qum after he returned to Iran in 1979.

10. Shi'i communities and states often officially cursed Abu Bakr and 'Umar in their

Friday noon services, while the Sunnis reciprocated by cursing 'Ali and Husayn in their noon services.

11. *Shirking,* or denying one's religious faith, remained the one unforgivable sin for Sunnis.

12. The nature of Buyid Shi'ism is unclear; apparently, it was predominantly Zaydi.

13. Daylam is modern Gilan; Tabaristan is modern Mazanderan.

14. The word *taqiyyah* expresses the act of dissimulating, or denying one's true identity. Sunni, on the other hand, regard any denial of one's religious belief as *shirking,* the one unforgivable sin.

15. Called Qarmatians after the missionary activities Hamdan Qarmat organized and conducted; and called Isma'ilis after those who recognized that the imamate passed through Isma'il rather than through his half-brother, Musa al-Kazim, the Imam of the Twelvers.

16. I refer to the Qarmatians based in this region as centered in al-Hasa/Bahrain. Many accounts refer to them as located in "Bahrain," but the large island known in modern times as Bahrain was then called Uwal, and was just one part of an earlier and larger Bahraini state.

17. Fatimids moved their capital from Ifriqiyyah (Tunisia) to newly constructed Cairo in 973.

18. For example, Arab nationalist groups like al-Qahtanyyi, al-Ahd, al-Fatah, al-Baath, the Free Officers' Society, and the Muslim Brotherhood.

19. Saladin was actually a Kurd rather than a Turk, but he arrived in Egypt as a subordinate of a Turkish sultan. The officers and troops he commanded were predominantly Turks and Circassians.

20. Although on a few occasions a Christian served as *vizir* (first minister with extraordinary administrative powers) of the Fatimid empire, the *vizirs'* powers over secular matters in no way compromised the Fatimid imams' ultimate authority, which also encompassed secular matters.

21. Also known as Abu al-Hasan 'Ali ibn Ahmad al-Ta'i.

22. *Wahhid* is the Arabic word for the number 1 (one).

23. *Ijtihad* means an independent analysis or interpretation. Sunni Islam generally opposed individual interpretation and relied upon *ijma'*, or accumulated consensus of present and past sources (*Sunna* means 'tradition').

24. A *mujtahid* is one who practices *ijtihad,* interpreting Islamic doctrine by the application of knowledge and reason.

25. While this basic procedure for education had existed much earlier, the term *mujtahid* apparently did not come into use until the nineteenth century.

26. There had been a long-standing tradition that secular authorities could not take people into custody who sought sanctuary and protection on religious property.

27. *Waqfs* were religious endowments, mostly of land, but they could be of almost anything of value.

28. Reza changed the official name to Iran ('land of the Aryans') on March 21, 1935.

29. There was strong suspicion that Kashani's activities had inspired the attack on the Shah's life on February 4, 1949.

30. He had distributed some Crown lands on earlier occasions.

31. Much of the success of SAVAK (the internal security force) depended on Iranians' believing they were more omnipresent than they were capable of being.

CHAPTER 5. CONFRONTATION WITH MODERN SECULARISM

1. Few political or ethnic entities outside of Europe met the modern definition of a "nation," which requires recognized borders and central institutions.

2. *Islamist,* a usage of fairly recent origin, designates one who advocates the creation of an Islamic society, that is, one which conforms to Islamic principles and laws. The term came into usage primarily to replace the term *fundamentalist,* which many Muslims believed often carried derogatory connotations.

3. *Salafiyyah* is derived from the Arabic verb "to precede."

4. The German word *zeitgeist,* which means "spirit of the time," seems particularly appropriate for the Nasser era, which truly possessed a special spirit of its own.

5. Sayyid Qutb, *Milestones* (Lahore: Kazi Publications), 80. (Hereafter, *Milestones.*)

6. *Milestones,* 10.

7. *Milestones,* 11−12. Islamists in Iran found this appealing but understandably emphasized the unique qualifications of Iran to become an Islamic republic and lead an Islamic Revolution.

8. *Milestones,* 6−47.

9. *Milestones,* 57.

10. *Milestones,* 61.

11. *Milestones,* 111.

12. *Milestones,* 115.

13. The 'Alawi were a Shi'i sect found primarily in northwest Syria and south central Turkey. Traditionally the least developed and most maligned group in the Middle East, the 'Alawi fall beyond the confines of Islam in most respects because of their largely secret religious beliefs. Their prominence in the Baath party allowed them to dominate Syria, especially after Hafiz al-Assad became president in 1970.

14. Religious endowment.

CHAPTER 6. SHI'I RESPONSE TO SECULARISM

1. The occurrence of the name "Sadr" among prominent Shi'i dates to its use from the eleventh century as an honorific title for religious scholars. Musa al-Sadr was, however, a close cousin of Muhammad Baqir al-Sadr of Iraq, one of the most distinguished modern Shi'i scholars, who was put to death by the Saddam Hussein regime in 1980.

2. In essence, the Iran Freedom Movement was a continuation of the National Front Movement of the 1950s associated with Mohammad Mossadegh.

GLOSSARY

Abbasid dynasty   Islamic caliphal dynasty (750–1258) with its capital usually situated at Baghdad.

abu   meaning "father of"; frequently used in Arabic names.

Abyssinia   the modern state of Ethiopia, located in west-central Africa.

'Alawi   a Shi'i sect of several million, concentrated primarily in northwest Syria and south-central Turkey. Their largely secret religious beliefs put them beyond the confines of Islam in most respects. Traditionally the least developed and most maligned group in the Middle East, their prominence in the Baath party allowed them to dominate Syria, especially after Hafiz al-Assad became president in 1970.

Alid   refers to association with 'Ali, who was Muhammad's cousin, adopted son, the Fourth Caliph, and First Imam of various Shi'i sects. "Alid imams" refers to successors of 'Ali.

Allahu akhbar   an oft-repeated Arabic phrase which means "God is great."

AMAL   militia force of the Movement of the Disinherited which Shi'i leader Imam Musa al-Sadr founded in Lebanon in 1974.

ayatollah   "sign of God"; the highest rank in Twelver Shi'i Islam.

bab   "door"; 'Uthman al-Amri called himself "The Bab" to the Hidden Imam. Three other individuals served as the Mahdi's "Bab."

bani   "sons of"; often designates a tribe, such as Bani Ta'i tribe of the Nefud region.

bast   practice of taking refuge or seeking sanctuary in a religious building, practiced particularly in Iran.

bidah   "forbidden."

Buyids   a Shi'i group which controlled most of Persia and Iraq from 945 to 1055.

Byzantine Empire   the eastern portion of the Roman Empire, which continued to exist for about one thousand years after the western portion disappeared. Islamic entities replaced it in many areas, and the Ottoman Turks
administered the coup de grace in 1453.

clan   the members of an extended family within a tribe, which is a band of
related clans.

Companions   the first converts to Islam who accompanied Muhammad from
Mecca to Medina.

al-Darazi   the principal popularizer of the concept that al-Muslimun al-
Hakim, the sixth Fatimid Caliph of Egypt, was God's embodiment on
earth. He disappeared in 1019. See *Druze.*

darwishe   the Persian word for members of Sufi religious orders. More popu-
larly known in English as "dervish."

dhimmi   "People of the Book"; Christians and Jews within the Islamic empire
who enjoyed a special protected status.

Dhu al-Hajja   a period from the eighth to the thirteenth day of the twelfth
month during which the *hajj* is performed.

Druze   a religion which grew out of Isma'ili Shi'ism; based on the divine nature of al-Hakim, the sixth Fatimid caliph of Egypt (996–1021). The formal name for this religion is *al-Tawhid.* The popular name Druze derives
from Muhammad al-Darazi, al-Hakim's most famous proselytizer.

Emigrants   earliest Muslim converts who accompanied Muhammad on the
hijra to Medina in 622. Their observations were vital in establishing the
authenticity of *hadith* or *sunna* (traditions) that recorded the Prophet's behavior and comments.

faqir   a member of a Sufi order who submits to the leadership of his master or
shakh.

Fatimids   Isma'ili Shi'i dynasty centered in Egypt from 969 to 1171. Their
empire encompassed North Africa, Greater Syria, and both sides of the Red
Sea. Aggressive promulgators of Isma'ili Shi'ism.

Fiver Shi'i   Shi'i sect which believes that Zayd ibn 'Ali ibn Husayn, who was
the grandson of the Imam Husayn and half-brother to the Fifth Imam, was
the Mahdi.

ghazis   warriors who conduct military activities specifically in support of
Islam.

hadith   accepted accounts of what the Prophet Muhammad said and did. The
body of *hadith (sunna)* is a major component of Islamic law. Shi'i Muslims
regard the life and comments of their imams as *hadith,* and, consequently,
as part of their law.

hajji   a Muslim who has performed the *hajj,* or pilgrimage, to Mecca.

Hamas   Movement of Islamic Resistance; originated in the Gaza Strip in January 1988 as an extension of the Muslim Brotherhood. It declared that Palestine was an Islamic *waqf* which all Muslims were obligated to recuse from Israeli occupation. It continued to hold that position after the PLO made peace with Israel and withdrew clauses in its charter that called for the destruction of Israel.

hanifs   pre-Islamic Arabs who believed in one God but did not embrace any particular religion.

Hashim   the clan of the Prophet Muhammad in the Quraysh tribe.

Hejaz   the region along the west coast of the Arabian peninsula which includes the holy cities of Mecca and Medina.

hijra   known in the West as the hegira; the movement of Muhammad and the other Muslims from Mecca to Yathrib (later Medina) in 622 C.E. Muslims regard that year as the first of the Islamic calendar because as a result of the move Islam had a solid, friendly base for further growth.

husayniyyah   a gathering in which people proclaimed the virtues of the martyred Imam Husayn, held in Shi'i communities since at least the tenth century.

Husayniyyah Irshad   a type of religious discussion group which emerged in Iran in the 1960s. These groups became popular because they used innovative approaches and addressed nontraditional subjects.

ijma'   "source of emulation"; the principal means of amending Sunni Islamic law.

ijtihad   personal interpretation of Islamic law. Shi'i Islam depends heavily on this practice, which Sunni Islam traditionally allows on a very moderate scale.

al-Ikhwan al-Muslimun   the Muslim Brotherhood which Hasan al-Banna founded in 1928.

imam   (1) nonclerical leader of prayer in a Sunni mosque; (2) one of certain specified individuals who according to Shi'i Islamic belief had the special guidance of God to enact his will on earth. Various sects have differed as to the identification of the Imams and whether their number was twelve, seven, or five.

imamate   refers to the concept of imams, which is central to all Shi'i sects of Islam.

International Islamic Congress   an organization created by the Revolutionary Command Council of Egypt in 1955, with headquarters in Cairo, to enable the otherwise secularly oriented Egyptian regime to reach out to the world's Muslims.

Intifada   "Uprising"; here, all references are to the uprising against Israeli occupation which began in December 1987 in Palestine.

intizar   Shi'i Muslim expression referring to the act of waiting for the Mahdi.

Irshad   See Husayniyyah Irshad.

Islam   "Submission to the will of God."

Islamic Jihad   name used by various loosely defined groups which originated in Lebanon and Palestine during the 1980s. All had in common the use of kidnapping and other forms of violence to achieve their often obscure goals.

Islamic *waqf*   Hamas declared Palestine an Islamic *waqf,* which the organization and all other Muslims were obligated to save from Israeli domination and partition; see *waqf.*

Islamist   a usage of 1980s origin to designate one who advocates the creation of an Islamic society, which conforms to Islamic principles and laws. The term came into usage primarily to replace the term "fundamentalist," which many Muslims believed carried derogatory connotations.

Isma'ili   the branch of Shi'i Islam that believes in Seven Imams.

isnad   the chain of transmission of traditional accounts *(hadith)* of the life of Muhammad.

jahiliyyah   traditionally referred to the "age of ignorance" which prevailed before the Prophet Muhammad brought the message of Islam. By the late twentieth century, the term came to refer to any society, at any time where Islamic law did not prevail.

jihad   variously translated as "holy war," "struggle," or "striving"; all have in common the connotation of overt action in behalf of Islam. This spectrum can encompass simple missionary activity as well as violent acts.

Kaaba   a cube-shaped structure in the court of the Great Mosque at Mecca. In it is the Black Stone, which has been considered sacred for centuries. The Kaaba determines the *qibla,* or the direction Muslims face when praying. Muslims believe Adam built the first temple for prayer on this location and that Ibrahim (Abraham) rebuilt it later.

Karbala   city in present-day Iraq, southwest of Baghdad, that was the scene of the Umayyad killing of the Imam Husayn and his followers in 680. Many Shi'i Muslims perform pilgrimages to the magnificent shrine to Husayn at Karbala.

khutba   sermon at Friday noon prayer service that traditionally includes a favorable comment about the head of government.

kiswa   the black, gold, and white cloth that covers the exterior of the Kaaba. A new one is made each year.

Literacy Corps   a major part of Shah Mohammad Reza's White Revolution in 1962. The objective was to raise the level of education of every citizen of Iran. Many Shi'i clergymen saw it as a triumph of secularism and a threat to the clergy's traditional role in Iranian education.

madrasa   an Islamic religious school.

Mahdi   like Qa'im, refers to the Imam Shi'i expect to return and bring perfect justice on earth.

al-Mahdi   a messiah concept in Islam, usually associated with various Shi'i sects which hold different views on the identity of the Mahdi and the details of his expected return and role in society.

Mamluk   "owned one"; a class of slaves which various Islamic regimes trained as soldiers and administrators. They obtained power and controlled large areas for significant periods of time.

marji-i-taqlid   "source of emulation"; a title bestowed upon a preeminent Twelver Shi'i ayatollah. During most periods no ayatollah achieves this distinction.

matn   content or subject matter of a *hadith* which follows the *isnad,* or chain of transmission.

mawali   an Arabic term for early non-Arab converts to Islam.

mihrab   some kind of physical marking in a mosque that indicates the direction to face *(qibla)* during prayer.

minaret   normally a narrow tower attached to a mosque from which the *mu'adhdhin* call Muslims to prayer.

minbar   a set of steps with a platform at the top where the *imam* may stand to deliver a sermon *(khutba)* at the Friday noon prayer.

Monophysite   belief that Christ was only divine, as opposed to being both human and divine.

monotheists   those who believe in one God.

Mount Hira   mountain near Mecca where at the age of forty Muhammad received the call to prophecy during the month of Ramadan in 610. A heavenly messenger, later identified as the Archangel Gabriel, informed him of his call.

mu'adhdhin   one who calls Muslims to pray, usually from a minaret (known in the West as "muezzin").

Muhammad al-Muntazar (al-Mahdi)   the Twelfth Imam, who Twelver Shi'i believe went into occultation (became invisible) in 874. They expect him to return to earth to provide perfect justice.

Muhammad ibn al-Hanifiyyah   son of Imam 'Ali (Fourth Caliph) and Khawala of the Hanif tribe. Many regarded him as the Mahdi.

Muhammad ibn Isma'il   nephew of Musa al-Kazim, the Seventh Imam, the heir of Musa's older brother Isma'il ibn Ja'far, who had been designated as the Imam before his premature death. The Hidden Imam of most Isma'ili Shi'i.

mujtahid   a Twelver Shi'i ayatollah who has the authority to practice *ijtihad,* or personal interpretation of the *shari'a.*

Muslim   one who submits to God's will.

muwahhidun "Believers in The One." This is the term Druze apply to themselves to emphasize their monotheism and the unity of everything under God.

Najaf location of the tomb of the Imam 'Ali (Fourth Caliph), the inspiration for all Shi'i Islam, partisans of 'Ali. This city southwest of Baghdad became the center of Shi'i scholarship.

nass refers to the practice that each Shi'i imam designates his successor while he is still alive.

Pahlavi dynasty which began in 1925 when Shah Reza (1925–1941) replaced the Qajar dynasty of Iran with his own. His son, Shah Mohammad Reza, reigned from 1941 to 1979, when he was overthrown by the Islamic revolution inspired by Ayatollah Khomeini.

People of the Book also called *dhimmi,* "protected ones"; Christians and Jews, who enjoyed a privileged status because they believed in the One God and possessed holy scriptures.

PLO Palestine Liberation Organization; chartered in 1964 as the umbrella organization of various Palestinian groups which sought to regain control of Palestine from Israeli occupation.

polytheists those who believe in more than one god, usually many.

Qa'im another word for the Mahdi, the imam who Shi'i expect to return and bring perfect justice on earth.

Qajar Iranian dynasty which governed from 1794 to 1925.

Qarmati an Isma'ili Shi'i sect which operated from Hasa/Bahrain and controlled large segments of the Arabian peninsula from 900 to approximately 1077.

qibla the direction Muslims face (toward Mecca) when praying.

qiya "analogy"; archive providing precedent for Sunni Islamic judges to refer to in making decisions.

Qur'an, Holy Qur'an means "recite" or "recitation." Muslims regard it as the word of God. Composed of 114 *suras*, or chapters.

Quraysh the dominant tribe in Mecca beginning in the sixth century A.D. The Hashim clan of Muhammad belonged to this tribe.

raka each sequence during an Islamic prayer that results in prostrate worshipers on hands and knees with forehead and nose against the ground or floor.

Ramadan the ninth month of the Islamic lunar calendar during which Muslims fast from sunrise to sunset and perform other religious duties to renew their religious performance.

RCC Revolutionary Command Council; the name the Free Officers' Society assumed after overthrowing King Farouk of Egypt on July 23, 1952.

Rightly Guided Caliphs Abu Bakr, 'Umar, 'Uthman, and 'Ali; these four were the only caliphs who had personally known the Prophet and, therefore, knew how he had behaved and what he had intended.

sadakat voluntary contribution Muslims can make beyond the obligatory *zakat;* has enabled Islamic communities to establish mosques, schools, hospitals, and other institutions of social and cultural importance.

Sadr an honorific title for religious scholars in Iran during the eleventh century. Usage of this name became frequent among prominent Shi'i scholarly families. In modern times the illustrious Musa al-Sadr of Lebanon was a close cousin of Muhammad Baqir al-Sadr of Iraq, one of the most distinguished modern Shi'i scholars, whom Saddam Hussein's regime killed in 1980.

Safavid Iranian dynasty which began early in 1500 and endured into the eighteenth century, shaping the future of Persia. Developed on the foundation Safi al-Din established in the thirteenth century. Safi al-Din joined the Zahidiyyah Sufi order, which took his name after he became its leader. Esma'il was the first Safavid Shah (1500–1524).

salaf the Arabic verb "to precede."

salafiyyah name given to modern Islamist activists, who generally believe that the future of Islam is best secured by emulating its earliest roots.

salat "prayer."

SAVAK Iranian internal security force whose success depended on Iranians' believing they were more omnipresent than they were capable of being.

Sevener Shi'i those who believe their Seventh Imam, Muhammad ibn Isma'il, was the Hidden Imam. The Twelvers maintain that Isma'il ibn Ja'far was the Seventh Imam.

shahadah the Islamic confession of faith, "There is no god but God, and Muhammad is His Prophet."

shari'a "straight path"; Islamic law.

shaykh an honorific title designating a high leadership role. In the Islamic context, it frequently refers to a leader of a Sufi order or sectarian unit.

Shi'i also frequently Shi'ites or Shi'ah. The branch of Islam descended from the supporters of 'Ali. The three major branches or sects are the Twelvers, Seveners, and Fivers. The numbers indicate the number of imams they venerate.

shirk the one unforgivable sin in Sunni Islam, which means to deny the existence of God or to ascribe anything else as equal to God.

shura "consultation." There is a strong movement in contemporary times to pressure avowedly Islamic governments into adopting this approach as a means of instituting representative government.

siyam "fast"; Muslims fast during the month of Ramadan, which is the ninth month of the Islamic lunar calendar.

Sufism   an approach to Islam which emphasizes direct spiritual union between believers and God. The term derives from early ascetics' rough
woolen clothes *(suf)*. A practitioner of Sufism is a Sufi.

sunna   "tradition"; pre-Islamic Arabs believed strongly in conforming to
their traditions. Accepted accounts of Muhammad's behavior and sayings
constitute the *sunna* of Islam, a main source of Islamic law. Sunni Muslims
make up more than 80 percent of all Muslims.

sura   chapter of the Qur'an.

al-Tawhid   "the One." Druze use this term to refer to their religion; it emphasizes their monotheism and the unity of everything under God.

Trinity   Christian belief that God the Father, God the Son, and God the
Holy Spirit are equal and the same. Muslims regarded this as assigning partners to God and, therefore, as shirking.

Twelver Shi'i   the main branch of Shi'ism, which believes in twelve imams
beginning with 'Ali and ending with Muhammad al-Muntazar (al-Mahdi,
the Hidden Imam), who went into occultation in 874.

'ulama   a body of educated scholars who have authority to adjudicate questions related to Islamic law and theology. After the earliest days of Islam,
when the *'ulama* was at Medina, no single group performed this role. Regional *'ulama*s made necessary rulings. The upper clergy of Shi'i Islam constitute their *'ulama,* although each is qualified to make a ruling without con-
sulting his peers.

Umayyad   Islamic caliphal dynasty (661–750) with its capital at Damascus.
Descendants of Muhammad's relative Umayya, who was the great-grandfather of 'Uthman, the Third Caliph (644–656).

umma   Muslim community; can apply to a Muslim community of any size,
from the most local congregation to the entirety of the world's Muslims.

umrah   the lesser pilgrimage to Mecca. Umrah pilgrims *(hajji)* perform the
same activities as for the *hajj,* but only a pilgrimage on the eighth to thirteenth days of the twelfth month is an acceptable *hajj.*

vizir   principal minister of a government.

Wahhabi   those who accept the leadership of Muhammad ibn 'Abd al-Wahhab, the late eighteenth-century Islamist of the Arabian peninsula who attempted to resurrect a strict Islam based on the practice of its earliest days.
Movement closely associated with the influence of the al-Saud family in
Arabian affairs.

waqf   Islamic endowment which believers establish to fund mosques, shrines,
schools, and the livelihood of the clergy.

White Revolution   an extensive program which Shah Mohammad Reza began in 1961 to modernize Iran. The Literacy Corps, which sought to ex-

pand education, was particularly provocative to Iran's *'ulama,* because it threatened to reduce their role in education.

wuquf   "the standing"; that part of the *hajj* which celebrates the Prophet's last sermon in Mecca.

Yathrib   the original name of the city which became better known as Medina.

zakat   alms which provide the revenues of each *umma,* fixed at the annual rate of 2.5 percent of a believer's net worth.

zandaqa   a movement in the late eighth century to preserve Persian cultural traits in an Islamic society dominated by Arabs.

SELECT BIBLIOGRAPHY

A few thousand books on Islam are presently in print in English. Many other worthwhile books are no longer in print but are available in libraries and through brokers and out-of-print specialists. The following brief list contains books currently in print and, in most cases, the citation lists their most recent publisher and date of publication. The list includes sound books and represents a reasonable spectrum of the books on Islam.

Abduh, Muhammad. *The Theology of Unity.* North Stratford, UK: Ayers Company, 1980.

Ahmed, Lelia. *Women and Gender in Islam.* New Haven: Yale University Press, 1992.

Algar, Hamid. *Islam and Revolution: Writings and Declarations of Imam Khomeini.* Berkeley: University of California Press, 1981.

Arberry, Arthur J. *The Koran Interpreted.* New York: Collier Books, 1980.

Ayalon, David. *Studies on the Mamluks of Egypt (1250–1517).* London: Variorum, 1977.

Bulliet, Richard W. *Islam: The View from the Edge.* New York: Columbia University Press, 1994.

Chauduri, K. N. *Trade and Civilization in the Indian Ocean. An Economic History from the Rise of Islam to 1750.* Cambridge: Cambridge University Press, 1985.

Daftary, Farhad. *The Isma'ilis.* Cambridge: Cambridge University Press, 1992.

Donner, Fred M. *The Early Islamic Conquests.* Princeton: Princeton University Press, 1981.

Esposito, John L. *Islam: The Straight Path.* New York: Oxford University Press, 1988.

———. *The Islamic Threat: Myth or Reality.* New York: Oxford University Press, 1992.

Hawting, G. R. *The First Dynasty of Islam.* Carbondale: Southern Illinois University Press, 1986.

Hodgson, M. G. S. *The Venture of Islam.* 3 vols. Chicago: Kazi Publications, 1996.

Holt, P. M. *The Age of the Crusades: The Near East from the Eleventh Century to 1517.* London: Longman, 1986.

———. *The Cambridge History of Islam.* 2 vols. Cambridge: Cambridge University Press, 1970.

Inalcik, Halil. *The Ottoman Empire: The Classical Age 1300–1600.* New Rochelle: Caratzas, 1973.

Irwin, Robert. *The Arabian Nights: A Companion.* London: Allen Lane, 1994.

Jayyusi, Salma K., ed. *The Legacy of Muslim Spain.* Leiden: E. J. Brill, 1992.

Keddie, Nikki R. *An Islamic Response to Imperialism: Political and Religious Writings of Sayyid Jamal ad-Din al-Afghani.* Berkeley: University of California Press, 1968.

———, ed. *Religion and Politics in Iran: Shiism from Quietism to Revolution.* New Haven: Yale University Press, 1991.

Keddie, N. R., and B. Barton, eds. *Women in Middle Eastern History: Shifting Boundaries in Sex and Gender.* New Haven: Yale University Press, 1991.

Kennedy, Hugh. *The Early Abbasid Caliphate.* London: Longman, 1986.

———. *The Prophet and the Age of the Caliphates.* London and New York: Longman, 1986.

Lapidus, Ira M. *A History of Islamic Societies.* Cambridge: Cambridge University Press, 1988.

Lyons, M. C., and D. E. P. Jackson. *Saladin, the Politics of Holy War.* Cambridge: Cambridge University Press, 1982.

Momen, Moojan. *An Introduction to Shi'i Islam.* New Haven and London: George Ronald, 1985.

Morgan, David. *Medieval Persia 1040–1517.* London: Longman, 1988.

Roemer, H. R. *The Cambridge History of Iran.* Vol. 6. P. Jackson and L. Lockhart, eds. Cambridge: Cambridge University Press, 1986.

Said, Edward. *Orientalism.* New York: Random House, 1979.

Schimmel, Annemarie. *The Mystical Dimensions of Islam.* Chapel Hill: University of North Carolina Press, 1975.

Voll, John O. *Islam: Continuity and Change in the Modern World.* Syracuse: Syracuse University Press, 1982.

Waines, David J. *Al-Islam: An Introduction to Islam.* New York: Cambridge University Press, 1996.

Watt, W. Montgomery *Muhammad, Prophet and Statesman.* London: Oxford University Press, 1964.

———. *Muslim Intellectual: A Study of al-Ghazali.* Edinburgh: University of Edinburgh Press, 1963.

Wendell, C. *Five Tracts from Hasan al-Banna (1906–1949): A Selection from the Majmuat Rasail al-Imam al-Shahid Hasan al-Banna.* Berkeley: University of California Press, 1978.

INDEX

Abbasid: caliphate, xvii–xxi, 66, 135;
dynasty (750–1250), 59–64; end of
Egyptian dynasty, 68–69; legal devel-
opment, 40; progenitors of dynasty,
20–21; relations with Qarmati, 82–
85; relations with Shi'i, 73–77
'Abduh, Muhammad, xxii, 99, 123
Ablution, 28
Abraham, 28, 33, 35–36, 39, 142
Abstract depiction, 48
Abu al-'Abbas al-Saffah, xvii, 59–60
Abu al-Hassan Bani-Sadr. See Bani-Sadr,
Abu al-Hassan
Abu al-Khattab, 'Umar ibn (Caliph
'Umar), xv, 8, 48, 49, 52, 71, 73, 78,
81, 135, 144
Abu Bakr, 10, 135, 144: caliphate, xv,
48–49; conversion, 7; first caliph, 25;
relations with Shi'i, 71–78
Abu Hanifa, 40, 75
Abu Hatim al-Khatib, ix
Abu Jahal, 14
Abu Lahab, 8
Abu Sufyan. See Ibn Harb, Abu Sufyan
Abu Tahir Sulayman, 84
Abyssinian, xiii, 3–8, 29
Acre, xx, 63–64
Adam, 33–39
Afghanistan, 49, 89
Africa: Fatamids, 61–62; Isma'ili, 81–

83; spread of Islam, 56–58; Yemen
trade, 21
Ahmad ibn Hanbal, 40, 98
Ahmad ibn Tulun, xvii, 61
Aishah, xvi, 24, 53, 134
Al-Adid, 85
Al-Akhram, al-Hasan ibn Haydara, 86
Al-Askari, Hasan, 77, 135
Al-Azhar University, 103
Al-Aziz (975–996), 85
Al-Banna, Hasan, xviii, xxiv, 100–102,
104, 106
Al-Bistami, 45
Al-Bukhari, Isma'il, 41, 135
Alcohol, 116
Aleppo, 110–111
Aleppo Artillery School, xxvii, 110
Al-Farabi, Abu Nasser, 45
Algeria, 83, 106
Al-Ghazali, Abu Hamid, xix, 44–46
Al-Hajj, 57, 134
Al-Hakim, al-Muslimun (996–1021),
xviii, 86, 140
Al-Hallaj, Mansur, 43
Al-Hanifiyyah. See Muhammad ibn
al-Hanifiyyah
Al-Hasa, xix, 82, 84, 85, 136
Al-Hira region, 6
Al-Hudaybi, Hasan, xxiv, 104
Al-Husayni, Haj Amin, 112

'Ali, Caliph/Imam, xvi, 42, 59, 60, 61,
82, 123, 135, 136, 139, 143, 144; cali-
phal candidate, 48–57; conflict with
Mu'awiyyah, 53–56; conversion, 7;
death, 55; destroyed Kharijites, 53–
58; Imam concept, 71–80; Muslim
champion, 12–18; relation to Mu-
hammad, 6–25; Shi'i movement, 53–
56, 71–80, 134, 145, 146; shrine, 73
'Ali al-Rida, 50, 51, 74, 77, 135
Al-Junayd, 45
Al-Kazin. See Musa al-Kazin
Al-Khatib, Abu Hatim, ix
Al-Khattab. See Abu al-Khattab, 'Umar
ibn
Al-Lat, 23
Al-Mahdi, 81, 143, 146; Fatamid belief,
83; new concept, 75; occultation, 77
Al-Makki, Abu Talib, 45
Al-Malik, 57
Al-Manar, Abu, xxiii, 99–101
Al-Mansur, Abu Ja'far, xvii, 59
Al-Muhasibi, 45
Al-Mu'izz, Caliph, xviii, 84–86
Al-Mustansir, Caliph, 85
Al-Mutawakkil, Caliph, 60
Al-Najjar, 11, 12
Al-Rashid, Harun, xvii, 60, 77, 134
Al-Rida, 'Ali, 50, 51, 74, 77, 135
Al-Sadiq, Ja'far, 75, 135
Al-Sadr. See Musa al-Sadr
Al-Saffah, Abu al-Abbas, xvii, 59–60
Al-Shibli, 45
Al-Tawhid, 86–87, 140–146
Al-Turabi, Hassan, 112
Al-Wahhab, Muhammad ibn 'Abd, xxii,
97
Al-Walid, Caliph (705–715), 57
Al-Zakiyyah, Muhammad ibn 'Abdullah
al-Nafs, xvii
AMAL, 115–127, 139
Amina, 4
Amir ibn al-As, 20, 49, 55
Anas, Malik ibn, 40, 75
Anatolia, 68
Angels, 46

Animals, 34–37, 48
Aqaba, xv, 23
Arabic culture, 47
Arabic language: hadith, 40; Islam spread,
55; Qur'an, 37; spread of, 47
Arab nationalism, xxvi, 103–118
Arabs: adjustments to Islam, 21–23;
Arabization of others, 47; beliefs be-
fore Islam, 2–10; capacity for memo-
rization, 37; domination of Islam,
49–52; non-Arab influence on Islam,
58; Shi'i appeal, 85–86; spread be-
yond Arab region, 60–70
Art, 38, 46
Ataturk, 90, 106
Attributes of Tyranny, xxiii, 100
Aus, 9
Authentication (hadith), 41
Awdah, 'Abd al-Aziz, xxvii, 114
Ayatollah: defined, 89–94; Khomeini,
126–131; secondary to laymen, 120
Ayn Jalut, xx, 64
Azerbaijan, 67

Baath, xxiii, 106–115
Bab, 78–79, 139
Badr, Battle of, xiv, 12–18
Baghdad: Abbasid capital, 59–64; Bagh-
dad Pact, 92; center of Islamic world,
73; Mu'tazila, 38; Qarmati influence,
84–85; Sufi activities, 43–45; Turk-
ish-Persian struggle, 67–70
Baghdad Pact, 92
Baha'i, 92
Bahrain, xix, 80–85
Balkans, 65
Bani al-Nadhir, xxiii, 18
Bani al-Najjar, 11
Bani Kinana, 17
Bani-Sadr, Abu al-Hassan, xxvi, 120,
125–126, 128, 130, 131
Basra, 53, 72
Battle of: Badr, xiv, 12–14; the Camel,
53; Chaldiran, xxi, 68; the Ditch, xiv,
17–19; Hunayn, xxv, 23; Marj
Dabik, 68; Mota, xiv, 20–23;

Nahrawan, xvi, 53; Nihavand, xv, 49; Qadisiyyah, xv, 49; Sharur, xxi, 67; Siffin, xvi, 53; Tours/Poitiers, xvi, 58; Uhud, xiv, 15–16

Beauty, 37, 48

Bedouin, 2–12, 15–17

Berber, 57, 83

Bilal, 14, 29

Black Sea, 63

Black Stone: icon of "The God," 4–5; among many gods, 21–22; Qarmati theft of, xviii, 84; role in pilgrimage (*hajj*), 35–36

Bogle, Andrew and Rhett, x

Book of Life, 39

Books of Wisdom, 87

Booty, 14

Boycott, xiii, 8

Buddhism, 65

Bursa, xx, 65

Buyids: control Persia and Iraq, 79; emergence in Persia, 62; overthrown, 85

Byzantine: control of Persia and Iraq, 79; emergence in Persia, 62; overthrown, 85

Byzantine Empire: beginning of Islam, 48–49; Muslims attack in Africa, 57; Ottomans overthrow, 65–70; reduced threat, 23; religious diversity, 78

Cairo: Abbasid caliphate, 69; Druze origin, 86; Fatamid caliphate, 84; founded, 61; Mamluk conquest, 68; Muslim Brotherhood, 101

Caliph: Abbasid in Egypt, 68–69; origin, 25; resistance to, 48; Rightly Guided, 55; Umayyad and Abbasid, 55–64

Caliphate or the Supreme Imam, xxiii

Calligraphy, 38, 48

Camel, Battle of the, xvi, 53

Capital: Abbasid auxiliary, 59; Baghdad, 45; Cairo, 84; Damascus, 56, 71; Istanbul, 66; Medina, 49; Qayrawan, 83; Samarra, 73; Tabriz, 67

Caravan, 4–9, 12–15

Caspian Sea, 67, 80–84

Caucasus, 63

Cavalry, 16, 63–64

Chain of transmission (*isnad*), 41, 142

Chaldiran, Battle of, xxi, 68

Chamran, Mustapha, 130

Children, 6, 113–116

China, 4

Christians: Arab, 5; cultural chasm, 95; *dhimmi* (protected ones), 49, 58; and free will, 38; in Nawful clan, 9; and Ottoman Turks, 66–67; People of the Book, 18; as potential Muslims, 22; pre-Islamic in Arabia, 3; relations with Turks and Mongols, 62–64; after spread of Islam, 24

Circassians, 63

Circumambulation, 35

City of the Prophet, 11, 21

Clergy: absence of, in mainstream Islam, 29; benefit from discontent, 109–118; and Iranian Islamic Revolution, 120–131; oppose change, 96; role among Shi'i, 87–94

Clinics, xxiii, 102–114

Clothing: in Iran, 120–131; in Islam's resurgence, 109–110; in Palestine, 116; Reza's changes, 91

Communists: influence on Bani-Sadr, 124–125; in Iran, 91; in Syria, 106

Companions: distrust of Umayyads, 56; role in *hadith,* 41; role in Islam, 10; yearn for simplicity, 58

Consensus: *ijma'* in Sunni Islam, 40–42; unessential to Shi'i, 89

Constantinople, xx, 66

Constitutional Movement in Iran, 90

Contracts, 1, 39

Converts: accelerated pace, 20–22; changed Islam, 70; disgruntled, 58; ended for Druze, 86; lack of instruction, 24–25; role of Sufi, 44; strident in new faith, 7; subvert Treaty of Hudaybiyyah, 19; warriors, 8; in Yathrib, 10–12

Cossack Brigade, 90

Cousins: Muhammad and 'Ali, 6;
Muhammad and Mutin ibn 'Adi, 9
Creation: Islamic concept, 39; Islamic
art, 48; rejection of Darwinism,
101–103
Crusader, 62–64, 85
Custom, 6–27, 31–33

Damascus: Arab control, 49; Abbasids
abandon as capital, 61; Baath Party,
111; center of Islam, 71–75; Muslim
Brotherhood, 103; Seljuks oust cru-
saders, 63; Umayyad capital, 56–57
Dancers, 42
Darwinism, 106
Date palm, 9
David, 39, 114
Daylam, 79–84, 136
Death of: 'Ali, 55; Hasan al-Banna, 101;
Husayn, 57; the Imams, 73–79;
Muhammad, 24–25, 48–49, 71;
Muhammad ibn Isma'il, 81; Muham-
mad Rashid Rida, 99; Nasser, 107,
108; Qutb, 104; Sadat, 104; Saladin,
64; Sufi saints, 44; Timur, xx, 65;
'Umar, 52; 'Uthman ibn 'Affan, 52
Deity, 3, 27
Devil, 35–36
Dhu al-Hajja, 34, 140
Dialectic, 123
Ditch, Battle of the, xiv, 17–19
Dome of the Rock, 46
Dress Law, 91

Eastern Bloc, 108
Education: al-Ghazali's role, 45; call for
reform, 99; during Intifada, 114;
among Iranian laymen, 125; among
Islamists, 101–109; Twelver clergy
and, 88–94; and unfulfilled expectations, 119
Egypt: Abbasid control, 61; Arab nationalism, 108; British control, 96; end of
Abbasids, 64; Fatamid control, 62, 79,
82–85; Islamic conquest, 49; Islamic
revival, 98–104; Mu'awiyyah control,

55; Ottoman control, 68; resentment
of Arabs, 52; under Saladin, 63; trade
with Mecca, 4–5
Egyptian Debt Commission, xxii, 98
Emigrants, 8–11, 18
Encyclopedia of Islam, 125
Equality, xxvi, 34
Euphrates River, 49, 53
Exile of: Ayatollah Kashani, 91; Ayatol-
lah Khomeini, 94, 120, 128; Muham-
mad 'Abduh, 99

Fadayan-e Khalq, 131
Families: Abbasid, 20–21, 54–64; 'Alid
lineage, 73–83; call for sacrifice, 105;
Hashim, 4; Islam divided, 14; Islamic
obligations, 31–36, 40; Muhammad,
7; Ottoman, 70; Palestinian in In-
tifada, 113; role in society, 10–12;
Safavid, 70; Shi'i, 59; trauma of con-
versions, 8; Umayyad, 56
Fast, 27, 31–33
Fatimah, xvi, 6, 71, 77, 78, 135
Fatimid: Shi'iism, 82–86; Shi'i lineage,
80; spread of empire, 61–64
Festivals, 44
Fidayeen al-Islam, 92
Final Judgment, 7
Five Pillars, 27–36, 109
Fiver Shi'i, 73, 140
Food: al-Ghazali's difficulty, 45; during
hajj, 34; and Muslim Brotherhood,
102; in Qur'an, 39; during Ramadan,
32; role in Battle of the Ditch, 17
Forgery, 41
Frankish empire, 56
Free Officers Society, 102

Gabriel, Archangel, 7, 35–36, 143
Gadhafi, Mu'ammar, xxvi, 106
Gaza, xxvii, 113–117
Gender, 114
Generosity, 31, 39
Geometrical figures, 48
Ghassanid Arabs, 49
Ghatafan, 17, 20

Ghazan Khan, xx, 64
Ghazi, 65–68, 140
God, The, 4–5, 48
God's Messenger, 17, 20–28
Grand Mosque, 35–36, 46
Grand Mufti of Jerusalem, 112
Great Britain, xxii, 92–103
Greater Syria, 15
Greek philosophers, 45
Gulf War, 116, 132
Gurgan, 84

Hadith; al-Ghazali's use of, 45; central to
    Sunni belief, 55; criticized in Iran,
    120; defined in note, 27; against ex-
    travagance, 36; female modesty, 110;
    Islamist use of, 97–98; in prayer, 30;
    role in law, 40–42; Shi'i use of, 88;
    unnecessary for imams, 80
Hama: Baathist Brotherhood conflict,
    107–111; near Salamiyyah, 81
Hamas (Movement of Islamic Resis-
    tance), xxvii, 112–117, 126, 140, 142
Hamza ibn 'Ali, 8–9, 86
Hanifid, 80
Harun al-Rashid, xvii, 60, 77, 134
Hasan al-Askari (Eleventh Imam), 77,
    135
Hasan ibn 'Ali: accepted payment, 55–
    56, 59, 73–75; grandson of Muham-
    mad, 71; son of 'Ali and Fatimah, 6
Hasanid, xvii, 80
Hashim clan: claim to caliphate, 48–59,
    71; lineage, 4; poor, 2; reaction to
    Islam, 7–9
Hashimite, 55–59, 81
Hawazin, 23
Health Corps, 93
Hebrew, 37, 39
Hegira, xiv, 10–12
Hejaz: defined, 4; Muslim control, 20–
    23; role in trade, 5
Helema, 6
Hell, 7–8, 36–42
Helpers: defined, 10; discontent, 56–58;
    role at Badr, 13–14

Hidden Imam: Bab's relation to, 78; re-
    lation to *ulama,* 88; role in Isma'ili
    Shi'iism, 81; Shi'i urged to act, 121
Himyar, 23
Hira, 6, 53
Hisham, Caliph, 59
Holy Land, xx, 64
Horses, 4, 13–17
Hospitality, 17
Hospitals, 31, 112
Hulegu, xx
Hunayn, Battle of, xv, 23
Hungarian, 65
Husayn ibn 'Ali, xvi, 135, 136; central
    to Shi'iism, 77–79; claim to Imamate,
    71–75; conflict with Mu'awiyah,
    55–57; death, 57; grandson of
    Muhammad, 6; *hadith* for Shi'i, 42;
    influence on Islamic Revolution,
    122–123
Husayniyyah Irshad, xxiii, xxv, xxvi,
    122–124, 125, 129, 141
Hussein, Saddam, 116
Hygiene, 34, 120
Hypocrites, 12

Ibn Anas, Malik, 40, 75
Ibn Ayyub, Salah ad-din. *See* Saladin
Ibn Badis, 'Abd al-Hamid, 100
Ibn Harb, Abu Sufyan, 13–17, 21, 50,
    52, 56
Ibn Haritha, Zayd, xiv, 6, 15, 20
Ibn Isma'il. *See* Muhammad ibn Isma'il
Ibn Ja'far. *See* Isma'il ibn Ja'far
Ibn Sina, 45
Ibn Ubay, 'Abdullah, 12
Ibrahim (d. 763), xvii
Ibrahim (father of Isma'il). *See* Abraham
Ibrahim Yazdi, 130
Id al-Adha, 35
Id al-Fitr, 33
Idolatry, 38–39
Ifriqiyyah, xviii, 83, 136. *See also* Tunisia
Ignorance: blamed on Iranian clergy by
    Shari'ati, 122; as concern of reform-
    ers, 99–107; of Islam in the West, 47

Ihram, 34
IIC (International Islamic Congress),
xxiv, 103
Ijma': al-Kawahibi, 100; consensus, 42;
role in law, 40; Wahhabism, 98
Ijtihad: acceptable to reformers, 98; central to Shi'iism, 88; defined, 42
Illiteracy, 37–38, 42
Imamate: appeal and development, 72–81; among Druze, 86; 'Ubayd Allah's claim, 83
Imams: alternative to caliphate, 55; central to Shi'iism, 71–84; immune from questioning, 42; occultation, 61; prepare for return, 123
Incoherence of the Philosophers, 45
India, 4, 57–65
Indus River, 49, 57
Infallibility of imams, 61, 79, 80, 83
Innovation, 15–17, 55
International Islamic Congress, xxiv, 103
Intifada, xxvii, 114–116
Iranian Islamic Republic, 125, 131
Iran-Iraq war, 113, 132
Iran's Islamic Revolution, 108–132;
influence on Islam, 108–109
Isaac, 39
Ishmael, 39. *See also* Isma'il
Islamic community: defined, 22; early discontent, 53, 71; selection of caliph, 48
Islamic duty, 33
Islamic expansion: from Atlantic to India, 57; under Muhammad, 24; widespread, 47–49
Islamic law: Hasan al-Banna, 101; in Iran, 90; Qur'an and *hadith,* 39–41; right to punish, 53; role of Ja'far al-Sadiq, 75
Islamic principles, 40
Islamic Republic, 129–130
Islamic Republic Party, 130–131
Islamic Revolution. *See* Iran's Islamic Revolution
Islamic year, 35

Islamists: defined, 97; in Egypt, 100–105; Iranian, 118–132; Palestinian, 114–115; spread, 108
Isma'il (son of Abraham), 33, 35, 36
Isma'il ibn Ja'far, 77, 80–81, 135, 143
Isma'ili Shi'ism, xvii–xviii, 134, 135, 136, 140, 142, 144, 145; conflict with Sunni, 61–63; Isma'ili Imam, 77–86; success, 70; various forms, 77–86
Isma'iliyyah, xxiii, 101
Isnad: defined, 41; Shi'i reject, 80
Israel: conflict with Palestinians, 113–117; defeat of Arabs, 108
Istanbul, xxi

Jacob, 39
Ja'far al-Sadiq, 75, 135
Janissaries, 44
Jerusalem, xiv, xv, xix; al-Ghazali's visit, 46; change of *qibla,* 18, 20; crusader control, 62; grand mufti of, 112; Muslim conquest, 49; Saladin control, 63
Jews: in Arabia, 3–5; oppose Muhammad, 18–19; in Yathrib, 9–10
Jihad: in Lebanon, 127; in Intifada, 114–116; Ottoman, 66; Sayyid Qutb, 105
Jordan, 20, 106–116
Judaism: in Arabia, 5–10; Islam differed, 20–28; new attitudes toward, 110; similar to Islam, 29
Judgment Day: forgiveness, 82; Mahdi concept, 81
Jurisprudence, 40, 87

Kansu al-Gauri, xxi, 68
Karbala: death of Husayn, 57; shrine, 90; survivor, 75
Kashani, Ayatollah, 91–92, 136
Kazimayn, 77
Khadija, xiii, 6–8
Khalid ibn al-Walid, 20, 49
Kharijites, xvi, 53–58
Khaybar Jews, xiv, 19–24
Khazraj, 9, 11

Khomeini, Ayatollah Ruhollah, xxv–
    xxvi, 94, 116, 120, 126–131, 135
Khutba, 30, 142
Khuzistan, 81
Kin, 63
Kinda, 23
Kingdom, the, 34, 132
Kinship, 8–11, 56–59
Kiswa, 35, 133
Kufa, 53–59, 72–84
Kurds, 47
Kutama Berber tribe, 83
Kuwait, 116

Lakhmid Arabs, 5–6, 49
Landholders, 92
Lebanese civil war, 113–115
Lebanese Sunni Muslims, xxvi, 127
Lebanon: Baathists, 106–108; Druze
    presence, 87; Islamist activities,
    113–127; Kashani exile, 92; Shi'i
    control, 80
Legislative Council, 99
Levitation, 44
Libya, 106, 127
Light, 43–46, 83
Literacy Corps, 93, 146
Loans, 39
Lunar calendar, 31–32, 144

Madrasa, 88, 142
Madrid peace conference, 117
Mahdi: Bab, 78; Druze concept, 86;
    Fatamid Shi'iism, 83; Muhammad
    al-Hanifiyyah influence, 75; Muham-
    mad ibn Isma'il, 81–85; numerous,
    80–81; promise to return, 79; Qar-
    mati concept, 83–84; Shi'i *ulama* as,
    87; Twelver, 77; 'Ubayd Allah, 83
Malik ibn Anas, 40
Mamluk Abbasid Caliphate, xxi, 66
Mamluks: conflict with Ottomans, 67–
    69; defined, 63–64; Egypt, 63–64
Marj Dabik, Battle of, 68
Marriage, 2–8, 135

Marwa, 36
Marwan I, 56–57
Marwanids, 56–58
Marx, Karl, 124
Marxism, 121
Mathematicians, 45
Matn, 41, 143
Mecca, xii, xiii–xv, xviii, xxiii, xxvi, 24,
    46, 71, 132, 134, 140–144, 146; con-
    flict with Medina, 52, 57; conflict
    with Muslims, 12–22; domination
    of Islam, 49; and *hajj,* 27, 33–35, 44;
    Arab control of, 65; Muhammad's
    pilgrimage, 20; Muslims triumph, 22;
    Ottoman control, 69; Qarmati raid,
    84; *qibla,* 10, 27, 29; religious center,
    1–2; role in Arabia, 1–10; seat of
    Islam, 4–10; Shi'i alternatives, 75;
    Sufi disregard, 44
Mecca: Mother of Cities, xxiii, 100
Meccan families, 7–8, 14
Medina, xv, xvi, 23, 140, 141, 146; al-
    Ghazali's visit, 46; as an Arab anchor,
    65; capital of Arab empire, 49; City
    of the Prophet, 21; in early Shi'i
    struggles, 71, 73, 75, 81; Muham-
    mad's arrival, 11; Muslim discontent,
    52; role in conflicts, 57, 59; role in
    hajj, 36. *See also* Yathrib
Mediterranean Sea, 48, 82
Mehmed II, the Conqueror, 66
Merv, 77
Messenger of God, 7–9, 22–29
Messiah, 39, 78, 135
Milestones, 104, 137
Mina, 35, 36
Minbar, 30, 143
Miracle, 37
Mirhab, 143
Modesty, 110
Mohammad Reza, 91, 125, 142, 144,
    146
Mojahedin e Khalq, 131
Monetary settlement, 40
Mongols: compared with Reza, 90;

conquests, 64–66; conversion to
Islam, 70
Monophysite, 3–5
Monotheists: Arab attitudes, 3–8; Muslims tolerated, 17–18; in Yathrib, 10
Monthly Religious Society, xxv, 120
Morocco, 106
Moses, 28, 39
Mosque: first in Yathrib, 11; Grand
Mosque of Mecca, 35–36; Mosque
of the Prophet, 46; in notes, 132–143; Umayyad Mosque, 45; worship,
29–31
Mota, Battle of, xiv, 20–23
Mount of Mercy, 35
Mount Uhud, 15. See also Uhud,
Battle of
Movement of the Disinherited, 127, 139
Mu'awiyah: challenged 'Ali, 53; first
Ummayad, 55–56; relations with
Hasan and Husayn, 75
Mu'awiyah II, 56, 57
Muezzin, 29, 143
Muhammad: at Badr, 12–15; birth, 4;
caliphate, 55; calling, 7; conversions,
16–25; death, 24; at The Ditch, 17;
family's role, 48–53; Ghazali revered,
45; hadith, 40–42; hajj, 35; hegira,
110; marriage, 6; Messenger of God,
27–28; Qur'an, 36–37; relations
with Hashims, 6–12; relations with
Meccans, 6–25; Shi'i claims, 60–70;
success, 24–25; at Uhud, 15–17
Muhammad 'Ali, 63, 96
Muhammad al-Muntazar: in occultation, 77; Twelfth Imam, 61; widely
accepted, 79
Muhammad ibn al-Hanifiyyah, xvi, 75,
79, 135, 143
Muhammad ibn Isma'il, xvii, 61, 143,
145; claim to Imamate, 77; Isma'ili
Mahdi, 81–85
Muharram: death of Husayn, 57; importance for Shi'i, 75; in Iran, 122
Mujtahid, 88–91, 136–143
Mulla, 88, 136

Murder, 40
Musa'ab ibn 'Umayr, 10
Musa al-Kazin, 77, 80–81, 135, 136, 143
Musa al-Sadr, xxv, xxvi, 127, 137, 139,
145
Music, 43–44, 116
Muslim: defined, 36; first converts, 7–8;
obligations, 27–35; rise to prominence, 10–23; Sufi alternatives, 44–47; under attack, 64–69
Muslim Brotherhood: Iranian influence,
126; origin and belief, 100–104;
Palestine, 112–115; spread, 106–107;
Sudan, 112; Syria, xxvi, 102–108,
110–111
Mu'tazila movement, 38
Mutin ibn 'Adi, 9
Muwahhidun, 86, 143
Muzdalifah, 35

Nahrawan, xvi, 53
Najaf: 'Ali's tomb, 73; Khomeini, 94;
Shi'i tombs, 75; ulama, 91
Nass, 80, 81, 144
Nasser, Gamal Abdel, xxiv, 93, 103, 104,
107
Nasserists, xxv, 107
National Front movement, 121–124,
137
Nawful clan, 9
Nefud, 6, 23
Nejd region, 23
Nemeiri, Ja'far, xxvii, 112
Neuphle-le-Chateau, 128
New Testament, 37
Niche of prophecy, 46
Nihavand, xv, 49
Nishapur, 45–46
Noah, 39
North Africa: Fatamid dynasty, 61–62;
Isma'ili expansion, 81–83; Muslim
conquest, 49; Muslim expansion, 57
Nur al-Din, 63

Obligatory duties, 27, 33
Occultation: defined, 135; Muhammad

al-Muntazar, 77; new concept, 75;
Twelver Shi'i, 79–83
Oil wealth, 108
Old Testament: discrepancies in Muham-
mad's accounts of, 18; family in, 11; as
part of Islam, 39; prophets of, 28
Olson, Robert, ix
One God: concept in Arabia, 1–7;
Muhammad's mission, 22–24; rela-
tion to Mecca, 35
OPEC, 93
Orphan, 11, 21
Orthodox, 5, 44
Osmanli, 65
Ottoman Empire: expansion, 68–69;
Islamic reformers attacked, 100; role
of Sufi, 44; Western influence, 96
Ottoman (Osmanli) Turks, 65
Oxus River, 49, 57

Pahlavi. See Mohammad Reza; Reza Khan
Palestine: Arab nationalism, 106–108;
Crusaders, 62; Fatamid control, 61–
63; Intifada, 113–117; Mongol inva-
sion, 64; Muslim Brotherhood, 102;
'Ubayd Allah in, 83
Palestine National Authority, 117
Palestine National Council, 113
Palestine war of 1948, xxiv, 102
Palestinian resistance, 112–117
Palm, 9, 37
Pan Arabism, 107
Paradise, 36, 42–44
Paris, 94, 121, 129
Party of God, 127
PDFLP, 112
Pear tree, 128
Pensions, 52
People of the Book: dhimmi in Islamic
Empire, 49; Muhammad's protection,
18; special status, 28
Persian Empire: conflict with Ottomans,
69; Islamic expansion, 48–49;
Mu'awiyyah's government, 56;
Twelver Shi'i role, 69–72
Persian identity, 69

PFLP, 112
Pilgrimage: Battle of the Ditch, 17;
Mamluk control, 68; Muhammad's,
19–24; obligation, 27–35; Qarmati
attacks, 83–84; raid during, 12; tra-
dition in Arabia, 1–5; Yathrib resi-
dents, 10
PLO, 112–117, 141–144
Poetry, 37, 43
Poets, 15, 16
Poll tax, 22–24
Polytheism, 3–7, 21–27
Population: Arabs beyond Arabia, 52;
Hejaz, 1–10; Iranian Shi'i clergy, 70;
Iraqi Shi'i, 94; Islamic distribution,
47; Meccan converts, 21; Muham-
mad and Yathrib, 121; Muhammad
domination, 23; Muslim Brother-
hood courted, 105–109; Northern
Arabs, 59; Ottoman management,
66; Palestinian, 116–120
Prayer: hajj, 35; obligation, 28–32; qibla,
18; Wahhabi, 78
Prophecy: absence of, 24–25; Arabic,
37; Muhammad's call, 7; Seal of, 55;
Shi'i approach, 80; Sufi, 46
Prophethood, 9
Prophet's Mosque, 36
Pyrenees, 58

Qadisiyyah, battle of, xv, 49
Qajar, 89–91, 144
Qarda, xiv, 15
Qarmat, Hamdan, 82
Qarmatians, xviii–xix, 82–85
Qaynuqa, xiv, 18
Qayrawan, 83
Qibla: in hajj, 35–38; from Jerusalem to
Mecca, 18–20; in prayer, 24
Quba, 11
Qum, 77, 94
Qur'an: al-Banna, 101; al-Wahhab, 97–
98; first revelation, 7; Iranian clergy,
120; in Islam, 30–32; Isma'ili, 80; in
law, 36–40; modesty, 110; Sayyid
Qutb, 104; Shi'i, 55; Sufi, 42–46

Quraysh: 'Ali opposed, 52; caliphate, 48;
conflict with Shi'i, 58; dominance in
Mecca, 2–4; Nawful clan, 9
Qutb, Sayyid, xxiii–xxvi, 104–106, 109,
115
Qutbzadeh, Sadeq, 130

Rabin, Yitzhak, xxvii, 117
Ramadan fast, 3, 31–33
Rayy, 84
Razmara, 'Ali, 96
Reagan, Ronald, administration, 132
Reason: al-Ghazali, 45–46; no conflict
with faith, 94; Shi'i jurisprudence, 87
Red Sea: Fatamid empire, 61–64; trade
route beside, 8–15
Refugees, 10–11, 115
Religious courts, 91
Revelation: al-Ghazali, 46; limited in
Sunni Islam, 26; Muhammad's, 6–7;
Qur'an, 37; regarding unbelievers, 19;
and Shi'i Imams, 78
Revenues, 31, 4
Revolutionary Command Council
(RCC), xxiv, 103
Revolutionary committees, 130–131
Reza, Mohammad, 91, 125, 142, 144, 146
Reza Khan, 90–91, 136, 144
Rida, Muhammad Rashid, 99
Rightly Guided Caliphs, 55–59, 144
Rioting, xxv, 107
Rural tribes, 2, 15–19

Sadakat, 31–32, 145
Sadat, Anwar, 104, 111
Saddam Hussein, 116
Safa, 36
Safavid dynasty, 44, 67–70
Saiqa, 112
Saladin, xix–xx, 63–64, 85, 136
Salafiyyah: al-Banna, 100–101; Palestine,
117; Sayyid Qutb, 105–109; Sudan,
112
Salah al-Din ibn Ayyub. See Saladin
Salat, 27, 145

Salman, 17
Samarra, 73–77, 134
Sarah, 36
Satan, 38–42
Saudi Arabia, xxii, 132; government of,
34
SAVAK, 125, 137–145
Second Congress of Islamic Societies,
xxv, 121
Secularism: Baath in Syria, 106–108; in
Iran, 90, 91, 119–132; Ottoman and
Persian, 96; in Palestine, 112; RCC
in Egypt, 103
Selim I, xxi, 68
Seljuk Turks, 62–63, 85
Selma, 11
Sermon (khutba), 30
Sevener Shi'i, 72, 145
Shahadah, 27, 145
Shah Nasir al-Din, xxii, 98
Sharia: defined, 36; structure, 41–42
Shari'ati, 'Ali, xxiii, xxv, xxvi, 120, 121–
124, 126
Sharif of Mecca, 69
Sharur, Battle of, xxi, 67
Shaykhs, 43–44, 87
Shirking, 27, 136, 145–146
Shrines: 'Ali, 73; Husayn, 75; Kaaba, 33;
Kazimayn, 77; Qum, 77; Sufi, 49;
Wahhabi disapproval, 98
Sicily, 61, 83
Siyam, 27, 145
Slaves: early converts, 8; freeing, 31;
kindness to, 40; from raids, 15
Slums, 119, 126
South Tehran, 119
Soviet Union, 92–107, 132
Spain, 59–69
Spirituality: al-Banna, 101; among
Arabs, 6; Iranian clergy, 91; Iranian
Shi'i, 69; Medina's role, 73;
purification, 38; Ramadan, 32; Sayyid
Qutb, 105; Sufi, 43–46
Straight Path, 30
Street politics, 128

Sudan, xxvii, 102–112
Suez Canal, xxiv, 101–103
Sufi: missionaries, 44; orders, 43–44, 145; "saints," 44; Way, 43; worship, 43, 44
Sufyanids, 56
Sulayman, Abu Tahir, 84
Suleiman the Magnificent, xxi, 69
Sunna: Arab traditions, 5; Islamic tradition, 36; role in law, 40–41; Umayyad defined, 55–56
Sunni Islam: and Sufism, 45; Seljuk revival, 70, 85; Shi'i challenge, 73; spread Islam, 61–67; Sunni judges, 42
Supreme Guide, 104
Sura, 7, 30,
Syria: Arab conquest, 49; Arabian trade, 3–15, 21–23; Baath, 111–113; Battle of Mota, 20; Druze, 87; Fatamids, 61–65, 79; Isma'ili, 81–89; Jews expelled to, 18; Muslim Brotherhood, xxvi, 102–108, 110–111; Ottomans triumph, 68; Seljuks, 61–65; Social Nationalist Party, xxiii; Umayyad center, 53–55

Tabaristan, 80–84, 136
Tabriz, xxi, 67–68
Tabuk, 23
Ta'if, xiii–xv, 9–12, 23
Talha, 53
Tariq, 57, 134
Taxes, 22, 48–49, 58
Tehran, 94–111, 119–122
Thaqeef, 23
Third Crusade, 63
Tigris River, 59, 69
Timur, xx, 65
Tolerance, 86, 109
Tombs, 44
Torah, 30
Tours/Poitiers, Battle of, xvi, 58
Trade: of Iran, 90; of Mecca, 1–23
Tradition: Arabian, 1–18; hadith, 40–41;

inflexibility, 55; Iranian clergy, 120; Shi'i occultation, 86; Shi'i martyrdom, 67
Tribes: Arabian, 23–24; Aus, 9–11; Bani Saad, 6; Berber, 83; Jewish, 18–22; Khazraj, 9–11; Muhammad among, 21–23; Quraysh, 2–6
Trinity, 3–5, 146
Tudeh party, 91, 124
Tulun, xvii, 61
Tulunids, 61
Tunisia: Islam triumph, 49; Isma'ili, 80–83; Muslim Brotherhood, 106. See also Ifriqiyyah
Turkey: Khomeini exile, 94; model for Reza, 90; Muslim Brotherhood, 106; Ottoman conquest, 65–70
Turkomen, 89
Turks: Iranians fear, 125; rise of influence, 60–70; support for Sunni Islam, 85–86
Tus, 44

'Ubayd Allah, xvii–xviii, 57, 82–84
Ubayy, 12
Uhud, Battle of, xiv, 15–17
Ulama: defined, 42; Iranian, 100; Shi'i, 88–91
'Umar. See Abu al-Khattab, 'Umar ibn
'Umayr, Musa'ab ibn, 10
Umayyad Caliphate, xvi–xvii
Umayyad dynasty, 21, 56
Umayyad Mosque, 45
Unions, 114
United Nations, 113, 114
United States: in Iran, 91–93; and Israel, 108–109
Universalist, 70, 97
Universal religion, 132
'Uthman al-Amri, 78, 139
'Uthman ibn 'Affan (Third Caliph), xv–xvi, 37, 52–53, 55–57, 72–73, 78, 134, 144, 146
'Uthman ibn Talha, 20
Uwal, 85, 136

Veiling, 35
Vizir, 135

Wahhabi, 97–98, 146. See also Al-
   Wahhab
Wailing Wall, 112
Waqf, 117, 141–146
War: 1967, 107; 1973, 107
Weapons, 48, 107, 126
Weather, 4, 32
West Bank, 115
Western dress, 109–110
Whirling, 43–44
White Revolution, 93–94, 120, 142–146
Widows, 31, 39
Wine, 39
Witnesses, 39, 44
Women: hajj, 35; Muslim Brotherhood,
   109–110; and raiding, 15; of unbe-
   lievers, 19
Wuquf, 35, 146

Yarmuk, xv, 49
Yathrib, xiii–xiv, 14, 22, 147; base of

operations, 15–19; in early Islam, 2,
   4, 5; before hegira, 9–12; remained
   Prophet's capital, 21. See also Medina
Yazdi, Ibrahim, 130
Yazid, xvi, 56–57, 75
Yemen: Fatamid, 61–62; Mamluk, 64;
   Qarmati, 82; Shi'i, 80; trade, 3–24
Young Ottoman, 100
Young Turk, 100
youth, 77, 109–112

Zahidiyyah Sufi order, 67
zakat, 27–32, 145–147
Zamzam, 36
Zandaqa, 60, 147
Zayd ibn 'Ali ibn Husayn, 140
Zayd ibn Haritha, xiv, 6, 15, 20
Zaydi Shi'iism, 59, 73–79
Zionism, 112
Zuhra clan, 4
Zybayr, 53, 56